Kentucky's Cookbook Heritage

Kentucky's Cookbook Heritage

Two Hundred Years of Southern Cuisine and Culture

John van Willigen

University Press of Kentucky

Paperback edition 2019

Scholarly publisher for the Commonwealth,
serving Bellarmine University, Berea College, Centre College of Kentucky, Eastern Kentucky University, The Filson Historical Society, Georgetown College, Kentucky Historical Society, Kentucky State University, Morehead State University, Murray State University, Northern Kentucky University, Transylvania University, University of Kentucky, University of Louisville, and Western Kentucky University.

Editorial and Sales Offices: The University Press of Kentucky
663 South Limestone Street, Lexington, Kentucky 40508-4008
www.kentuckypress.com

Unless otherwise noted, photographs are from the author's collection.

Library of Congress Cataloging-in-Publication Data

Van Willigen, John.
Kentucky's cookbook heritage : two hundred years of southern cuisine and culture / John van Willigen.
pages cm
Includes bibliographical references and index.
ISBN 978-0-8131-4689-8 (hbk. : alk. paper)—ISBN 978-0-8131-4691-1 (pdf)—ISBN 978-0-8131-4690-4 (epub)
1. Cooking, American—Southern style. 2. Cooking—Kentucky—History. 3. Cookbooks—Kentucky—History-19th century. 4. Cookbooks—Kentucky—Bibliography. I. Title.
TX715.2.S68V38 2014
641.59769—dc23 2014016214

ISBN 978-0-8131-7849-3 (pbk. : alk. paper)

This book is printed on acid-free paper meeting the requirements of the American National Standard for Permanence in Paper for Printed Library Materials.

Manufactured in the United States of America.

Member of the Association of University Presses

Contents

Introduction

Cookbooks as the Key to Kentucky Foodways and Culinary History

Kentucky cookbooks (that is, collections of recipes produced by Kentucky authors or groups) provide a glimpse of what Kentuckians ate, how they prepared food, the cooking technology used, and the social setting of food preparation and consumption at the time of the book's compilation. Tapping into this potential resource requires careful analytical reading, however. As John Egerton notes, "Cookbooks tend to keep their social and cultural clues discreetly buried between the lines, but when they can be uncovered they may be useful barometers of a society's tastes and priorities and values" (1993, 17). This book is based on a close reading of a selection of Kentucky-published cookbooks from the past and the present.

It is clear that cookbooks and their recipes have changed considerably in terms of diversity and format. The first noticeable change is that the rate of publication has increased over time. There were few nineteenth-century cookbooks, although this started to change after the Civil War. During World War I, the Depression, and World War II, few cookbooks were produced. By the 1950s, there was a large increase in the number of cookbooks published, followed by another substantial surge starting in the 1980s. More recent increases reflect readers' growing interest in food writing, which is associated with changes in the style and content of cookbooks. These changes are the result of many factors, including the development of new dishes, evolving recipe formats, new food preparation technology, shifting availability of ingredients, increased presence of branded or processed foods, growing interest in saving time when cooking, new knowledge about cooking techniques, greater cultural diversity in Kentucky communities, and changes in the meaning and politics of food.

Many of the changes in cookbooks and their recipes can best be understood in terms of the transformations occurring in the American food system. The two overarching changes are that consumers are less involved in producing food and that food must travel a longer distance. Using the idea of a watershed as a metaphor, culinary historian Ann Vileisis (2008) speaks of the "foodshed," or the area from which we obtain our food. In the 175 years covered by this book, the limits of the foodshed have changed for many Kentuckians—from the garden spot near the house, adjacent fields and pastures, and the cellar to faraway and largely unknown locations. This has had important consequences. People now have less knowledge about where their food comes from, how it is produced, who the producers are, and whether it is wholesome and safe to eat. A major part of our culture has been taken from us. One of the consequences is a loss of knowledge and skill. One might say that, in certain realms, we have been decultured. At the same time, we have obtained new food knowledge. I may not know how to slaughter and dress a chicken, but I have a working knowledge of nutrition and I can prepare a credible pad Thai. Some argue that our interest in cookbooks is related to our separation from food production.

It is not often a cookbook's goal to depict or explain history, but in the process of providing lists of ingredients and instructions for cooking them, it may reveal traces of history. Further, it is interesting to place cookbooks in their social context and to think about how they reflect their times. Often this is quite obvious in the recipes, but it may require a careful reading, rereading, and interpretation. When I originally conceived of this book, I thought in terms of excavating an archaeological site. Cookbooks are like archaeological strata. Each one reflects something of the era in which it was created. It does not provide a complete picture of what life was like; rather, it offers a complex and hard-to-fathom tracing of reality as it existed for its creator. When archaeologists excavate a site, they may not find much to work with, and they are often hard-pressed to understand the meaning of the artifacts they do uncover. So it is with cookbooks: although much can be learned through the study of cookbooks and their recipes, they are of limited use for understanding foodways.

Working with Liberty Hall's early-nineteenth-century manuscript cookbook. (John van Willigen)

One limitation is the problem of historical lag. With regard to using cookbooks and recipes to study culinary history, Karen Hess notes, "The lag between practice and the printed word is one of the most frustrating aspects of work in the discipline of culinary history" (Hess 1992, 44). Hess goes on to cite the example of johnnycake and other corn-based, hearth-baked breads of the early colonial era, noting that 175 years elapsed between the earliest preparation of these foods by American cooks and the recipes' appearance in the historical record. This is not to say that these recipes did not exist, but they were most likely kept in people's heads or sometimes written out by hand. In fact, most recipes are not written; they are stored deep in memory or improvised, based on the cook's creative vision and knowledge of the fundamentals of cooking, as well as what is in the pantry. A lot of cooking is "done by ear," to use Marion Flexner's phrase describing the method of the African American cooks who worked for her family (Flexner 1941, x). Those wonderful cooks internalized the principles of preparation that produced the results they were interested in.

So while there might be a recipe, it is probably not written down and perhaps not even memorized: it just is.

Even written recipes were rarely published in cookbooks, as it was common for families to keep their own handwritten books of recipes. Reliance on these manuscript cookbooks was very common. As Mary Tolford Wilson notes in reference to the early American colonial era, "Unless she was illiterate or unusually shiftless, the homemaker of course had her own written collection of receipts, medicinal as well as culinary, gathered from family and friends" (1984, viii). While reviewing the cookbook collection at Frankfort's Liberty Hall, a historically important home built in 1796, I found a number of manuscript cookbooks. The oldest recipes were dated 1812, and it was obvious that others had been added through the years, many of them copied from other publications. Along with the recipes, there were many other kinds of notes, as well as an effort to index the materials. These early manuscript cookbooks were often passed from mother to daughter. In one case, culinary historian Karen Hess compiled a manuscript cookbook of Martha Washington's (Hess 1981) and later re-

The restored kitchen at Riverside Historic Site in Jefferson County. (John van Willigen)

leased it as *Martha Washington's Booke of Cookery and Booke of Sweetmeats* (Hess 1996), with the addition of extensive historical annotations. In a case closer to home, the family that occupied the historic Riverside farm passed down a collection of recipes dating from about 1890 and written on a simple notepad. Riverside, which was built in the nineteenth century on the Ohio River in southwestern Jefferson County, is now part of metropolitan Louisville's park system. The Riverside recipes are believed to come from Nannic Storts Moremen, who, along with Israel Putnam Moremen, owned the farm. Some of these recipes are included in a booklet titled *Riverside Receipts* (Linn and Neary 1999), published as part of the interpretive program at Riverside. Following is Riverside's recipe for rice pudding.[1]

Grandma's Pudding (1890)

> Bake in a yellow earthen dish with not-too-hot-a-fire. Into the baker put a quart of new milk, a scant cupful of rice, two tablespoonfuls of sugar, a quarter of a teaspoonful of salt, half a cupful of large Eayes (brand name) raisins. After stirring well to dissolve the sugar, she grated some nutmeg on top. When a scum began to form upon the milk, she skimmed it in, and as fast as it formed, did so again. She did not let it brown until the rice began to thicken; then she let it brown on top. About an hour and a half was allowed for it to cook. When she lifted it from the oven and set it in the spring house to cool, it was delicious and seemed filled with cream. (Linn and Neary 1999, 19)

This recipe reveals some of the food preparation technology of the time. Note that it calls for "new milk." About twelve to twenty-four hours after a cow is milked, the liquid separates into cream and milk. New milk refers to the liquid before that separation occurs; thus, new milk has a high butterfat content. (Today, homogenization breaks down the fat globules, which eliminates the butterfat's separation from the rest of the milk.) Morning milk probably has the same meaning as new milk. In addition, the recipe gives no indication of the oven temperature, as the wood-burning ovens of the era did not have thermostats. Finally, the reference to a springhouse indicates that containers of milk were placed in springwater to keep them cool.

Many of Kentucky's history archives have manuscript cookbooks from different periods. For instance, University of Kentucky archivist Deirdre A. Scaggs and Andrew W. McGraw wrote *The Historic Kentucky Kitchen: Traditional Recipes for Today's Cook* (2013), based on manuscript cookbooks in the university's special collections. Besides creating manuscript cookbooks, cooks often added their own recipes to printed cookbooks, old and new. It is typical to find recipes written down or pasted into antique and vintage cookbooks. Cookbooks served as little box files for recipes.

Manuscript recipes allowed sharing among friends and neighbors.[2] Years ago, swapping recipes was something like friending someone on Facebook. Sharing recipes linked people together, created common memories, and provided an affiliation. On top of this, it was useful for cooking. This worked in both social time and social space. One intriguing question is how people decided which recipes to share. A quick review of community cookbooks shows that people tended to contribute recipes from loved ones, famous food writers or other celebrities, or famous restaurants: think Mom's stack cake, Cissy Gregg's dumplings, or the Beaumont Inn's corn pudding.

Another limitation of using cookbooks to understand culinary history is that these books can have very long lives. For one thing, some of the better-known "national" cookbooks stay in print for many years, although they may exist in various editions. Related to this is that families often retain and use cookbooks over a long period. I bought a copy of the 1888 edition of *Housekeeping in the Blue Grass* a few years ago, and inside I found recipes from 1945 and 1962 that had been clipped from the newspaper. There was also a bill of sale for $1.60 for the cookbook dated February 1943 from W. K. Stewart Company in Louisville.

Cookbooks and recipes also vary in terms of the "taste" reference group they are written for. Recipes and their ingredients contain "prestige markers": some cookbook writers serve as arbiters of what is considered "good taste," and others make a point of selecting the everyday. Whether a recipe calls for Velveeta pasteurized processed cheese or Kenney's artisanal aged Cheddar says something about the recipe writer's position in the hierarchy of taste and perhaps his or her ideology of food. These meanings change over time. What was either high or low prestige at some point in the past can have a different meaning years later. Changes in the status of biscuits and cornbread are good examples. Another case of food being a marker of prestige is the iconic Kentucky dish called the Hot Brown sandwich. Fred K. Schmidt, a chef at the Brown Hotel, developed the recipe in 1926 and served it to the hotel's late-night dinner-dance clientele as an alternative to ham and eggs. The current Brown Hotel recipe specifies Pecorino Romano cheese in a white sauce made with heavy cream, yet one can find recipes in community cookbooks based on Velveeta or generic cheese. Basically, the Hot Brown is an open-faced sandwich of sliced turkey on toast, covered with a Mornay sauce and crossed strips of bacon, and garnished with sliced tomatoes.

It is also possible to use the prestige of both recipes and ingredients ironically. What comes to mind are recipes for tiramisu that use Twinkies and Cool Whip rather than ladyfingers and mascarpone, or even dump cake or pig pickin' cake recipes. This means that recipes and cookbooks can vary in terms of how they function as prestige markers and the extent to which they deploy irony.

The relationship between cookbooks and foodways is anything but direct. The recipes selected for inclusion in a cookbook do not necessarily represent what people really eat; the recipes may be incomplete depictions, one or two times removed from the carefully prepared dishes actually served at the table. In a similar vein, while it is safe to say that everybody eats, not everybody cooks, and very few people write cookbooks or even recipes for that matter. Cookbooks are a distillation of what those writers know about cooking and nutrition and what they think is important. Beyond this, their understanding of the audience's knowledge of cooking is critical. Often, but not always, early published recipes included little information about procedure. This is usually seen as evidence that the cookbook users already knew the process, so it was not necessary to repeat it. More recently published recipes tend to include far more procedural instructions.

One interesting aspect that is often not reported in cookbooks is the source of a recipe. And when a source is described, it is often done inconsistently. In the case of *The Kentucky Housewife*, the earliest published Kentucky cookbook, the author cites the source of only one recipe out of about 1,300. In contrast, in most community cookbooks the recipes are signed, and a few are also attributed to other individuals. For instance, *Heritage Cooking Crittenden County, 1792–1992* includes "Mamaw Duncan's Chicken Casserole," a recipe contributed by Marcia Lewis of Sturgis, the daughter-in-law of Helen Lewis, who was probably a member of one of the homemaker clubs that put the cookbook together. Even when there is some documentation of the source, the recipe's historical roots largely disappear. There seems to be a much greater tendency to list the source if the contributor was famous or a beloved relative. The contribution and inclusion of a recipe may be motivated by the desire to commemorate a particular person. Much of the rich narrative of Ronni Lundy's cookbooks, such as her *Shuck Beans, Stack Cakes, and Honest Fried Chicken: The Heart and Soul of Southern Country Kitchens* (1991), consists of stories of the people—often famous musicians—who devised the recipes. Fame also played a role in determining which recipes to include in *What's Cooking in Frankfort*, produced by the Daughters of the American Revolution in 1949. It starts with recipes "used by wives of our Governors." As the author states, "Our present beloved First Lady has kindly contributed one of Governor [Earle C.] Clements' favorites," reproduced below (Sutterlin 1949, 4).

Butterscotch Fudge Bars (1949)

½ cup butter
2 cups brown sugar (light)
2 eggs
2 cups flour
2 teaspoons baking powder
½ teaspoon salt
1 teaspoon vanilla
1 cup nuts

> Cream butter, gradually add sugar. Beat in eggs. Add dry ingredients, nuts and flavoring. Spread in well oiled pans. Bake 20 to 25 minutes at 375 degrees.

Clements was governor of Kentucky from 1947 to 1951.

As mentioned earlier, one theme developed in this book is that recipe format, precision in measurement, extent of culinary disclosure, and amount of contextualizing narrative have all changed over time. Changes in content and formatting began even earlier than the time frame considered here. For example, today we expect ingredients to be presented in the order of their use and in specific measured amounts. But according to food writer M. F. K. Fisher (1968, 6), this did not occur in cookbooks until the early nineteenth century. She notes that the first user of this innovation was William Kitchiner in *The Cook's Oracle*, originally published in England and appearing in an American edition in 1830. Most editions of this book include a statement on the title page that "the quantity of each article is accurately stated by weight and measure; being the result of actual experiment," reflecting the novelty of this innovation (Kitchiner 1830, i).

Another theme discussed at various points herein is that the cookbook enterprise has always been structured by gender. Cookbook writing has largely been the domain of women. In addition to the domestic sphere of child rearing and homemaking, the process of writing and compiling cookbooks was one area in which women were allowed to function more or less untrammeled, as evidenced by culinary history scholarship. The exhibit "The Old Girl Network: Charity Cookbooks and the Empowerment of Women," presented at the University of Michigan's Clements Library in 2008, is one example. Curated by eminent American culinary historian Janice Longone, the exhibit made it clear that involvement in the production of charity cookbooks allowed women to write, organize, market, and, above all, be in charge. Longone points out that the skills learned in the charity cookbook enterprise gave women a foundation to expand their realm beyond the domestic. The same can be said for the production of for-profit cookbooks.

Therefore, there are a limited number of Kentucky cookbooks written by men. According to my research, the first Kentucky cookbook written by a man was Tandy Ellis's little pamphlet titled *Camp Cooking*, published in 1923 (an interesting little book that is discussed in more detail later). The most famous male-written cookbooks are those produced by Duncan Hines of Bowling Green, starting in 1939. Like Hines, most male cookbook authors are celebrities, professional chefs, or entrepreneurs. Men contributed a few recipes to some community cookbooks—most often, recipes for game.

In addition to gender, social class and ethnicity are important factors in cookbook production. In the earliest periods, most cookbooks were written by upper-middle-class white women or compiled by groups of upper-middle-class white women associated with mainline Protestant churches in towns or cities. Thus, the considerable role of African Americans in the development of Kentucky foodways was hidden behind the white women who hired or, prior to emancipation, owned them. For the most part, these African American cooks were unnamed, although there seem to be a few signed recipes by African Americans that appeared in cookbooks as early as 1894. The earliest Kentucky cookbook authored by an African American was Atholene Peyton's *The Peytonia Cook Book*, published in 1906 in Louisville. Later in the twentieth century some African American women published their recipes through the agency of white women, and I found a few community cookbooks produced by African Americans. Therefore, our understanding of Kentucky foodways through cookbooks is influenced by the fact that cookbook production has always had a clear gender, class, and ethnic tendency.

Another part of the story is the contribution of Native Americans to Kentucky culinary history and their influence on Kentucky foodways. Although there were many Native American recipes, there were no early Native American cookbooks. The first European American pioneers in Kentucky ate a diet based on foods that were also important to the region's Native Americans. Both groups grew similar crops, and the pioneer farmers made use of Native American farming practices, such as the companion planting of corn, beans, and squash. Pole beans would climb up the cornstalks, while the squash plants shaded the base of the corn plants, preventing the growth of weeds. The beans also improved soil fertility through nitrogen fixation. As a result of this practice, today you can buy what are called cornfield beans in many farmers' markets across the state. The early European American farmers planted these crops in hills rather than rows—another Native American practice. And initially, both groups farmed based on hoe rather than plow cultivation. It is important to note that both exploited a wide variety of each of the three basic crops produced. Like the Native Americans, European Americans mastered the method of processing corn in alkali to produce hominy. Both were also hunters, which resulted in the addition of deer, bear, squirrel, rabbit, turkey, and waterfowl to their diet. Needless to say, both were subsistence farmers, using the food they produced for family consumption, not for the market.

There are many recipes of Native American origin in early cookbooks. These foods were especially important in the South and, along with foods of African origin, are one of the foundations of southern cuisine. Corn was the most important Native American food. Corn yields were much higher than wheat yields, and corn could be consumed in its milk phase as well as being processed as a mature grain. In addition, wheat required more careful soil preparation, and plantings in the rich, newly farmed Kentucky soil produced very leggy wheat stalks that would lodge or fall over. Early cookbooks often referred to cornmeal as Indian meal and included many different recipes for breads, ranging from hoecakes to light bread. Some cookbooks included recipes for roasting ears of corn, and early corn pudding recipes called for milk-stage field corn rather than today's canned sweet corn.

One problem is that the culinary relationship between Native American and Euro-American Kentuckians is not well understood. Most casual accounts rely on legends about the Pilgrims of New England or the Powhatan peoples of Virginia rather than the actual culinary transactions occurring in the Bluegrass State. The exchange of foodways between Native Americans and the European colonists spanned about 200 years. It started far away from this region and continued in the contact sites of what would become Kentucky. Clearly, much of the influence was indirect, as there is archaeological evidence of European cultural influences far earlier than the appearance of the first Europeans in Kentucky.

Having a comprehensive list of Kentucky cookbooks was important for this project, although compiling such a list was challenging. It can never be complete: new cookbooks are always being written, many community cookbooks were printed in limited numbers and are difficult to find, and both old and new cookbooks are discovered all the time. The starting point for constructing the list was my own collection, which is continually growing with additions from used-book stores, library bookstores, antique stores, flea markets, and Ebay. This was supplemented by the list and description of cookbooks in John Egerton's classic *Southern Food: At Home, on the Road, in History* (1993). Egerton, from Trigg County, includes a lot of Kentucky content in his writing about foods of the South, and he certainly represents a go-to source for southern and Kentucky food. I regard his list as a "hall of fame" of Kentucky cookbooks, although it does not include anything more recent than 1993. The search went well beyond this, as described in the introduction to the annotated bibliography.

To review: There are two basic types of Kentucky cookbooks. Most numerous are cookbooks that were compiled by church groups, homemaker associations, garden clubs, hospital auxiliaries, historical and genealogical societies, service organizations, professional associations, volunteer fire departments, Junior Leagues, medical associations, parent-teacher associations, businesses, and other groups, usually to raise money for various projects and sometimes to increase awareness about a specific issue. Almost all the people involved in these projects were women. These are often called community cookbooks or sometimes charity cookbooks, and they account for the vast majority of the books on my list. The earliest community cookbook on the list is the classic *Housekeeping in the Blue Grass*, initially published in 1875 by the women's group of the Presbyterian Church in Paris, Kentucky, and republished a number of times (see chapter 2). Generally, these types of cookbooks are not self-consciously focused on Kentucky food (though there are exceptions). That said, most community cookbooks contain the recipes that were on cooks' minds and in their repertoires, so in this sense, they represent a regional cuisine. But it seems unlikely that the typical recipe contributor would ask herself whether her recipe represented the essence of the region's foodways. There are many reasons why recipes are contributed, and expressing culinary heritage is just one of them. In some ways, random contributions may represent actual foodways better than recipes that are thought to reflect a region's food traditions. Although one can discuss regional differences in food, there is considerable risk in mythologizing what people actually eat. There are subtle differences between what people really cook and eat and what people say about cooking and eating.

The second kind of cookbook, also important, is that written by food writers, chefs, restaurateurs, and celebrities with Kentucky ties. The earliest, published in 1839, is *The Kentucky Housewife* by Mrs. Lettice Bryan, who was born in Boyle County (see chapter 1). A few of these cookbooks were clearly intended as compilations of Kentucky foodways, such as *Out of Kentucky Kitchens* by Marion W. Flexner (1949), *Charles Patteson's Kentucky Cooking* (1988), and Sharon Thompson's *Flavors of Kentucky* (2006). Others are focused on the general category of southern foods rather than Kentucky foods. Examples of these are Camille Glenn's *The Heritage of Southern Cooking* (1986) and Ronni Lundy's *Butter Beans to Blackberries: Recipes from the Southern Garden* (1999). But both Glenn and Lundy have clear Kentucky ties: Glenn was raised in Dawson Springs in Hopkins County and worked in Louisville, and Lundy was raised in Louisville and spent significant time in Corbin in southeastern Kentucky.

A few cookbooks started as community cookbooks and evolved into the second type. The best example is Irene Hayes's *What's Cooking in Kentucky* (1965), which is still in print. This comprehensive cookbook was compiled to raise money for a church building fund in Hueysville in Floyd County and grew from there. A few cookbooks focus on Appalachia but have clear eastern Kentucky roots, including Sidney Saylor Farr's *More than Moonshine: Appalachian Recipes and Recollections* (1983) and Mark F. Sohn's *Mountain Country Cooking: A Gathering of the Best Recipes from the Smokies to the Blue Ridge* (1996). Other regional cookbooks focus on Louisville or the Bluegrass, and a few have a southern or western Kentucky orientation. Some cookbooks are linked to specific restaurants or chefs. Examples include Richard T. Hougen's *Look No Further: A Cookbook of Favorite Recipes from Boone Tavern Hotel, Berea College, Kentucky* (1955) and the more recent *Jonathan's Bluegrass Table: Redefining Kentucky Cuisine* (2009) by Jonathan Lundy, the owner-chef of his eponymous Lexington restaurant. Always interesting are celebrity cookbooks, which include *The John Jacob Niles Cookbook* (Rannells 1996), Naomi Judd's *Naomi's Home Companion: A Treasury of Favorite Recipes, Food for Thought, and Kitchen Wit and Wisdom* (1997), and Loretta Lynn's *You're Cookin' It Country: My Favorite Recipes and Memories* (2004). There are also some "single-ingredient" cookbooks, including Elizabeth Ross's *Cornmeal Country: An American Tradition* (2004) and Albert Schmid's *The Kentucky Bourbon Cookbook* (2010).

Chapter One

The First Kentucky Cookbook

Antebellum Hearth Cooking

The earliest Kentucky cookbook is *The Kentucky Housewife*, written by Lettice Bryan and published in 1839. Its content reflects the foodways of the region's upper-class white households in the decades prior to the Civil War. The recipes were designed to be prepared on an open, wood-fired hearth, and the ingredients consist mostly of foods produced in the household's gardens, orchards, and pastures. There are also recipes for game. Some ingredients, such as sugar and various spices, had to be obtained from great distances and were no doubt used sparingly. In reading the recipes, one is made aware of the labor involved in producing the food and preparing it for use. Many ingredients required processing in the home. Convenience was not an attribute of food, and self-sufficiency was an important part of Kentucky foodways. One indication of this is the lack of branded food products referred to in the recipes. These kinds of foods, so common today, began to appear in a limited number of recipes after the Civil War. Although *The Kentucky Housewife* was probably intended as a comprehensive cookbook, it certainly has a southern cast and contains some foods clearly associated with the South, including the earliest published recipe for cobbler.

Like most other cookbooks, *The Kentucky Housewife* adapted to the social forms of the region. Its presumed audience consisted of the mistresses of large households, who often had cooks on staff and other kitchen help. This means that although the mistress had considerable knowledge of cooking, she was primarily a manager of staff, equipment, and ingredients and less actively involved as an actual cook. Although only one sentence in *The Kentucky Housewife* expresses it directly, it is clear that in many cases the cooks and other kitchen staff were enslaved women and men. As a result, in addition to its value as a cookbook and its usefulness as a source on culinary history, it is a document about slavery.

While relatively little is known about Mrs. Bryan, a few things can be said. She was born Lettice Pierce in 1805 near Danville in Boyle County[1] and was married to Virginia-born Edmund D. Bryan in Adair County in 1823. She died in 1877 while in Macoupin, Illinois, and was apparently buried at Cave Hill Cemetery in Louisville. Her family had originally migrated from Virginia and appeared to be well-off. Her name appears in the 1850 U.S. Census records of Washington County, Kentucky, along with those of her husband and their six children; Edmund Bryan's occupation is listed as physician.[2] Mrs. Bryan may have been a resident of Cincinnati during the time her husband was attending medical school at the Medical College of Ohio in that city; he graduated in 1835.[3] The cookbook was registered with the district court of Kentucky and published in 1839 by Shepard and Stearns in Cincinnati.[4] At the time, Cincinnati was growing rapidly, based on intense industrialization. Much of the boom was attributable to livestock slaughtering, which provided feed stock for the cooking fat, soap, and candle industries, in addition to the meatpacking potential. The venerable Cincinnati-based firm of Procter and Gamble, founded in 1837, produced soaps and candles made from animal fats and, much later, Crisco.

The Kentucky Housewife is one of the three "southern housewife" cookbooks. Although these cookbooks do not constitute a series, they are sometimes written about together in culinary histories. The others are *The Virginia Housewife or Methodical Cook* by Mary Randolph, originally published in 1824 (Fisher 2006; Randolph [1860] 1993), and *The Carolina Housewife* by Sarah Rutledge, published in 1847 (Rutledge [1847] 1999). None of these books should be thought of as limited to the states in their titles, as Mary Randolph, Lettice Bryan, and Sarah Rutledge were clearly more cosmopolitan. In his introduction to the University of South Carolina Press's 1991 edition of *The Kentucky Housewife*, Bill Neal states that Mrs. Bryan's book is less original than the other two but is nevertheless fully developed with service ideas and suggestions for food to accompany the large number of recipes. The three "housewife" books are thought to be the earliest American regional cookbooks; although there are earlier American cookbooks (Fisher 2006), the housewife cookbooks are important. Damon Lee Fowler (2008), a prominent cookbook author and advocate for the southern food tradition, cites four cookbooks that provide "the largest surviving record" of classical southern cooking: the volumes by Randolph, Bryan, and Rutledge (all antebellum) and *Mrs. Hill's New Cookbook* by Annabella Hill, published in 1867. According to Fowler, the Hill volume has a western Georgia focus.

A number of earlier and historically important cookbooks were produced in colonial America. The first cookbooks used in the colonies were written by English authors and were either imports or American reprints of English books. The best known of these is *The Art of Cookery Made Plain and Easy* by Hannah Glasse, which was originally published in 1747. This cookbook was widely used in England and, as such, expresses English foodways. The first cookbook written by an American was Amelia Simmons's *American Cookery, or the Art of Dressing Viands, Fish, Poultry, and Vegetables, and the Best Modes of Making Pastes, Puffs, Pies, Tarts, Puddings, Custards, and Preserves, and All Kinds of Cakes, from the Imperial Plum to Plain Cake: Adapted to This Country, and All Grades of Life*, published in 1796 in Hartford, Connecticut (Simmons [1796] 1984; Fisher 2006). In contrast to the Glasse volume, the recipes in Simmons's modest little book make use of American ingredients, including corn, cranberries, turkey, molasses, squash, and potatoes.[5]

The Kentucky Housewife is comprehensive, as it contains more than 1,300 recipes. The recipes are presented in block format, which means that the ingredients and procedures are contained in a single narrative. This format was used until the innovative cookbooks of the Boston Cooking School, which presented the ingredients list separate from the description of the procedure. This pattern became the standard (with some exceptions) and is still used today. It is usually attributed to Mrs.

D. A. Lincoln and her *Mrs. Lincoln's Boston Cook Book: What to Do and What Not to Do*, published in 1884. Bryan's discussion of the cooking process includes considerable detail. While most of the book is devoted to food preparation, she includes recipes or advice for food processing and preservation, food for the sick, household remedies, cosmetics, and household cleaning agents. The sources of the recipes are not indicated, with one exception. In that case, Bryan identifies the source as the *British Encyclopedia.*

The Kentucky Housewife has multicultural roots. Besides its apparent British foundations, it includes foods of both African and Native American origin. There are recipes for okra, eggplant, and yams, on the one hand, and for turkey, cranberries, corn, beans, and squash, on the other. Just a few recipes have a specific ethnic identity, such as the Dutch *oley koeks.*

The recipes are generally vague and even elusive about the quantity of ingredients, and they use a combination of measurements—some familiar to contemporary cookbook readers, some not. In addition to the familiar cups, quarts, and tablespoons (although we cannot assume that these are the same as the measurements used today), there are references to "bird-based" measures, such as a lump of lard or butter the size of a hen's egg or a partridge's egg. Handfuls are also used. That said, many recipes do not specify any amount. These practices continued to the end of the nineteenth century, when many of these names for measures were abandoned.

More generally, *The Kentucky Housewife* reflects foodways based on high levels of self-sufficiency, with much evidence of home gardens and animal production. I am not speaking of pioneer households on the frontier, but in the 1830s the nation's food system was still based almost entirely on local resources. It had yet to undergo the spectacular transformation in production and transportation that so dramatically reduced the cost of food and increased its availability over the next seventy-five years. People relied on local mills for meal and flour, and there was no centralized production and distribution of livestock, as evidenced by the instructions for slaughter embedded in some recipes. There are many recipes for food preservation, and other recipes include information relevant to harvesting from the garden. No branded or packaged foods are used in the recipes, and commodities like sugar were expensive and required home processing. Although canned foods were available as early as 1810, Mrs. Bryan does not include any canned foods in her recipes. This book was published before the invention of baking powder, and some of the recipes call for its ancestors pearlash and saleratus.

The next generation of Kentucky cookbooks underwent a significant transformation, as the Civil War was a major stimulus for food processing and preservation. The next Kentucky cookbook, *Housekeeping in the Blue Grass*, was published in 1875. It contained much less about food processing, fewer food preservation recipes, and even a limited number of recipes that include canned foods and branded products. As the role of processed foods increased, food processing companies had an impact on the content of cookbooks in the late nineteenth century. The home economists and cooks who worked for these companies created recipes that used the companies' products; these recipes were then distributed by the companies themselves and incorporated (to an extent) into newly authored cookbooks.

Mrs. Bryan's recipe instructions, however, reflect the fact that much food was grown or raised at home rather than purchased at the market. For instance, in the recipes that involve meat, it is clear that the animal must be slaughtered. Some of the recipes actually indicate that the meat is to be slaughtered at home, and many call for the animal to be "freshly killed." Home butchering is part of the culinary story of *The Kentucky Housewife*. Under the general remarks on pork, Mrs. Bryan exhorts the reader, "In cutting up meat, be careful to cut it smoothly: to have it rough and haggled does not only spoil the looks of it, but flies are much more apt to get into it than when cut smooth" (1839, 92). The proximity of field or garden can be seen in the instructions for butter beans: "They should be full grown and the pods yellow on the vines before they are gathered; then hull or shell them out, and dry them perfectly in the shade" (ibid., 210). There are also instructions for drying and pickling various foods, curing meats, and saving seeds. Nevertheless, foods imported from elsewhere do appear in the recipes, and they call for a number of exotic ingredients, including staples such as sugar and many spices of tropical origin. Mrs. Bryan even includes six recipes for large batches of curry powder.

Cooks using *The Kentucky Housewife* must have spent a great deal of time preparing the ingredients to make them usable in the recipes. I am not talking about slaughtering a pig here, but far more complex processes such as preparing sugar, butter, and cheese. Refined sugar was imported from the Caribbean and was kept in the pantry in the form of a loaf; because it was so expensive, it was often locked up in a sugar chest. After boiling the juice from the sugarcane to reduce its water content, refiners poured the sugar-saturated liquid into conical iron molds, where the sugar crystallized. These cone-shaped loaves varied in size (a small one weighed about three pounds) and state of refinement, and they were often wrapped in blue paper to make the sugar look whiter. Brown sugar was also used as a sweetener, as was molasses and honey. Mrs. Bryan makes no mention of sorghum, which was apparently introduced to Kentucky cooks in around 1850 (Roberts 2011, 14). In her general instructions about cake making, Mrs. Bryan advises, "Weigh your sugar and break up, spread it out on a cloth, crush it to a fine powder with a rolling pin, pass it through a sieve and put it into a bread pan" (1839, 275). Kitchens were equipped with shears or nips to cut sugar from the loaf. Shortly after publication of *The Kentucky Housewife*, the price of sugar began to drop dramatically, and the use of sugar became more common.

Mrs. Bryan also includes advice for making butter and preparing it for use in cooking. Her general discussion of cake making includes the following: "Weigh your butter, wash it in one or two cold waters, and work it with a wooden spaddle[6] till firm, draining every particle of water from it" (1839, 275). The water in the butter is related in part to the churning process. Similarly, she starts her Almond Cheese Cake recipe with a long discussion of how to produce suitable cheese, beginning with rennet: "If you have the liquid preparation of rennet, turn your milk to a curd with some of that. . . . But if you have not got the preparation, cut a piece of dried rennet two or three inches square, according to the strength of it; put it in a cup, pour over it two or three spoonfuls of wine, and twice as much warm water, and set it by till next day. Then make a quart of sweet milk over lukewarm, pour in the rennet water, cover it, and set it by the fire, where it will keep warm, till the curd forms" (ibid., 288). *The Kentucky Housewife* is one of the few cookbooks that includes a recipe for preparing rennet, an essential ingredient in cheese making.[7] Rennet is a substance produced in the stomachs of young, unweaned calves; it curdles the milk the calf consumes, starting the process of digestion. The dried rennet Mrs. Bryan refers to is a piece of a calf's stomach.

Calf's Rennet (1839)

> Take the rennet from the calf as soon as it is killed, empty it of its contents, and hang it in a cool, dry place for four or five days. Then turn the inside out, slip off the curd with your hand, fill the rennet with salt, having mixed with it a very little saltpetre, and lay it in a stone pot. Sprinkle over it a teaspoon of vinegar and a handful of salt, cover it, and set it in a cool dry place for several weeks. Then hang it up, dry it thoroughly, and it will keep good a year or two. When you wish to make use of it, cut a piece the size you wish, put it in a cup, pour on a few spoonfuls of wine or brandy, cover it well with lukewarm water, and the next day the liquid will be fit for use. It is an excellent plan to keep rennet ready prepared; being always in readiness, it will be found a great convenience. Cut off a piece six or eight inches square, put it in a small jar, or wide-mouthed bottle, pour on a pint of water, half a pint of brandy, and stop it securely. Shake it up each time before you use it; a table-spoon of the liquid will be sufficient to turn a quart of milk, if the rennet is good. (Bryan 1839, 73)

Consistent with the emphasis on self-sufficiency, recipes for preserving food abound in *The Kentucky Housewife*. There are instructions for drying a wide array of fruits, such as peaches, cherries, cranberries, and apples; drying vegetables such as pumpkins and green beans; saving seeds; curing ham; and corning and pickling beef and pork. Mrs. Bryan also provides instructions for preserving eggs.

To Keep Eggs (1839)

Eggs will keep good for some time, buried in charcoal or wheat bran, after greasing them a little with mutton tallow; but I believe the general opinion of those who have tried it is, that to keep them in lime-water is the best way they can be preserved. To half a bushel of water add little over a pint of unslaked lime,[8] and as much coarse salt, and when the whole is dissolved, put in the eggs; be very particular that you do not put in one that is cracked, as it will spoil the whole; there should be plenty of water to cover them well; if the brine is too strong with the lime, it will eat the shells; this of course can be easily detected; if the eggs are fresh and whole, and water to the proper strength, it is said they will keep good for years. (Bryan 1839, 224–25)

The self-sufficiency theme is also evident in the large number of recipes for cooking game, including venison, rabbit, squirrel, wild duck, woodcock, feelark,[9] snipe, and "any sort of small birds" (Bryan 1839, 130).

To Roast Woodcocks, Feelarks or Snipes (1839)

Pluck them carefully, touch a slip of writing paper to a blaze of fire, and hold them immediately over it to singe off the little hairs that adhere to the skin; wash them very clean in cold water, and if practicable, let them lie in sweet milk and water at least one hour before they are cooked. Season them inside and out with salt, put in each a lump of butter, rolled in bread crumbs, and seasoned with a little pepper; rub them over with butter, and roast them before a brisk fire, which will cook them in a few minutes; them serve them up, garnish with little mounds of ripe, soft peaches, having them mashed fine; add to the drippings, some drawn butter, chopped asparagus, or parsley and pepper, and serve it in a boat, to eat with the birds. (Bryan 1839, 130)

Hearth Cooking

The recipes included in *The Kentucky Housewife* are geared toward cooking at a hearth or fireplace. It is the only cookbook included here that is based on this technology. Cooking was done on the hearth well into the nineteenth century, yet by the time *Housekeeping in the Blue Grass* was published in 1875, wood and coal cookstoves were the norm. In fact, wood-burning cookstoves were available before the publication of *The Kentucky Housewife*, but they are not apparent in the recipes. The use of wood-fired fireplaces shaped the cooking strategies as well as the cooking implements and recipes of this era. Some argue that the upper-class households of the region were slow to adopt innovative wood- and coal-burning cookstoves because they had servants—either enslaved or hired—to do the much more demanding work of hearth cooking.

Before returning to Mrs. Bryan's recipes, a discussion of fireplaces and hearths is in order. Fireplaces varied in size, design, and associated tools and utensils through time and based on the resources of the home owners. The physical evidence in Kentucky is largely limited to the elaborate hearths of the few remaining stately homes from that era.[10] The typical hearth was far simpler. Most fireplaces served the dual purpose of heating and cooking, although sometimes the kitchen was detached from

Cooking with coals in a Dutch oven and skillet at Liberty Hall, 2013. (John van Willigen)

the rest of the house. In the earliest pioneer log cabins, the fireplace was built at one end of the one-room structure. In what architectural historians call saddlebag houses, the fireplace was located in the center of the room and had two sides. Typically, hearths and chimneys were built of locally available stone, often limestone or river cobbles; however, in the earliest pioneer period, chimneys were often constructed of mud and sticks.

These fireplaces could be quite large, often requiring a long "backlog" in the rear of the fireplace. Over time, these logs would burn through and be replaced. A man from Adair County reported in a 1966 interview, "This old fireplace was so big that they would bring in what they called a back log, and my grandfather would roll it into the house with big wooden sticks and roll it o'er to the fireplace and put it up on these big stove irons" (Montell and Morse 1976, 47). Daniel Drake, who grew up in Mayslick in the 1790s, recalled that, thanks to his lack of planning, "I often had to cut off a large backlog in a cold winter morning, before a fire could be made" (1870, 261). According to Drake, buckeye was the preferred tree for backlogs, which could be four or five feet long, because buckeye did not burn easily and the logs lasted a good long while.

There was great variation in the size and elaborateness of fireplaces in early Kentucky. Those used for cooking were generally much larger than those used for heating alone. In large mansions, cooking fireplaces might be located in alcoves, and the brick floor of the fireplace was often enlarged to allow cooking on the hearth floor, with coals taken from the fire with a shovel. Designs changed over time and became more fuel-efficient and convenient. People of more limited means continued to make do with simple hearths and basic equipment.

Archaeology of a Hearth

Located on the Ohio River in Jefferson County is the historic site called Riverside, mentioned earlier. The focal point is the Farnsley-Moremen brick farmhouse (still standing) that was built in 1837, just two years before *The Kentucky Housewife* was published. Archaeologists from the Kentucky Archaeological Survey discovered the foundation of the sixteen- by seventeen-foot frame building that served as the detached kitchen, as well as the remains of the hearth it contained. At the time, it was common for the kitchen to be detached from the main house; this reduced the risk of fire, lessened the impact of kitchen heat during the summer, and served to separate the people of the household from the enslaved African American staff. Through their excavation and careful analysis, the archaeologists were able to reconstruct the kitchen building. The brick hearth was five and a half feet wide and two feet deep. The bricks used to construct the chimney foundation and the hearth were handmade and fired at Riverside. The burned fragments of firewood included sycamore, white oak, yellow poplar, and hickory (Linn and Stottman 2003). Among the artifacts found in the excavation were fragments of andirons—sometimes called firedogs. Firewood was placed on the andirons to allow a draft under the logs and to keep the burning wood in its proper place (Cebulska 1976). The size and shape of the hearth clearly showed how it was used. Cooking was done with hot coals rather than flames. The hot coals from the log fire were distributed to different places on the spacious hearth to heat individual utensils—in effect, creating many "burners." Thus, the cooking fire was much more like the one used to cook hamburgers on the backyard charcoal grill than the roaring fire depicted on Christmas cards.

In the deposits covering the remains of the hearth, the researchers found fragments of ceramic cookware and a trammel.[11] The presence of a trammel implies the use of an iron hearth crane to swing large cast-iron pots over the main fire. Clues to the types of food cooked included the remains (bones) of pigs, cows, sheep, and chickens (likely raised on the farm), as well as animals that were hunted, such as turtles, quail, and squirrels. Plant remains were also found, including corn, barley, peaches, black walnuts, and hickory nuts.

Using the Hearth and Managing the Fire

The application of heat was accomplished in a number of different ways. First, convection heat was provided by the fire itself to heat pots and pans suspended over it. The fire also supplied radiant heat that could be used to cook with the help of spits. Spits were usually placed in front of the fire rather than over it. Reflector ovens—sometimes called tin kitchens—were also designed to be placed in front of the fire. As was apparent at Riverside, another method was to shovel coals from the fire to the space in front of the fireplace and heat food in utensils. These coals were inevitably consumed, so the heat they provided started to decline immediately. The coals had to be shoveled back into the fire when cooking was done or replenished if the cooking was to continue. Last, some foods were cooked directly in the ashes. According to my reading, Mrs. Bryan includes only one recipe for direct cooking in *The Kentucky Housewife*, where she advises wrapping mackerel in fish paper and roasting it in "wood ashes on a clean hearth" (1839, 147). Similarly, hot ashes were used to roast ears of green corn in their shuck, winter squash, and sweet and Irish potatoes in season (Montell and Morse 1976, 48). Simple cornbreads called ashcakes could also be cooked this way, either placed in the ashes or on a specially cleared area on the hearth.

With hearth cooking, cooks had to be skilled in managing the fire and its heat. This involved complex knowledge of the factors that control the amount of heat produced. The distance of the pot from the heat source; the fuel's size, extent of ash covering, and wood type; and the amount of draft were important factors. When coals are referred to in *The Kentucky Housewife*, they are often described as "clear," which presumably means without a lot of ash. Cooks had to know that wood chopped to kindling size burned quicker and hotter than large logs. They could also control the heat by reducing or increasing the amount of embers allocated to a particular pot. Newly placed logs created cool spots in the fire and could be used to shield a pot from the heat. The last factor that controlled the heat was the amount of draft.

In earlier and simpler times, cooking utensils were suspended over the fire from a device called a lug pole. Because the early ones were made of wood, they gradually weakened and required replacement. In fact, they would sometimes break during cooking, sending pots into the fire with disastrous results. Cooks were at considerable risk of being scalded if the lug pole broke. An important improvement over the lug pole was the crane, mentioned earlier. These hinged, wrought-iron frames were firmly attached to the fireplace masonry, allowing the cook to swing the pot in or out of the fire and providing more heat control and safer and more comfortable cooking. These cranes were often used to suspend large pots of simmering water, as cooking in boiling water was a common method that required less attention than other techniques. With the use of the crane, a cast-iron cauldron could simply be swung over the fire, making heat regulation less of a challenge. This method was used in many recipes for pudding.

The Kentucky Housewife includes more than fifty pudding recipes featuring a wide range of ingredients, including sweet potato, white potato, and various fruits such as orange, lemon, plum, apple, cherry, cranberry, whortleberry, quince, raisin, and pear. A number of recipes are based on rice or bread; others are based on squash, coconut, almond, custard, or cornmeal. Although the majority of the recipes are for baked puddings, a number of Mrs. Bryan's recipes are for boiled puddings prepared in a cloth pudding sack. Mrs. Bryan advises, "For boiled puddings, you should have very thick cloths, made of German sheeting, or a remarkably thick linen, as a thinner article will admit the water and spoil the pudding. The cloths should be dipped into boiling water and dusted with flour before the puddings are put in. Tie a string tightly round the cloth, to exclude every particle of water, leaving plenty of room in it for the pudding to swell. They should be boiled in a large quantity of water, which must be boiling when the pudding is put in. Add no water except from a boiling kettle" (1839, 232). Here is one of Mrs. Bryan's boiled pudding recipes.

A Raisin Pudding (1839)

Beat six eggs very light, and stir them into a quart of sweet milk, with a large spoonful of mixed mace and cinnamon, a grated nutmeg and a glass of white wine, adding by degrees enough flour to make it into a common pudding batter. Seed, cut and dust with flour a pound and a half of raisins (Sultana raisins are preferable, having no seed); stir them gradually into the other ingredients, giving all a hard stirring at the last. Put it into a pudding cloth, having first dipped it into boiling water, and dusted it with flour; tie a string firmly round end of the cloth, leaving plenty of room for the

> pudding to swell, and dusting the tying place with a little dry flour, to secure it against the admission of water, which would spoil the pudding, if suffered to approach it. Put it in a large pot of boiling water, and boil it gently and steadily for several hours, turning it over several times, and replenishing the pot with water from a boiling kettle. When it is done, turn it smoothly into a dish, sprinkle over it some preserved raisins, finely shred; grate on some loaf sugar, and eat it warm, with wine sauce, or white wine and sugar. (Bryan 1839, 241–42)

The cookbooks of the nineteenth century contained many pudding recipes that used various cooking procedures in addition to boiling in a bag. Cookbooks published later had fewer boiled pudding recipes, and contemporary cookbooks have few pudding recipes of any kind.

Kitchen Utensils, Hearthside

Cooking in the coals was accomplished with a number of special utensils. Most of these were probably made of cast iron, but utensils made of copper, tin, and other metals are mentioned in recipes. These cooking vessels tended to have rounded bottoms rather than the flat bottoms that were typical of pots used with woodstoves (not to mention today's induction ranges). We still use some of these utensils in today's kitchen, while others are obsolete. The most important were gridirons, Dutch ovens, and skillets specially adapted to hearth cooking, called spiders. These were supplemented with trivets and salamanders.

Gridirons are open iron frames with legs and handles; they were usually used to cook meats in the coals of the hearth. Good cooks ensured that the gridiron was hot and well greased before use—accomplished by putting lard in a linen covering and rubbing it on the gridiron.

Broiled Beef Steaks (1839)

> Place a gridiron over a bed of clear coals, and clean and grease the bars well. Having prepared your steaks as for frying, with the exception of seasoning them, broil them on the gridiron till thoroughly

> done, turning them over frequently; then transfer them to a hot dish, sprinkle them immediately with salt and pepper, and put on a few spoonfuls of melted butter, and you may slightly acidulate them with flavored vinegar, or lemon juice, if you like them so. (Bryan 1839, 40)

Dutch ovens are large, round, covered kettles with legs that allow them to be placed in the coals. The lids were usually constructed with a flange so that hot coals could be placed on the cover, thus cooking the food from both top and bottom. Dutch ovens were often used for baking, sometimes with a water bath, as well as for frying and simmering. Mrs. Bryan describes part of the process of making "light white bread" after combining the flour, yeast, salt, and water or milk: "Knead it till it becomes smooth, but no longer; put it in an oven that has been cleaned, greased and rubbed with dry flour; throw a few embers about it, to warm it slightly, but not so much so that you may bear your hand on it without burning you. Cover the oven, set it by the fire where it will keep a little warm, and do not disturb it more than to turn it round occasionally till it rises to double the original height; then heat it gradually and bake it with a moderate heat" (1839, 317).

Newly manufactured and vintage Dutch ovens can still be bought for campfire cooking. The Lodge Manufacturing Company and others make Dutch ovens with and without legs. One central Kentuckian, interviewed in 1965, recollected that his mother "had a big cast-iron container with a lid, called an oven. She used coals of fire under the oven and on top of the lid to bake things inside" (Montell and Morse 1976, 48). This strategy appears in Mrs. Bryan's recipes for wheat bread and, with the addition of a water bath, custards. In the following recipe, the term *oven* refers to a Dutch oven.

Baked Custard (1839)

> Boil a quart of sweet milk, flavor it with anything you please, and set it by to cool. Beat eight eggs very light, and when the milk is cold, mix them with it, adding four ounces of powdered sugar. Stir it till well mixed, put it in custard cups, filling them quite full; set them

> in an oven, pour round them hot water, but not enough to reach to tops, lest it gets in, and spoils your custards. Having heated your lid, put it on the oven, throw some coals on, and under it, and bake the custards till thick, and of a light brown. When cold, grate nutmeg over them, and send them to the table with a teaspoon for each cup. (Bryan 1839, 320)

Also common were long-legged frying pans with round bottoms and long handles, which allowed them to be used in wood coals arranged on the hearth. Although some historical literature calls these pans *spiders*, Mrs. Bryan does not use the term; nor does it appear in the other "housewife" cookbooks. Typically, contemporary collectors of antique pans use this term. In some places, *spider* refers to the flat-bottomed iron skillets used on the flat tops of woodstoves.[12] Here and there, in other historical Kentucky cookbooks, one can find recipes for spider cornbread. Mrs. Bryan calls these pans frying pans; she also refers to stew pans, soup pans, sauce pans, and porridge pots, as well as unspecified pots and pans.

Fried Steaks of Veal (1839)

> Cut them from the fillet or leg, having them tolerably small and about half an inch thick; beat them evenly, not tearing them in the least, lay them for a minute or two in a pan of fresh water or milk, which will improve them greatly; then squeeze them a little, spread them out smoothly, sprinkle them with salt and black pepper, and dust them with flour. Have ready a frying-pan of boiling lard, place it over a bed of clear coals, and put in your steaks side by side, not crowding them too much, a fault that is often practiced. As soon as they are a nice brown on both sides, put them into a warm steak dish by the fire, thicken the gravy with a little flour, cream and chopped parsley, or minced onion, give it a boil, stir in gradually the juice of half a lemon; pour it over the steaks and send them up warm. (Bryan 1839, 64)

Among the other utensils used were trivets and salamanders. Most often, a trivet functioned to raise a kettle above the coals. Alternatively, a trivet could be placed inside a Dutch oven to raise the food off the bottom of the pot, as might be desirable with a pan of biscuits. The salamander, a special-purpose tool, is a heavy iron plate with a long handle. The salamander was heated up and then placed over the food (such as meat) to brown it. Only a few recipes in *The Kentucky Housewife* call for a salamander, and Mrs. Bryan suggests that a hot shovel could be used as well (1839, 67). Today, the term *salamander* refers to the industrial-strength browning ovens used in restaurants, and in some contemporary setups, a handled iron called a salamander is used as an alternative to a propane torch to caramelize the sugar in crème brûlée. The following recipe for burnt custard is the English version of the familiar French dish crème brûlée.

Burnt Custard (1839)

> Beat the yolks of ten eggs and the whites of five to a froth, stir in a quart of milk, add four ounces of powdered sugar, a little grated lemon, and boil it in a pitcher as before directed. [In an earlier recipe for vanilla custard, Mrs. Bryan instructed: "Put it in a pitcher, set it in boiling water, and simmer it gently till thick and smooth, stirring it all the time; then remove it from the fire and set it to cool."] When it is quite cold, put it into cups, pile on each the beaten white of eggs, grate on some loaf sugar, and brown them delicately with a salamander or red hot shovel, by holding it a little above them. (Bryan 1839, 324)

Some fireplaces were equipped with built-in brick ovens for baking cornbread, biscuits, and loaves of bread. The presence of a brick oven indicated the family's wealth and distinction. Usually a fire was built in the oven, which heated the bricks; the coals were then removed, and the food was cooked on the residual heat. As a result, bread was always baked with steadily declining heat. Baking was also accomplished with tin reflector ovens or Dutch ovens, as mentioned earlier.

As one might expect from such an early regional cookbook, *The Kentucky Housewife* achieves several "firsts." According to Damon Lee Fowler, it contains the earliest recipe for the iconic southern dish cobbler, which Mrs. Bryan calls "a peach pot-pie."

A Peach Pot-Pie (1839)

> A peach pot-pie, or cobler, as it is often termed, should be made of clingstone peaches, that are very ripe, and then pared and sliced from the stones. Prepare a pot or oven with paste, as directed for the apple pot pie, put in the prepared peaches, sprinkle on a large handful of brown sugar, pour in plenty of water to cook the peaches without burning them, though there should be very little liquor or syrup when the pie is done. Put a paste over the top, and bake it with moderate heat, raising the lid occasionally, to see how it is baking. When the crust is brown, and the peaches very soft, invert the crust on a large dish, put the peaches evenly on, and grate loaf sugar thickly over it. Eat it warm or cold. Although it is not a fashionable pie for company, it is very excellent for family use, with cold sweet milk. (Bryan 1839, 268)

Here, *oven* refers to a Dutch oven, and *paste* means pastry dough. In the apple pot pie recipe referred to, a small Dutch oven or porridge pot is buttered and floured before lining and covering the fruit with rolled-out pastry dough. Mrs. Bryan instructs us to "bake it with moderate heat, having a fire both on and under the oven" (1839, 267–68).

Some cooking was done with radiant heat in front of the fire using spits or reflector ovens. Spits could be turned by hand or by a number of different devices, all called jacks. Jacks were powered in different ways, including by a spring-driven device resembling clockworks or by the draft in the flue of the fireplace.

Roasting Meat

The Kentucky Housewife has much to offer in terms of technique for cooking meat on a hearth. Mrs. Bryan starts at a basic level, instructing her readers how to skewer the meat on a spit without mutilating it. She advises, "Be careful not to run it through a nice part of [the beef roast], or through a part that will be exposed when served" (1839, 28). The spit may have been attached to the front of the andirons or to a special rack placed in front of the fire (not over it). Basting was an important part of the cooking process, and the recipes often mention the need to place a pan under the meat to catch the drippings. For roasting beef, Mrs. Bryan instructs, "Stir as much salt as you think it will take to season it well, in a little cold water, with a small portion of pepper, and baste the beef with it frequently till you have used up the brine, or till the meat is sufficiently seasoned; then discontinue it, and baste with a mixture of fresh lard and hot water, until a sufficient quantity of essence has flown from the meat into the dripping-pan; then baste bountifully with it, till the meat is done" (ibid.). The spit had to be turned occasionally, and the fire needed to be tended so that it was "clear and steady," with little smoke or blazes. With large pieces of meat, there was the risk that the outside would be overcooked and the inside would still be too rare. To avoid this, Mrs. Bryan suggests covering the outside of the roast with white paper. In her recipes for roasting beef, the meat is evenly dusted with flour from a "dredging box" late in the cooking process, after removing the paper.

Mrs. Bryan gives no roasting times or temperatures; she suggests using a fork to see how the juices are running. "In the place of counting the hours by the clock, you will find it best to notice the fire and what you are cooking" (1839, 29). Cooking in the days of *The Kentucky Housewife* was not a "set it and forget it" affair. Fires had to be tended more or less constantly, spits had to be turned, and fuel had to be added. Between periods of cooking, the fire would usually be allowed to subside (to conserve fuel and reduce the risk of burning the house down) but not go out. Glowing embers might be preserved in a corner of the fireplace and then brought to life with wood shavings and kindling.

As the final step in the roasting process, Mrs. Bryan instructs readers to "turn the spit very fast for a few minutes to raise a froth, basting the meat all the time with melted butter, which will make the froth much higher, lighter and more delicate every way, than to baste with hot drippings" (1839, 29). Typically, the fat in the drippings pan was skimmed, and the remaining gravy was seasoned and served as an accompaniment to the meat. Various ingredients were used to flavor gravies, including wine and ketchup. Brown flour—wheat flour that has been toasted—was often used to thicken gravy. Mrs. Bryan describes the process of making brown flour: "Put [the flour] into an oven that is moderately heated, set it over a few coals, and keep stirring it as you would coffee to brown it evenly and prevent its burning. As soon as the whole is of a light brown, take it up, cool it, put it up in dry bottles, and cork them tight. It will be found a very convenient article, being always in readiness" (ibid., 163). A similar recipe for browned flour appears in Marion W. Flexner's *Dixie Dishes* (1941, 3) and in Naomi Judd's *Naomi's Home Companion* (1997), under the name "Polly's Toasted Flour." Damon Lee Fowler discusses it under "Southern Browning" in his encyclopedic *Classical Southern Cooking* (2008, 210).

In addition to gravy making, the drip pan comes into play when cooking vegetables. Mrs. Bryan suggests that after cooking white potatoes flavored with butter, cream, salt, and pepper, place them in the drippings pan to allow the juices to flavor the potatoes.

The roasting process is nicely described in the following recipe.

To Roast a Pig (1839)

A pig for roasting should be recently killed, very fat, and not too large to lie in a dish. Having it neatly prepared, rub a little salt on the inside of it, cut off the feet close to the joints, skewer the legs to the body, and fill it with a stuffing, made of bread crumbs, fresh suet, or butter, pepper, sifted sage, grated nutmeg, and lemon, and made sufficiently moist with the yolks of eggs. Then rub it over with lard, truss it for the spit, pin white paper over it and roast it before a clear, brisk fire, basting it with salt-water and pepper, till well seasoned, and then with cold lard till it is done. While the pig is roasting, boil the feet, heart and liver, mince them fine, and reserve them for the gravy. When the pig is done, dust a little flour very evenly over it, having removed the paper, and baste it well with butter; let it remain a few minutes on the spit, and if it is small serve it whole, garnished with slices of lem-

> on; but if it is rather large to serve whole, take off the head, separate the chop from the face, split the pig lengthwise, from one end of the chine to the other, press it open, and lay it in a dish with a part of the stuffing laid around it, and the head and chop placed on each side. Having skimmed the drippings, put the mince into it, with a lump of butter, rolled in flour, a handful of shred parsley, and a glass of Madeira; serve it in a gravy boat. (Bryan 1839, 94)

The strategies for roasting in *The Kentucky Housewife* are particularly interesting in a historical context, as they contrast with cooking methods from more recent times. As Anne Mendelson states, "Roasting in the original sense—a dry-heat method requiring free circulation of air around meat on an open rack or spit before the heat source—had disappeared from American homes as enclosed ranges replaced open hearths in the course of the nineteenth century" (1996, 135). As late as 1884, *Mrs. Lincoln's Boston Cook Book* defined roasting as "cooking before an open flame" (Lincoln 1884, 20). By this standard, today's roasts should be called "bakes." In fact, Mrs. Bryan includes recipes for both roasting and baking meats, with roasting done on a spit and baking done in an oven. Her "To Roast a Pig" recipe (above) is followed in the text by a "To Bake a Pig" recipe (1839, 94). This method is discussed in the next chapter, which focuses on recipes geared toward cooking with woodstoves.

The Quest for Flavor

Recipes in *The Kentucky Housewife* make extensive use of a wide variety of herbs, spices, juices, wines, spirits, and other elements to enhance flavor. Herbs mentioned in the recipes include parsley, thyme, sweet marjoram, summer savory, sage, sweet basil, and rosemary. Also in the inventory are spices such as pepper, allspice, nutmeg, mace, cinnamon, cloves, cumin, cardamom, ginger, and turmeric. Some of these are processed into spice mixtures, flavored vinegars, sauces, and "catchups" (as Mrs. Bryan spells it) to be added to gravies and sauces. She uses various kinds of mustard, including mustard seeds, ground mustard seeds, and something called "made mustard," which is used as a dressing for chicken salad. Mrs. Bryan provides six recipes for curry powders. The ingredients for the first one are as follows: "coriander seeds thirteen ounces, black pepper two ounces, cayenne pepper one ounce, tumeric [*sic*], and cumin seeds each three ounces, and trigonella [fenugreek] seeds four drachms;[13] all to be pulverized and mixed together" (1839, 159). Mrs. Bryan's flavored vinegars are made with shallots, celery, red peppers, tarragon, and horseradish, and she notes that they "are particularly useful to flavor gravies, soups, and sauces" (ibid., 178). I provide one example here.

Tarragon Vinegar (1839)

> Pick the leaves of the tarragon from the stalks just before it blooms; spread them out on a cloth, and let them lie for two or three days to dry a little; then put them into a jar [of vinegar], close and set it by for one week; then strain and bottle it. If you wish it very strongly flavored with the tarragon, fill it up the second time with fresh leaves and soak them in the same manner. Any kind of nice sweet herbs may be soaked in the same manner for the purpose of seasoning. (Bryan 1839, 179)

Mrs. Bryan's commitment to ketchup was strong, and she includes recipes based on oyster, lemon, rum, lobster, mushroom, anchovy, fish, and walnut, along with an elaborate tomato-based preparation called "kitchen catchup" (see below). Ketchup was made to be bottled and "sent to table in castors, and sometimes sent in the small bottles in which they are put up" (1839, 171).

Kitchen Catchup (1839)

> Chop fine two quarts of ripe tomatoes, sprinkle them with salt and put them into a pan with one dozen minced onions, a handful of scraped horseradish, and boil them gently for one hour, adding no water, but stirring them frequently: then strain them, put the liquid into a pan with an equal portion of red wine; and half an ounce of black pepper, half an ounce of nutmegs and half an ounce of cloves.

> Cover the pan and boil it gently till reduced to half the original quantity: then cool and bottle it. (Bryan 1839, 174)

The Quest for Light Breads and Cakes

Mrs. Bryan employs a number of strategies to lighten baked goods. Many of her bread recipes use yeast, which is described as a bottled liquid. Her cake recipes often include egg whites beaten with an improvised whisk. Mrs. Bryan writes, "Beat the whites in an earthen dish to a stiff froth, using a broad-bladed knife, small hickory rods or a bunch of wire, bent in hoops or broken" (1839, 75). This is similar to today's practices, except that many more eggs are used in Mrs. Bryan's recipes. In the sixteen recipes that call for whole eggs, the average number used is just over a dozen; the maximum is twenty-eight eggs. Among the recipes that use just the egg whites, the average is eighteen egg whites, with one recipe requiring twenty-four whites. This is a lot of eggs, but it is important to remember that eggs were smaller then.

The Kentucky Housewife was published about thirty years before a true baking powder was available on the market. Until then, other chemical leavens were used. A few of Mrs. Bryan's cake recipes include saleratus as an ingredient, and one recipe says that pearlash can be used. Pearlash, which appears more frequently in earlier cookbooks, is potassium carbonate, or potash. It is obtained by running water through wood ashes until the resulting solution is thought to be saturated, and then boiling it down to a dry state. This "make-do" pioneer process became the foundation of the American chemical industry, as both pearlash and saleratus were utilized in soap and glass making and played an important role in the export market.

In terms of baking, both pearlash and saleratus give off the gas carbon dioxide when mixed with an acid, acting as a leavening agent. In this regard, saleratus has an advantage because it gives off twice as much carbon dioxide as pearlash. On the downside, the potassium carbonates have a strong aftertaste, described as bitter and soapy. In fact, saleratus was initially used not as a leaven but to help neutralize the sour taste found in sourdough bread (Ciullo 2006). In the process, bakers discovered it was a good leaven. The name *saleratus* means "aerated salt," reflecting how it is made, which involves exposing a carbonate compound to carbon dioxide. Confusing the issue is that saleratus can refer to either potassium bicarbonate or sodium bicarbonate. Most of us have sodium bicarbonate—or baking soda—on our pantry shelves. Baking soda, or bicarbonate of soda, represented an improvement because it does not have the bitter aftertaste of pearlash and the potassium version of saleratus. The following recipe for biscuits uses saleratus or, optionally, pearlash.

Saleratus Biscuit (1839)

> Sift a quart of flour, sprinkle into it a salt-spoonful of salt, and rub into it one ounce of butter. Pour half a tea-cupful of boiling water on a small tea-spoonful of saleratus, let it stand to dissolve, and then stir it into enough sour milk to make the flour into a soft dough. Knead it but very little, flour your hands, make it into small biscuits, and bake them in rather a hasty oven. In using saleratus or pearlash, for any kind of cake or bread, be sure to dissolve it in boiling water or sour milk, and make up the bread with sour milk; otherwise, it will not rise so well. Pearlash biscuit may be made in the same manner. (Bryan 1839, 304)

Although the content of baking powder can vary, it is often a mixture of sodium bicarbonate, an acid salt such as tartaric acid, and cornstarch to keep it dry and bulk it up. It is easier to use than baking soda. I discuss baking powder in more detail in the next chapter.

Mrs. Bryan's Ongoing Influence

In addition to being an important historical document, *The Kentucky Housewife* continues to have an influence on cuisine. Recipes from Mrs. Bryan's book are published on the Internet and in historically oriented southern cookbooks such as Damon Lee Fowler's *Classical Southern Cooking* (2008). Fowler's cookbook is an excellent source of iconic southern recipes and culinary scholarship and includes a number of recipes adapted from Lettice Bryan's book. Here is one of them.

Lettice Bryan's Fried Cabbage

1 small, fresh cabbage
2 tablespoons lard or unsalted butter
¼ cup water
Salt and whole black pepper in a peppermill

1. Pull off the tough, dark outer leaves of the cabbage and discard them or set aside for soup. Wash it under cold, running water and cut it in half lengthwise. Cut out the core and slice each quarter across into thin strips no more than a quarter of an inch wide.

2. Put the cabbage, fat, and water into a large, heavy lidded skillet and cover tightly. Turn on the heat to low. Cook slowly, stirring from time to time, until the cabbage is very tender, about ¾ to 1 hour. If it gets too dry, add a few spoonfuls of water, but no more than is necessary.

3. When the cabbage is very tender, remove the lid and raise the heat to medium high. Cook, stirring constantly, until all the moisture is evaporated and the cabbage is evenly golden, being careful not to let it scorch. Turn off the heat, season with salt and pepper, and serve warm. Serves 4. (Fowler 2008, 217)

Fowler's recipe adaptations are quite simple. He abandons Bryan's block format for the modern system of listing ingredients separately and in sequence, followed by a more detailed and systematic description of procedures. He also provides actual measures; for example, "enough lard or butter to season it well" (Bryan 1839, 192) becomes "2 tablespoons." The increase in heat is absent in the original, as is the warning about scorching.

The Social Context

The Kentucky Housewife is intended to be a cookbook for a supervisor of a large upper-class household with a kitchen staff, which often included enslaved persons. Slavery is not addressed directly in the book but is referred to in passing. In her brief discussion of management, Mrs. Bryan observes that households "have established rules for domestics and slaves to be governed by." She comments that an effective household manager should "fail not to give [the staff] such advice as is really necessary to promote their own welfare." She advises the household manager to "examine frequently your cupboard and other household furniture, kitchen, smokehouse, and cellar, to see that everything is in its proper place, and used in the right manner, that nothing be lost, or wasted by the neglect of hirelings or servants." She goes on: "Attend to the giving out of your meals, and proportion the seasonings to each dish yourself. This may be done at an early hour; and with the proper instructions to the cook, the lady may be relieved of further trouble during the day" (1839, vii).

Mrs. Bryan's upper-class audience is reflected in the large quantities yielded by the recipes and in some of the instructions she includes. For instance, she periodically concludes recipes with the phrase "send the dish to the table," which implies that the kitchen and its activities are separate from the dining room and that, in contrast to most readers' experiences, the cook did not necessarily eat the food. She also notes that some of the dishes are meant to be served at "fine suppers." For example, there is a recipe for a construction called a "jelly cone," based on gelatin and sponge cake. According to Mrs. Bryan, these "are only introduced at parties or fine suppers, and should be at least two on the table" (1839, 329). Yet Mrs. Bryan also displays a practical orientation against extravagance, which she reveals toward the end of her extensive introduction to baking cakes. "If these directions, together with what I will hereafter give in each receipt, be carefully followed and dexterously performed, you may safely calculate on having the best of cake, besides relieving yourself of the expense and inconvenience of hiring a cook expressly for the purpose" (ibid., 275).

Although expressed in a limited way, slavery was an important part of the social world of Mrs. Bryan's audience. Kentucky was a slave state even though it did not secede from the Union and become part of the Confederacy. In Kentucky there were both advocates of secession and a few abolitionists (e.g., Cassius M. Clay). Between these two extremes resided the majority of Kentuckians, who were both pro-slavery and pro-Union. Kentucky's brand of slavery was different from that which operated in the

Deep South; it resembled the pattern of slavery found in other border states such as Missouri. Kentucky slave owners believed they treated their slaves better than their counterparts in the Deep South did. Although some early scholarly writers accepted this view, contemporary historians reject it; nevertheless, it may linger in the public thinking. It is important to note that individual Kentucky slave-owning farmers held relatively few slaves. In almost all cases, they owned fewer than twenty slaves, the number used to define a plantation demographically. As a result, slave masters and their families worked more closely and were more familiar with the slaves they owned compared with slaveholders farther south. In addition, Kentucky farms were typically based on a mixed farming strategy rather than the Deep South's monocrop plantations based on cotton, sugar, or rice. This presumably gave the enslaved workers access to a wider variety of food. That said, the tobacco and hemp farming taking place in Kentucky, as well as the manufacture of hemp products such as rope, twine, and bags, was very labor intensive and made use of slave labor.

There was substantial variation in the percentage of enslaved peoples at the county level in Kentucky. The Bluegrass counties had higher slave populations relative to the state as a whole, with an average of 7 slaves per slaveholder in 1860. Woodford County had the highest percentage, with an average of 9.2 slaves per slaveholder and more than 52 percent of the county's total population enslaved, according to the 1860 census (Astor 2012, 22). In Boyle County, where Mrs. Bryan was born, the average was 6.5 slaves per owner.

In addition to fieldwork, many enslaved women and girls did housework as cooks, washerwomen, child care providers, and maids. No doubt they were active users (but probably not readers) of the information provided in *The Kentucky Housewife* and the other cookbooks and manuscript recipes available at the time. The involvement of these women in cooking and other kitchen work went beyond the households of their owners. A feature of Kentucky and other slaveholding border states was the hiring out of slaves, often to non-slave-owning households. In his study of slavery in Bourbon County (in the Bluegrass), Keith C. Barton (1997) found that more than 60 percent of such hiring out involved enslaved women performing domestic services as cooks, laundresses, and child care providers. African American cooks played an important role in the development of American foodways (Wallach 2013, 45).

With the Emancipation Proclamation of January 1863, President Abraham Lincoln freed enslaved people in the states in rebellion. But because Kentucky had not seceded, its slaves were not freed until ratification of the Thirteenth amendment in December 1865.[14] One of the effects of the Civil War and the associated political turmoil was African American migration to towns and cities both in and out of state. Those African Americans who remained on the farms became more difficult to control. The postwar period was chaotic, and the white slave-owning class lost its slave labor, which devastated its farming and manufacturing enterprises and reduced the value of its capital wealth. The enslaved women and men who worked in the kitchens of large farms also left, radically challenging the white women who made up the readership of *The Kentucky Housewife*. Interestingly, nostalgic vestiges of slavery continued to appear in some Kentucky cookbooks at least through the 1950s.

To close, cooking *The Kentucky Housewife* way was hard work. Much of the cooking was done just a little above floor level, so the cook had to bend over to tend to the cast-iron pots, which were heavy and tiresome to handle. Control of heat levels required special skills and knowledge, and it took a lot of fuel (firewood) to prepare meals. In sum, hearth cooking was dangerous, unhealthy drudgery. Woodstoves would be a significant improvement, and they quickly replaced hearth cooking where they were available and affordable.

Chapter Two

The Needs of the "New Regime"

Post–Civil War Cookbooks

In the introduction to *The Kentucky Housewife: A Collection of Recipes for Cooking*, Mrs. Peter A. White includes the intriguing but cryptic statement that her cookbook will help "home life in Kentucky under the new regime" (1885, 3).[1] Although she provides no explanation, I think the "new regime" refers to the dramatic changes occurring in the white, upper-class households of the region after the freeing of enslaved persons and other stresses caused by the Civil War. These households had fewer staff after the war. They lost not only the physical help but also the knowledge of the formerly enslaved women, gained over years of service. One result was an increase in the number of cookbooks published during this period. John Egerton, speaking of the South in general, expresses the situation clearly: "One of the most fascinating and ironic indicators of the pervasiveness of this social pattern was the spate of post–Civil War cookbooks aimed at white women who found themselves quite literally help-less after the Civil War" (1993, 16). Toni Tipton-Martin's words resonate with Egerton's, as she states in the introduction to a reprint of *The Blue Grass Cook Book*, "the nation was in the throes of an entirely restructured social order." She goes on: "Black servants fled the hard and thankless work in Southern households for better job opportunities in the promised land of the North" (Tipton-Martin 2005, xxv). More and more, upper-class housewives were on their own. Culturally, the community's store of culinary knowledge was diminished with the loss of African American staff who understood both recipes and cooking techniques. According to Tipton-Martin, "Cookbooks appeared in record numbers," and "most of them appealed in one way or another to the emotional needs of frustrated housewives who had lost their help mates" (ibid.). This may have increased the need and hence the market for cookbooks. As Bourbon County native Nannie Talbot Johnson wrote in the early pages of *What to Cook and How to Cook It*, "This is indeed a day of cookbooks" (1899, 3).

In addition to these important social changes, there were substantial improvements in cooking technology. At the heart of these innovations was the increased availability of mass-produced and affordable wood- or coal-fired cookstoves, which had an almost revolutionary impact on food preparation (see O'Neill 2004; Groft 2005; Brewer 2000). Hearth cooking became uncommon, and cookbooks like Mrs. Bryan's *The Kentucky Housewife* fell out of favor, replaced by those that focused on woodstove cooking (see Fowler 2008). There were also changes in the design of pots and pans and food storage equipment. Another important advance was the advent of branded packaged goods and their inclusion in cookbooks from this period.

The starting point of our discussion of this era is an important central Kentucky charity cookbook, *Housekeeping in the Blue Grass*, produced by the Ladies of the Presbyterian Church of Paris, Kentucky, and first published in 1875. There were numerous (at least five) editions of this book; it was apparently published as late as 1905 with the same title. It seems that recipes in the new editions were treated as addendums, rather than making pervasive changes in the text. This cookbook was compiled, published, and sold by the Missionary Society to benefit the church. The preface says, "It was suggested, after mature consideration of ways and means, that we might not only greatly increase our funds, but also contribute to the convenience and pleasure of housekeepers generally, by publishing a good receipt book" (Presbyterian Church 1875, v). Before discussing this cookbook and its contents, I examine the early history of American charity cookbooks.

The 1888 edition of *Housekeeping in the Blue Grass.*

"HOUSEKEEPING IN THE BLUE GRASS."

A NEW AND PRACTICAL

COOK BOOK:

CONTAINING

NEARLY A THOUSAND RECIPES,

Many of them new, and all of them tried and known to be valuable—such as have been used by the housekeepers of Kentucky and other States; together with many Miscellaneous Recipes, useful in families, etc.

FIRST EDITION OF ONE THOUSAND SOLD IN LESS THAN THREE WEEKS AFTER ISSUE.

SECOND EDITION NOW READY.

WHAT THE PRESS SAYS OF IT.

This is one of the best and fullest books of recipes for cooking and other household purposes we have ever seen.—*Earnest Worker.*

It is a work of uncommon merit. The contributors are ladies of the highest social character, and what they have contributed can be relied upon with implicit confidence. This book will now be the standard for good eating, not only in Kentucky, but all over the West and South.—*Lexington (Ky.) Gazette.*

The Kentucky matron is the model housewife of the nation. No housekeeper in the land should be without this book.—*Kansas City Times.*

The work is worth double the price asked for it, to any housekeeper, and is far ahead of anything of the kind we have ever seen.—*Mt. Sterling Sentinel.*

Its recipes are practical; they have been tried by some of the best housekeepers in Virginia and Kentucky. They are adapted to southern articles of food and suited to southern tastes.—*Christian Observer.*

The book is pretty enough for the parlor table, and so useful that no one with a kitchen should be without it. We are sure it will take position as a standard work of its class.—*Louisville Commercial.*

It is the best—the very best recipe book we have yet seen.—*Carlisle Mercury.*

Beautifully bound in cloth, tinted paper, gilt side title, and interleaved with writing paper,

RETAIL PRICE. $1.50.

Liberal discount made to Missionary Societies, Agents and Booksellers. Sent by mail, post paid, on receipt of price.

All orders addressed to

MRS. N. T. MARTIN,
PARIS, KY.

Flyer advertising the second edition of *Housekeeping in the Blue Grass.*

Charity Cookbooks

The production of fund-raising cookbooks by "women's charitable organizations" began toward the end of the Civil War and accelerated dramatically in its aftermath (Longone 1997, 18). This occurred in both the North and the South. Initially these compilation projects were undertaken to raise money for veterans, widows, orphans, and other victims of the war. Margaret Cook's bibliography of charitable cookbooks (1971) cites her view that *A Poetical Cookbook* by Maria J. Moss, published in 1864 in support of a "sanitary fair" in Philadelphia, was the first of its kind.[2] By the mid-twentieth century there was a virtual flood of charity cookbooks, made possible by the marketing efforts of printing firms that had these books at the heart of their business plans. This trend continues to the present. Although it is not clear how many different cookbooks the women of the First Presbyterian Church of Paris produced between 1875 and today, their most recent, *Feeding the Flock*, was published in 2009 and pays homage to the original by reprinting its preface. As must be true of most regions in America, the fund-raising or charity cookbook is easily the most common type of cookbook published in Kentucky. Unfortunately, only a limited number of charity cookbooks can be found in libraries.

Charity cookbooks generally consist of recipes contributed from members of the community. For instance, the majority of recipes in *Housekeeping in the Blue Grass* are from Paris or Bourbon County (Paris is the county seat). Most of the rest of the contributors are from nearby communities in central Kentucky, and a handful come from other adjacent states. I list seven charity cookbooks published before 1900 in the bibliography—all of them church produced in Paris, Maysville, Louisville, Bowling Green, or Owensboro. The denominational breadth is quite narrow, being limited to mainline Protestant churches: Presbyterian, Methodist, Christian, and Baptist. The first cookbook from a Pentecostal Protestant church was produced more than ninety years later.

Because cookbooks of this type are group efforts, one could call them committee cookbooks. As a result, they tend to lack a clear culinary voice—for example, the formatting of recipes can vary. Charity cookbooks produced by the Junior League and similar efforts that appeared later in the twentieth century are exceptions, as they are produced with considerable editorial discipline.

Although they make interesting reading, these early charity cookbooks would require considerable adaptation if a twenty-first-century cook wanted to use the recipes. They tend to have very limited descriptions of procedures, with no specific times and temperatures. In a few cases I have found recipes consisting only of the word *take* and an ingredients list. *Take* is the right term. *Recipe* is derived from the imperative form of the Latin verb "to take." *Receipt*, which is used interchangeably with *recipe* in early cookbooks, has the same meaning, but the etymology is Greek. Both terms were originally used for medical concoctions and were abbreviated *Rx*. The simple instruction "take" makes it quite clear that the users of these cookbooks had lots of skills and knew how to apply them, making detailed discussions of procedures superfluous. Illustrating this common assumption is a charming quote from Bettie Sue Broaddus, who contributed her mother's recipe for hickory nut cake to *Recipes Old and New: A Community Cookbook*, published by the Estill County Historical and Genealogical Society in 2004. She writes, "Mama gave me no directions for mixing. She said, you know how to make a cake!" Nevertheless, Broaddus adds some instructions for the less experienced cook: "Just in case you are a beginner: Cream butter and sugar together. Add eggs, one at a time, mixing well after each one. Sift flour and baking powder together . . . " (Estill County 2004, 81).

Others have made their own observations about the lack of instructions. In referring to a late-seventeenth-century English cookbook, irrepressible food writer M. F. K. Fisher points out that much technique is taken for granted in cookbooks: "In mixing the cake, the mace and nutmegs which have been prescribed are not mentioned again. Any idiot knows that they could be sifted along with the flour, and that of course they would be grated or powdered . . . but as a spoiled idiot-child of the twentieth century I want to be told" (1968, 6).

Following is an example of a "no instructions" recipe from *Housekeeping in the Blue Grass*. Only a few of its recipes are this simple.

White Sponge Cake (1875)

> Ten eggs (whites only), one and a half tumblers of sugar, one tumbler (heaping) of flour, one teaspoonful cream of tartar, one teaspoonful essence of lemon. (Presbyterian Church 1875, 97)

A more typical and complex recipe is the one for Woodford pudding, which most assume is named for Woodford County, Kentucky. Recipes for Woodford pudding appear in other cookbooks more or less up to the present, and it is featured in John Egerton's seminal *Southern Food* (1993). It is a jam-flavored baked pudding that is almost like a cake and is served with a sauce. Butterscotch and vanilla are popular flavors, and both the pudding itself and the sauce can be spiced up with bourbon. The following recipe, contributed by Mrs. Amos Turney Jr., is typical of the era, with its obsolete measure of teacups and no precise temperature or cooking time cited.

Woodford Pudding (1875)

> Three eggs, one tea-cupful of sugar, one half tea-cupful of butter, one half tea-cupful of flour, one tea-cupful of jam or preserves, one teaspoonful of soda dissolved in three teaspoonfuls of sour milk. Cinnamon and nutmeg to taste. Mix all well together and bake slowly in a pudding pan. Serve with sauce. (Presbyterian Church 1875, 87)

The recipes in *Housekeeping in the Blue Grass* and other cookbooks of this era are sometimes vague about cooking times, most likely attributable to the variability of heat in woodstoves and assumptions about the cook's knowledge. That said, a few recipes gear their instructions to the daily flow of work. Mrs. Morris Gass advises that one should put "a little flour" in her recipe for salt-rising bread at "about 11 o'clock" (Presbyterian Church 1875, 53). In a recipe for Sally Lunn, Mrs. J. Payne adjusts the timing of mixing the dough—combining flour, butter, eggs, salt, milk, and "good yeast"—based on the season: "Make it up about nine o'clock in the morning in winter, and eleven o'clock in summer; work it over about four o'clock, and make it in a round shape into pans and bake for seven o'clock tea" (ibid., 57).

In addition to *Housekeeping in the Blue Grass*, a number of other cookbooks were produced by groups of women as church fund-raisers. *The New Kentucky Home Cook Book*, published by the women's group of the Methodist Episcopal Church South of Maysville, Kentucky, in 1884, was intended to help finance the construction of a parsonage. A somewhat expanded edition was published in 1885. Egerton comments, "This is a surprisingly broad and elegant assortment of culinary creations" (1993, 360). The following recipe for deviled eggs was contributed by Mrs. Robert Ficklin.

Deviled Eggs (1884)

> Take one dozen hard-boiled eggs; when cold, remove the shell, and cut lengthwise; take out the yelks,[3] and mash them well, with two tablespoons of butter, salt and pepper to taste, one heaping teaspoonful of mustard, and one level teaspoon of celery seed; moisten well with vinegar; replace the yelks, and press the two halves together. Place them in a dish, thin the rest of the yelks with more vinegar, and pour over the eggs. Grated cheese may be added to the filling, if desired. (Methodist Episcopal Church 1884, 184)

The Louisville Cookbook, Containing over Five Hundred Receipts, Some of Them Original, Many New, and All Thoroughly Tested, compiled by the First Christian Church Young Ladies' Missionary Society of Louisville, uses the block or narrative format. It includes a recipe for Saratoga potatoes—the prototype for today's potato chips. The recipe was submitted by Mrs. R. H. Wilson.

Saratoga Potatoes (1890)

> Peel and slice very thin six large Irish potatoes. Let stand in salt water ten hours or over one night; dry on towel. Have beef suet hot in deep vessel, suet not less than 2 inches deep. When smoking hot, drop in

> about one-half of potatoes at one time. Fry very quickly; take out when light brown on a dish and sprinkle with salt while hot, when cool they will be dry. (First Christian Church 1890, 52–53)

Celebrity Cookbooks

The late nineteenth century gave rise to the first celebrity cookbooks. *Mrs. John G. Carlisle's Kentucky Cook Book*, published in 1893, is the first cookbook listed in the bibliography to include the author's name in the title. The question is, who is Mrs. John G. Carlisle? As I learned, she was the wife of a well-known politician from Kentucky. John G. Carlisle, a Democrat, was Speaker of the House of Representatives from 1883 to 1889 and then served as secretary of the treasury in the cabinet of his political ally President Grover Cleveland. An elementary school in Covington is named for him. Mrs. Carlisle's compilation contains a few signed recipes, including one from Mrs. Grover Cleveland. The recipes use a mix of old and new measurements. Most are presented in a narrative format, but some consist of only lists of ingredients. Just one branded product, Cox's gelatin, is mentioned, along with a few canned ingredients, including French peas, mushrooms, and pineapple. Mrs. Carlisle's cookbook contains a number of baked and boiled pudding recipes, including the following.

Poor Man's Pudding (1893)

> One teacupful of shredded suet rubbed thoroughly into four cups of flour, two cups of New Orleans molasses, one cup of milk, into which put a teaspoonful of soda dissolved in hot water; one pound of currants washed and dried; one pound of raisins, stoned and chopped, one nutmeg, one large tablespoon of cinnamon. Put into a well floured pudding bag and boil for three hours. The water must be kept boiling hard or the pudding will be heavy. (Carlisle 1893, 121)

An interesting western Kentucky cookbook from this period is Mary Rochester Coombs's *Kentucky Cook Book*. It was published in 1894 by a Bowling Green printer, C. M. Coombs, probably her husband. The recipes have "been gathered up by myself, not from doubtful sources, but from those of my friends who have had long experience in household duties" (Coombs 1894, i). Mrs. Coombs uses both the older block format and the more modern practice of providing a list of ingredients separate from the instructions. A number of the recipes are signed, usually without comment. In some cases, Mrs. Coombs mentions the location of the recipe contributor. For example, a potato soup recipe is signed by Mrs. Gillette, from a cooking class held in Louisville, and a recipe for gumbo soup is signed by Mrs. Frank Williams of New Orleans. One recipe is attributed to Miss Parloa; this is presumably the noted cookbook author Maria Parloa, whose *Miss Parloa's New Cookbook and Marketing Guide* was first published in 1880. Most intriguing are the recipes for Kentucky corn dodgers and crackling bread signed by Mammy Charlotte, who, I believe, was an African American cook. If so, they could be the first published recipes attributed to an African American in a Kentucky cookbook. I don't mean to slight Mrs. Coombs's recipes, but I have included Mammy Charlotte's recipe for corn dodgers here.

Kentucky Corn Dodgers (1894)

> Make up one pint of meal, with one teaspoon of salt, a piece of lard the size of an egg, mix with warm water and sweet milk, (don't make too thin as you cannot handle to make nice smooth pones) work the mixture well, with your hand until perfectly smooth, then make into pones, put on a hot baker that is well greased, cook in a hot oven, put on top shelf and let brown first, (as it prevents cracking) then place at the bottom and finish cooking. (Coombs 1894, 88)

The unsigned recipe for pumpkin bread following this one simply instructs the cook to add a teacup of stewed pumpkin to the corn dodger recipe.

Single-Author Cookbooks

Mrs. Peter A. White's *The Kentucky Housewife: A Collection of Recipes for Cooking*, mentioned earlier in this chapter, is the first single-author cook-

Mrs. Peter A. White's *The Kentucky Housewife*.

book from this era included here. There are others. Although Mrs. White's book was published in Chicago, she was apparently raised in Lexington and wrote the book while a resident of Cincinnati.[4] Unlike the charity cookbooks of the era, Mrs. White's comprehensive volume demonstrates her sole authorship with its a uniform editorial voice. She presents the recipes in the modern format, starting with a list of ingredients. *Mrs. Lincoln's Boston Cook Book* had first utilized that innovation the preceding year. Careful measurement is an important feature of the cookbook. Mrs. White's introduction states: "Having always regarded a cookery book as a book for the kitchen, I have, in order to carry out my idea, not only been explicit in giving proportions, but have endeavored to express myself so simply that any cook who can read can take this book and be her own teacher" (1885, 8). The theme of "exact proportions" was featured in the advertising copy used by the publisher. That said, Mrs. White uses a diverse set of measures, mixing the modern and the obsolete. For example, on one page she uses the dessert spoon, cooking spoon, and salt spoon, as well as the familiar teaspoon. The book has an unusual publication history. The title was changed to *The Kentucky Cookery Book: A Book for Housewives* in 1891. It was apparently republished in 1903 as *The Blue Grass Cook Book*, with Genevieve Long listed as the author.

Most of Mrs. White's quick bread recipes include baking powder, but some make use of soda and cream of tartar or sour milk. These ingredients are usually accompanied by the admonition to "bake immediately." Actual cooking times are sometimes included. For example, she gives the following cooking times for vegetables, which seem very long by today's standards: "Peas and asparagus should be cooked one hour; beans, three hours; beets, two hours; turnips, two hours; potatoes, half an hour; cauliflower should be wrapped in a cloth and boiled two hours, and served with drawn butter" (White 1885, 59). Mrs. White's recipe for okra soup uses a time-of-day cooking format.

Okra Soup (1885)

One chicken, or a small knuckle of veal,
Two quarts of clear water,

Six large tomatoes,
Four large onions,
One quart of okra,
One bunch of parsley
Salt and cayenne pepper to the taste,
One teaspoonful of summer savory,
Half a teaspoonful of powdered allspice.

Put on the chicken, or veal, in the water and let it boil up twice, skimming carefully until all of the grease is taken off; add the tomatoes, parsley, onions, summer savory, allspice, cayenne pepper and salt. Put this on at breakfast time; at 12 o'clock, put in a separate saucepan the quart of okra, cut up in thin slices. Boil for an hour, or until perfectly tender. Half an hour before dinner strain the soup and add the okra. This is for a 2 o'clock dinner; if for a later dinner put on the meat and vegetables at 1 o'clock and the okra at 5 o'clock. (White 1885, 58)

Product Placement

In cookbooks of this era we find the earliest mention of branded commercial products. For the most part, these consist of basic ingredients such as flavorings, leavens, and gelatin rather than true convenience foods. *Housekeeping in the Blue Grass* (1875) specifically mentions and endorses Cox gelatin, stating unequivocally that "Cox is best." Also mentioned (and, by implication, endorsed) are Baker's chocolate, Burrows' ground mustard, Coleman's mustard, Maillard's vanilla chocolate, and Twin Brother's yeast. Mrs. White mentions Cox's gelatin, Fleischman's yeast, and Coleman's English mustard.

Packaging and the branding associated with it laid the foundation for advertising. The 1875 edition of *Housekeeping in the Blue Grass* includes more than thirty advertisements, some of which are for grocery stores. One advertisement for Dr. Price's cream baking powder assures readers that Dr. Price's product is "strictly pure" and that "it is not sold in bulk; buy it only in tin cans, securely labeled" (Presbyterian Church 1875, ii). Consumers seemed to fear that bulk ingredients could be easily adulterated or spoiled in other ways, so advertisements of this era often emphasized food purity and a clean production process.

In her history of American cookbooks, Carol Fisher (2006, 46) cites *Miss Parloa's New Cookbook and Marketing Guide* (1880) as one of the first cookbooks to endorse products, although *Housekeeping in the Blue Grass* was published a few years earlier. Maria Parloa (who contributed a recipe to Mrs. Coombs's cookbook) preceded Fannie Farmer as the principal of the famous Boston Cooking School, which actively engaged in product placement.

Cox's gelatin was an early convenience food. It was originally imported from England but was ultimately manufactured in the United States as well. Although contemporary food writers tend to disparage processed food (and rightly so), the 1875 edition of *Housekeeping in the Blue Grass* contains a recipe for making jelly out of calves' feet that clearly shows why cooks welcomed the availability of commercially produced gelatin (*The Kentucky Housewife* [Bryan 1839] has similar recipes).

Calves' Foot Jelly (1875)

> Split four feet and put the whole into a stewpan; pour one gallon of cold water over; boil till reduced to about one half then strain through a sieve, to remove the bones. When settled and cold, take off the grease from the surface and boil again with the following mixture; six eggs, whipped in a little water, two pounds of sugar, and the juice of four lemons; stir all well, removing the scum as it rises. When thoroughly skimmed, set by the fire and pour one pint of Madeira, or any other wine or liquor into it; filter through a flannel bag. (Presbyterian Church 1875, 125)

Calves' feet are also used to make the jellies included on a festive menu originally created by Fannie Farmer and described by Chris Kimball in *Fannie's Last Super* (2010). In the late nineteenth century, molded jellies were often served as desserts, and well-equipped kitchens had many decorative molds. The availability of gelatin converted an extraordinarily complex, messy, multistage task into a simple matter of ripping open a cardboard box (think Jell-O, which was widely available by 1904), pouring the contents into a pot of hot water, and stirring.

A few recipes in *Housekeeping in the Blue Grass* call for isinglass, another thickening agent that was used like gelatin. Isinglass is a powder prepared from the dried swim bladders of fish—originally sturgeon, but later cod, because it was much cheaper. (By the way, isinglass is still used to clarify beer.) *The Kentucky Housewife* also included some recipes made with isinglass. In fact, Mrs. Bryan made a big pitch for the superiority of Russian isinglass over the American variety. *Housekeeping in the Blue Grass* also includes a recipe or two that calls for Irish moss, which is derived from algae that is also the source of the thickener carrageenan. Carrageenan is still used in foods today; check the ingredients lists on various contemporary products, and sooner or later you will find carrageenan, but I have never seen isinglass listed. All the *Housekeeping in the Blue Grass* recipes that use these thickeners (calves' foot jelly, manufactured gelatin, isinglass, and Irish moss) are sweet dishes.

Developments in Cookstoves

As stated earlier, cooking was typically done on a woodstove. Wood-fired cookstoves constructed of brick, with iron cooktops, were first developed in the 1730s. Improvements in these early patterns were achieved by an American-born physicist, Benjamin Thompson (aka Count Rumford). His work in the 1790s led to more fuel-efficient fireplaces and ovens. Cast-iron cookstoves became available by around 1830, although they were smaller than later versions. Wood-burning cast-iron cookstoves became more common after the Civil War and reached a high point in their development in the 1890s. By that time, gas cookstoves and a supply infrastructure were becoming available.

The big advantage was that wood- and coal-fired cookstoves used fuel far more efficiently than fireplaces (Brewer 1990, 35). Cookstoves also reduced the workload by raising the cooking pots off the hearth's floor, making it much easier to move them from one source of heat to another. In addition, the fires of stoves required much less tending than fireplaces

A small woodstove at the McCreary County Museum in Sturges, 2013. (John van Willigen)

did. As a result, *Housekeeping in the Blue Grass* and the other cookbooks from this period contain fewer direct references to issues related to cooking fires compared with Mrs. Bryan's hearth-focused cookbook.

In this era there were hundreds of stove foundries in the United States, including in Kentucky. Some of the nineteenth-century Kentucky stove manufacturers were Baxter, Kyle and Fisher, Bridgeford, J. S. Lithgow, O. K. Stove, Progress, and Scanlon, all of Louisville; Bogenschutz in Covington; and Gladiator Stove in Russell in Greenup County. All the Kentucky stove manufacturers were located on the Ohio River. Woodstoves of this era were made of heavy cast iron, which increased transportation costs, so proximity to the river was an important consideration.[5]

Cast-iron stoves were often embellished with porcelain enameled surfaces, nickel trim, and other elaborate decorative elements. The heart of the woodstove was the firebox, which was usually situated at one side of the stove, with a door through which the fire could be stoked. Because the fire needed an adequate draft, there were adjustable vents to control the airflow into the firebox and a damper in the flue to control the heat and gases going up the chimney (the stove was connected to the chimney flue with a sheet-metal pipe). If the fire did not draw properly, the wood might smolder, and smoke could back up into the kitchen. If the stove drew too well, it would consume fuel too quickly and overheat.

Coal- and wood-burning stoves were superficially the same, but there were some differences. For one thing, wood could be burned in coal stoves, but coal could not be used in woodstoves. In coal stoves the firebox contained a grate on which the burning fuel rested. Typically, coal stoves came with a cast-iron handle that could be attached to this grate and used to shake the ashes into an ash box below. The ash box could be removed when it was full and dumped. Those that used coal would sift the ashes to recover unburned fuel. If woodstoves came with shaker grates, they were of a different design than those used in coal stoves.

The heat from the firebox was available for both the oven and the stove top. The stove top was flat and had two to eight removable round caps, usually eight inches in diameter. The caps were supported by a frame that could be lifted out, and each cap had a recess in which a cap lift-er could be inserted. Although these caps might have resembled burners, they did not work that way. The entire surface of the stove top was hot, although the heat level varied with the distance from the firebox. A skilled cook knew how to reduce the heat by moving a pot away from the firebox. The recipe for "Clear Beef Soup" in *Housekeeping in the Blue Grass* addresses this situation: "After it has been well skimmed, set the pot on the back of the stove and let it boil gently six hours" (Presbyterian Church 1875, 2–3). This reminds one of putting something "on the back burner."

Various options could be purchased with a basic stove. Many woodstoves were equipped with hot water reservoirs and places to keep food warm. The optional hot water reservoir was often located adjacent to the oven, on the side opposite the firebox. It was typical for stoves to have metal shelves or cabinets above the stove top at eye level. There might also be cabinets underneath the oven, used to store pots and pans.

A typical morning ritual was to start the fire with a corncob soaked with coal oil (Slade 2004, 3) under a crisscross of kindling topped by the fuelwood itself. The men and boys of the household had the task of keeping the wood box full, which involved chopping wood into pieces of various sizes (including kindling), as well as harvesting the wood in the first place. Farms might have woodlots specifically for this purpose. This required axes, saws, chopping blocks, and other tools.

During the winter, the stove provided a welcome source of heat. In rural settings, it was common to care for lambs, typically born in the early spring, by the heat of the stove. Some cooks would hang green beans to dry on the wall in back of the stove. In summer, it was common practice to fire up the stove for breakfast in the relative cool of the morning, cook dinner early, and then let the fire die out. Supper would consist of leftovers from dinner. During canning season and on wash days, this was not an option, and kitchens could get very hot.

Cast-iron wood-burning stoves required a lot of maintenance (U.S. Department of Agriculture 1915, 44). Ashes had to be emptied daily and disposed of. Because the stove was made of assembled parts, they had to be sealed periodically with special fireproof material; in addition, the vent pipe, heat passages, and chimney had to be cleaned of soot and creosote from time to time to preserve efficiency and prevent fires. This was often a springtime task for the man of the house. The black stoves required the application of a graphite or carbon black–based polish to prevent rusting.

Woodstoves could be dangerous. While in use, they presented a burn risk to those in the confined space of the kitchen. Because the surface got extremely hot, children had to be watched constantly. The stove had to be placed carefully to avoid burning the floor and walls of the home. The ashes produced also presented a fire risk. Finally, a stove could expose the occupants of the house to carbon monoxide if there were leaks in the stove, flue, or chimney.

The heat available for cooking varied, based on the amount and variety of wood used, when the fueling occurred, the setting of the dampers, and a pot's distance from the stove's firebox. There was a lever that shunted heat to the oven for baking. In contrast to gas and electric stoves, there was no thermostat to control the oven temperature, although some woodstoves had a thermometer on the oven door. The problem of maintaining an even temperature in a wood-fired oven is illustrated by the following warning in the cake section of *Housekeeping in the Blue Grass*: "Never allow the heat to diminish while cake is baking or it will fall." It also advises, "In baking cakes it is a good plan to fill a large pan with cold water and set it on the upper grate of the stove, to prevent them from burning or cooking too fast on top. Let it remain until the cakes are baked" (Presbyterian Church 1875, 96).

As mentioned in the preceding chapter, the transition from fireplaces to wood-burning (and gas and electric) stoves changed the practice of roasting meat. Originally, the meat was placed in front of the heat source, outside an oven, creating a dry cooking environment. With the woodstove, roasting involved cooking the meat in an enclosed space. Although the term *roasting* was still used, this was actually baking; nevertheless, people continued to refer to roasted chicken, pork, and beef (but, interestingly, baked ham). Baking created a moister atmosphere because, as the meat's internal temperature rose, the moisture in the meat was released in the oven as steam. The drippings often spattered inside the oven, causing smoke that flavored the meat. Cooks attempted to enhance this process by starting with a high initial temperature to sear the meat and using prepared browning agents, such as Kitchen Bouquet, to brown the drippings and improve the flavor of the gravy. Kitchen Bouquet (currently manufactured by the Clorox Corporation) was first sold in 1880. Worcestershire sauce may have been used in the same way.

Today, some people still use wood-fired cookstoves for various reasons, including a desire to be self-reliant and live "off the grid." There are firms that renovate and resell vintage woodstoves of various kinds. Wood-burning cast-iron cookstoves are still being manufactured in the twenty-first century; one of the oldest and largest cast-iron stove manufacturers is the United States Stove Company in South Pittsburgh, Tennessee. These firms make a variety of models—from very modern-looking woodstoves to those that resemble vintage stoves. In addition, some gas and electric stoves are manufactured to look like late-nineteenth-century woodstoves. There are also firms that convert old-time woodstoves to gas or electric for those who want to combine modern convenience with old-fashioned country charm.

This era brought considerable change in cooking technology, but it is important to keep in mind that the transition from fireplace to wood- or coal-burning stove was quite gradual and occurred at different times in different places. And although they are not mentioned in the Kentucky cookbooks of the late nineteenth century, gas and kerosene stoves were already available.

Chapter Three

A Turning Point

The Early Twentieth Century

This chapter focuses on two Kentucky cookbooks published in 1904: *The Blue Grass Cook Book* by Minnie C. Fox and *The Blue Ribbon Cook Book* by Jennie C. Benedict.[1] In many ways, Fox's book reflects a nostalgic culinary past, while Benedict's book looks toward the future. Both are important in terms of understanding the changing needs of households in this era, and both were written by a single author with her personal goals in mind. The contrast between the Fox and Benedict cookbooks reveals the influence of the emerging domestic science movement and the increased entrepreneurship of women. Following an examination of these two cookbooks, a number of committee-produced charity cookbooks and single-author cookbooks, including the earliest Kentucky cookbooks written by African Americans, are discussed.

Minnie Fox's *The Blue Grass Cook Book* is closely related to the earlier charity cookbook *Housekeeping in the Blue Grass.* It includes an introduction by her famous brother, journalist and novelist John Fox Jr. Two of his best-known novels are *The Little Shepherd of Kingdom Come* (1903) and *Trail of the Lonesome Pine* (1908). Both these regional novels were on *the New York Times* best-seller list. Another of Minnie's brothers, Rector Fox, had established the book's publisher, Fox, Duffield Publishing in New York, only the year before. The book is enhanced by photographs taken by Alvin Langdon Coburn, depicting African American cooks and other household staff at two Bourbon County estates: Auvergne and Mount

One of the Alvin Langdon Coburn photographs that shaped the interpretation of Minnie Fox's *The Blue Grass Cook Book*. (University Press of Kentucky)

Airy.[2] Minnie Fox lived a few miles away from Auvergne and was a good friend of the Clay family that owned the estate. Coburn, who was a well-known photographer of celebrities (his subjects included George Bernard Shaw, William Butler Yeats, Mark Twain, and Henry James), may have been a friend of John Fox Jr. His photographs were published in *The Blue Grass Cook Book* only a few years after his return from Paris, France, where he received his initial training in photography. Coburn was associated with two other famous photographers—Alfred Stieglitz and Edward Steichen. Although he destroyed much of his work toward the end of his life, there are collections of his prints at the University of Texas, the Metropolitan Museum of Art, and the National Gallery of Art. After World War I Coburn became a British subject and lived in Wales. The U.S. Postal Service honored Coburn by issuing a stamp based on one of his photos as part of a series commemorating important American photographers. Coburn's photographs figured prominently in the social interpretation of Fox's cookbook.

The relationship of Fox's cookbook to *Housekeeping in the Blue Grass* goes beyond their shared Paris, Kentucky, roots. The link is evident in the recipes. A few of the same contributors and their recipes are found in both books, although the recipes are presented somewhat differently. The Mrs. W. A. Johnson of Paris, Kentucky, who contributed a recipe to the Fox volume is likely Nannie Talbot Johnson, who published an important cookbook of her own in this era, *What to Cook and How to Cook It* (discussed later in this chapter). Both *Housekeeping in the Blue Grass* and *The Blue Grass Cook Book* reflect an upper-class, white sensibility. As Toni Tipton-Martin writes in the introduction to the reprint of the latter, "The book seems broadly representative of the culinary experiences of well-to-do white people in Kentucky a century ago" (2005, vii).

In these households much of the cooking was done by African Americans. Fox's cookbook makes their contribution to the development of cooking in Kentucky clearer than do other volumes published in this and later eras. This is accomplished by Coburn's photographs of African American cooks and references in the titles of a few recipes. For instance, the name Marcellus, an African American staff member at Auvergne, is mentioned in the title of six recipes, and his photograph is included. His recipe for potato soup is included here. Notice that it follows the so-called standard pattern of listing the ingredients first.

Marcellus's Potato Soup (1904)

> 3 large-sized potatoes,
> Butter,
> 1 cup of cream,
> Salt and pepper to taste.
>
> Cut the potatoes up in fine pieces and boil 2 hours in 2 quarts of water. Add seasoning and piece of butter size of an egg and 1 cup of cream. Serve hot. (Fox [1904] 2005, 41)

Tipton-Martin's introductory essay provides an interesting perspective on early Kentucky cookbooks in general as well as the specific circumstances of the Fox cookbook. Fox's book represents an attempt, albeit cautious, to acknowledge the contributions of African Americans to Kentucky foodways. This relationship is explored in much of Tipton-Martin's writing, where she points out that the role of African American cooks, who were often enslaved or indentured, was hidden and uncelebrated and that much of their culinary creativity and inventiveness was appropriated by white women. Under what Tipton-Martin calls the "Jemima code," the understanding was that these African American women were merely the providers of kitchen labor, not the active creators of a regional cuisine. As Tipton-Martin states, "The written word has been cruel to African American cooks, and that truth alone makes the unearthing and reproduction of *The Blue Grass Cook Book* a cause for celebration . . . it is a salutary redress to the African American descendants of generations of invisible cooks" (2005, v).

In contrast to Tipton-Martin's recognition of the cultural confiscation of African American cooks' culinary creativity, cookbook historian Anne Mendelson takes a more typical and far less nuanced view when she writes dismissively, "The nostalgia for survival of the slave-owning South is gratified in Minnie C. Fox's *Blue Grass Cookbook*" (1996, 115). Food historian Karen Hess generalizes the concern to southern cookbooks: "I should note that most of the recipes in all Southern cookbooks are, in fact, largely recipes gleaned by the writers from African American cooks, their own and others" (1995, 90). These assessments aside, Fox's cookbook begins to recognize the importance of African American cooks in the development of the region's cuisine (Tipton-Martin 2005, xix).

The Original Aunt Jemima

The original and ultimately iconic Aunt Jemima was born Nancy Green in Montgomery County, Kentucky. She was working as a maid when she was hired by a Missouri businessman to make pancakes using a mix he had developed for a display at the 1893 World's Columbian Exposition in Chicago. She subsequently became the advertising spokesperson for the pancake mix and related products, and as the stereotypical African American mammy, she was an instantly recognizable icon. She worked in this role until she was struck dead by an automobile in 1923.

The recipes in *The Blue Grass Cook Book* are presented with limited precision and instructions and a mixture of old English and standard American measurements. The formatting, as noted earlier, is somewhat more modern, in that some of the recipes start with a separate list of ingredients, followed by the instructions. Variation in the format is related to the book's hybrid nature—a combination of the individually authored and the community contributed. Included here is a recipe for poultry croquettes, a dish that was far more common in earlier cookbooks.

Very Fine Croquettes (1904)

1 pound of cooked turkey or chicken,
3 teaspoons of chopped parsley,
1 pint of cream,
1 large onion,
¼ pound of butter,

¼ pound of bread-crumbs,
Salt, pepper, and cayenne pepper to taste.

> Sprinkle the parsley over the meat and run through grinder twice. Boil the onion with the cream and strain onion out, and when cool pour cream over bread-crumbs, add the butter, and make a stiff mixture, then add salt, etc. Beat in the meat and mix all together.
>
> If too stiff, add a little cream and make as soft as can be handled. Put on ice to get stiff. Then roll and shape. Dip in egg, and roll in bread-crumbs, and fry in hot lard. (Fox 1904, 80)

To commemorate the republication of *The Blue Grass Cook Book*, the Southern Foodways Alliance held a luncheon during its 2008 field trip to Louisville. The menu included dishes inspired by recipes in the book and prepared under the direction of Todd Richards, then the executive chef at the Seelbach Hotel. Dishes included Bluegrass pea soup, green tomato pickle, smoked bacon and cheddar spoon bread, string beans, almond mandalines, brandied peaches, and Xalapa punch. In most cases, the recipes were modified somewhat from the original. For instance, the recipe for brandied peaches contributed by Mrs. John W. Fox (Minnie's mother) was turned into a salsa.

Brandied Peaches (1904)

> Pour hot boiling water over white clingstone peaches and rub the peeling off. Make a rich syrup of half a pound of sugar to a pound of fruit. Add water to sugar, and when the syrup boils up, drop the peaches in and let them cook till the fruit can be pierced with a straw. Remove the peaches and put in a jar. Let the syrup boil till very thick, and while warm add an equal part of brandy and pour over the fruit. Seal in glass jars. Ready for use at any time. (Fox 1904, 293–94)

In contrast to Fox's book, *The Blue Ribbon Cook Book* by Jennie C. Benedict makes the transition to a more modern presentation. Writing the book was

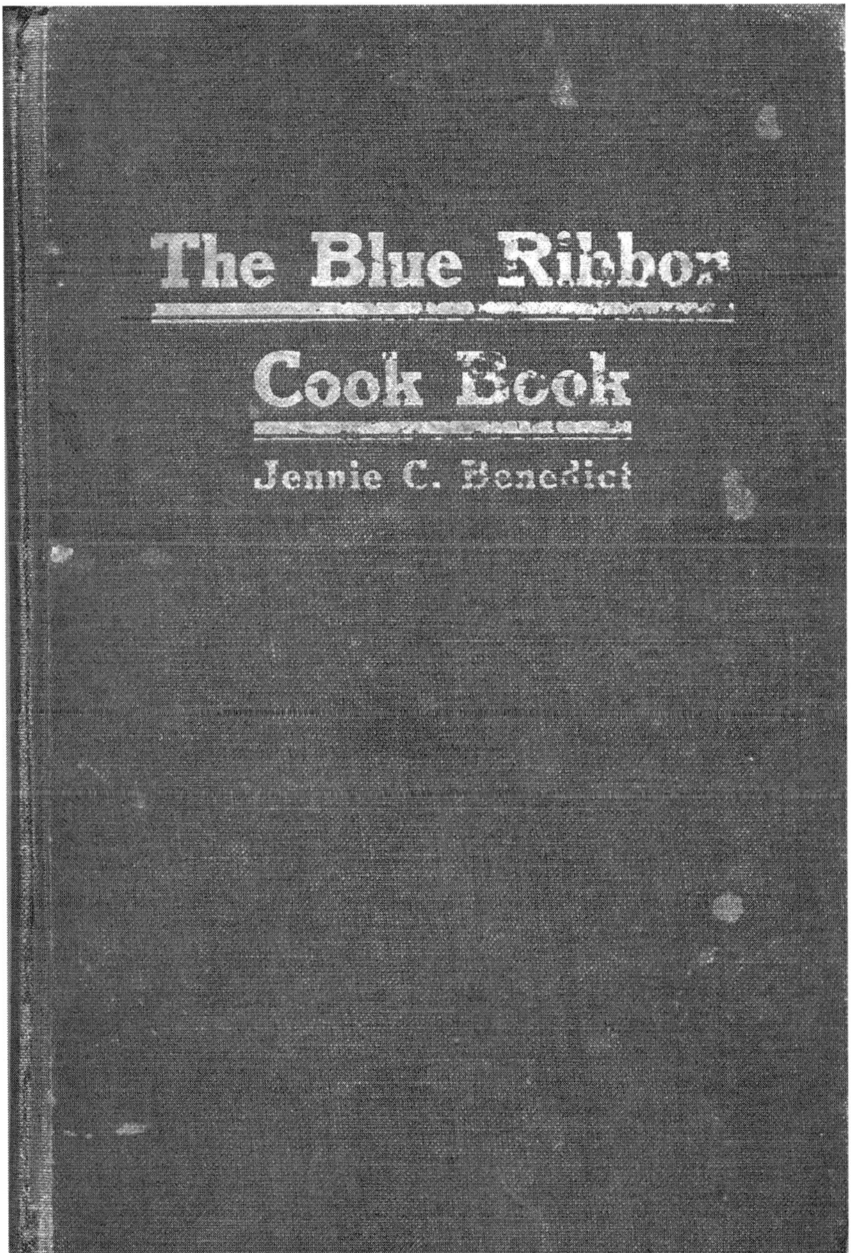

The 1904 edition of *The Blue Ribbon Cook Book*.

part of Benedict's robust entrepreneurial strategy, and she was influenced by the domestic science movement, which can be seen as a metaphor for the transformation of gender expectations and women's increased freedom from the constraints of the traditional patriarchal domestic sphere. These changes were national in scope, and Benedict's work, as well as other Kentucky cookbooks, was just one a manifestation of them. The cookbooks were an important part of the food-based entrepreneurial careers that women like Jennie C. Benedict, Nannie Talbot Johnson, and Atholene Peyton developed in the context of the domestic science movement.

Benedict's first cookbook, *A Choice Collection of Tested Receipts*, was published in 1897 and was used as the basis for a succession of editions with the *Blue Ribbon* title. In 2008 the University Press of Kentucky republished the 1922 (fourth) edition, with a spirited introductory essay by Louisville food writer Susan Reigler. The fifth and last edition was published in 1938. In contrast, other than its 2005 reissue, *The Blue Grass Cook Book* appeared only in 1904 and did not seem to have much presence in the market.

Jennie Benedict was born at Harrods Creek in 1860, and by 1900 she "had become Louisville's foremost caterer" (Reigler [1922] 2008, v). According to her memoir *The Road to Dream Acre* (1928), an important foundation for her cooking skills was the teaching of her old black mammy, who predicted Benedict would be a fine cook someday. This experience corroborates Tipton-Martin's ideas about the Jemima code. Similarly, the later cookbooks written by Marion W. Flexner—*Dixie Dishes* (1941) and her better known *Out of Kentucky Kitchens* (1949)—acknowledge the creative role of African American cooks in her household in a respectful and affectionate, though patronizing, way.

Benedict's father, who was also in the food business, encouraged her endeavors. One of her earliest businesses was making and selling lunches to schoolchildren. From there, she started to do catering, including for Derby Day. She ran the catering business from her home, taking orders for cakes, pies, sandwiches, and homemade candies and promoting her services with mailed circulars (Benedict 1928, 8). In her memoir she includes this tip for serving a crowd, which she seemingly can't help sharing with her readers: "Just here it may be of interest, and a help to many, to know that the meat from a three pound hen, and half as much celery as meat, will make a quart of chicken salad. A gallon of salad will serve thirty people. If a little lemon juice is added to the water in which the chicken is boiled, the meat will be bleached and tender" (ibid., 23). Benedict was clearly an entrepreneur—a very successful one—and fruitcakes were an important building block in her business. During the Christmas season she baked and sold them, often shipping them to her customers by mail. Here is her fruitcake recipe.

Fruit Cake (1904)

1 pound butter
1 pound sugar
1 pound flour
½ pound citron
½ pound candied cherries
12 eggs
2 nutmegs
½ glass of wine
½ glass of brandy
2 pounds raisins
1 pound currants
½ pound figs
½ pound pineapple
2 pounds almonds
1 tablespoon cinnamon
1 tablespoon allspice
1 cup molasses
2 teaspoons baking powder

Cream the butter and sugar together. Add New Orleans molasses, then eggs, which have been beaten separately, next the flour, which has been browned; then dissolve two teaspoons of baking powder in a cup of cream or new milk, and add to the mixture. Then add the

> spices which have been dissolved in the tumblerful of liquor. Chop fruit and nuts, dredge with flour, and put in the batter last. Bake slowly four hours. (Benedict 1904, 89)

Benedict reminds us in a footnote, "This is the recipe which gave me my start in business."

Benedict also opened a successful tearoom called Benedict's in the heart of Louisville, in the 400 block of South Fourth Street. It apparently became a landmark. One of the Little Colonel books—a sentimental, central Kentucky–sited series—mentions Benedict's tearoom (Johnston 1906). In addition to her success as an author and businesswoman, she made important contributions to Louisville by encouraging the development of health care facilities for women and the poor. In these ventures she was closely associated with Jennie C. Casseday, one of the leaders of the Women's Christian Temperance Union. Casseday was instrumental in creating the Louisville program of the King's Daughters health and social services, in which Benedict was active.[3]

Jennie Benedict's approach to food, in contrast to Minnie Fox's, was consistent with that of the national domestic science movement. From the standpoint of cookbooks (our primary concern here), a domestic science orientation involved more precision in the cooking process, greater awareness of nutrition and health, more concern for hygiene, and, to a lesser extent, the presentation of recipes to feed the sick and infirm. The clearest indicator of these changes was the advocacy of standardized measurements. "Exact measurement was the foundation for everything else that happened in the scientific kitchen, although there was not always agreement about how to reach exactitude" (Shapiro 2001, 108). In the cookbooks written by early advocates of domestic science (such as Mrs. D. A. Lincoln and Fannie Farmer), the use of level measurements in standardized containers, as well as the abandonment of "bird-based" measures, was advocated. The wide availability of more precise measuring cups and spoons in the 1890s made this possible.

Institutionally, the movement was related to the establishment of cooking schools for the general public, classes in cooking and nutrition in high schools, and academic programs in home economics at public land-grant universities such as the University of Kentucky,[4] as well as the writing of cookbooks. The cooking schools were an important institutional base of the movement. Initially, they were oriented toward training immigrant women to both provide better nutrition to their families and prepare for careers in domestic service. In Louisville the program was aimed at African Americans and immigrants. Nationally, the target audience for this training had to be augmented by middle-class women to ensure an adequate clientele for these services. The early manifestations of this movement occurred first in the Northeast, in cities such as Boston, New York, and Philadelphia. With some time lag, the movement extended to Kentucky—mostly in Louisville, but also in Lexington and then in rural communities.

The domestic science movement resonated with the women's movement in general, as well as with other social and technological changes.[5] The movement raised the prestige of women by supporting the professionalization of traditional domestic roles typically associated with women and the application of scientific knowledge to the domestic sphere. That is, cooking and meal preparation became more technical and entered the domain of the expert. The social changes included increased urbanism, changing expectations about gender roles, and a diminution in self-sufficiency among rural households. The technological changes included the availability of gas and later electric cooking, at least in urban areas, and a better scientific understanding of the role of proteins, fats, carbohydrates, and vitamins in the diet. Domestic science–oriented cookbooks such as *Mrs. Lincoln's Boston Cook Book* (1884) included extensive and scientifically based discussions of the nutritional aspects of food.

The best culinary practices were thought to be within the purview of professionals and academics, rather than the good cooks of a community. This is consistent with the proliferation of single-author cookbooks and the establishment of cooking schools and academic programs. According to culinary historian Janice Longone, the post–Civil War cooking school innovation was focused on large eastern cities (1997, 18). Today, the most famous (but not the first) of these schools is the Boston Cooking School, which was founded in 1879 under the direction of Mrs. D. A. Lincoln.[6] She was succeeded as principal of the school by Carrie M. Dearborn and then by the not yet famous Fannie Merritt Farmer. Apparently, the Boston Cooking School was the first to replace the block recipe format with the modern or standard format, which provides a separate ingredients list followed by a description of the procedure. Mrs. Lincoln herself was an early—perhaps the first—user of this format in *Mrs. Lincoln's Boston Cook Book: What to Do and What Not to Do* (1884), which was later reprinted as *The Boston Cooking School Cookbook*. Fannie Farmer is often associated with this innovative format, but she was not the first to use it; in fact, this format is found inconsistently in the Fannie Farmer cookbooks published by the Boston Cooking School. This pattern is used in most, but not all, contemporary cookbooks. A few Kentucky cookbooks use a format similar to that introduced in the second edition (first trade edition) of *The Joy of Cooking* (Rombauer 1936). Typically called the action method, it combines the procedures and the ingredients and uses typography and page placement to make the distinctions clear. According to Marion Rombauer Becker, daughter of *The Joy of Cooking*'s author, "Bold type carried ingredients in a chronological framework of light-face. You only had to run your eye down the bold items to see if you had suitable on hand. And you couldn't go wrong in procedure if you followed the sequence of preparation in light-face" (1966, 29). Irene Hayes uses a similar format in *What's Cooking in Kentucky* (1965), as do the cookbooks written by Bowling Green's Duncan Hines.

An important part of the institutional story of the domestic science movement was the creation of the previously mentioned land-grant universities and their home economics departments. Starting just before World War I, these organizations and their related extension services brought the values and technologies of the domestic science movement to rural Kentucky. This represented a push for improved nutrition, especially in rural settings. These programs organized homemaker associations that promoted various aspects of domestic life, including improved food preparation; these homemaker groups also produced cookbooks starting in the 1950s. On the downside, extension programs had the effect of devaluing traditional food preparation practices, resulting in what might be called a culinary disenfranchisement. This was guided by a pervasive gustatory ethnocentrism based on the depiction of locally produced food as impure and unhygienic and the assumption that local cooks did not know enough about the science of nutrition. The foodways advocated by the movement were oriented toward the British-inspired cuisine of New England.

On a somewhat smaller scale, the domestic science movement was also reflected in the Pure Food Expositions held in various cities, including Philadelphia, Boston, Baltimore, New York, Cincinnati, and Louisville (in early 1895). These events were often sponsored by local grocery retailing associations, and they exhibited the products of food manufacturers such as Knox gelatin, Baker's chocolate, Fleischman's yeast, and McCormick spices. These expositions also included cooking classes, the distribution of free samples, and entertainment. Clearly, there was a mutually supportive relationship between the domestic science movement and the food producing industry. There was also a close association between the domestic science movement and the cooking schools.

At the time, food that was processed and packaged in factories was touted as healthier than food produced on farms. These ideas are still used today to discourage institutions such as universities and hospitals from buying their food direct from the farmer. Laura Shapiro concludes, "Uniformity, sterility, predictability—the values inherent in machine-age cuisine—were always at the heart of scientific cookery, so the era of manufactured and processed food descended upon the domestic-science movement like a millennium" (2001, 191). Foodways, whether ethnic or rural, were dismissed as problematic on either health or nutritional grounds. Perception of these "deficiencies" mobilized the movement's reformist tendencies. The goal was to reform America one cook at a time. Although the cuisine advocated by domestic science was nutritious and efficiently prepared, it did not necessarily taste good. The emphasis seemed to be on whether the food was right to eat, rather than good to eat.

Jennie Benedict's career took flight at the Pure Food Exposition in Louisville. Carrie Dearborn, principal of the Boston Cooking School, was scheduled to do a domestic science demonstration at the exposition, but she became ill, and Benedict was asked to replace her. According to Benedict's memoir, Mrs. Dearborn's husband was so grateful that he offered Benedict admission to the Boston Cooking School. As a consequence, she attended a six-week course at the school—an important center advocating the domestic science approach. Following her Boston experience, Benedict was able to add the role of cooking instructor to her résumé.

The first classes Benedict taught were in Owensboro and Bowling Green, and they focused on gas cooking—specifically, natural gas, the newly introduced replacement for manufactured gas. The first natural gas pipeline reached Louisville in 1888, and shortly thereafter Benedict taught classes there. Her 1897 cookbook recommends a gas cooking stove, among other products, and includes an ad for a Louisville gas appliance dealer. The transition to gas is discussed more thoroughly later in this chapter.

The Boston Cooking School Cookbook endured through a number of editions, the last being published in 1990, when it was called *The Fannie Farmer Cookbook.* This long-running cookbook made the Boston Cooking School the most famous of the various cooking schools established in this era. The recipes are conveyed in such a way that even cooks with little experience could replicate them. These are not "ingredients only" recipes. Their use of standard volume measures and their concern for nutrition represent the domestic science turn in American cookbooks and in the history of American culinary affairs (Hess and Hess 2000, 124). Benedict's cookbook follows a similar pattern and is a central Kentucky manifestation of the domestic science movement and its approach to cooking.

The recipes selected by Jennie Benedict are a combination of regional and cosmopolitan. Although the description of procedure is robust, *The Blue Ribbon Cook Book* does not intentionally evoke a sense of place—that is, there is no narrative focusing on the origin and history of the recipes or on Kentucky life in general. Cookbooks with an explicit regional, cultural, and historical flavor do not appear until the 1940s. Consistent with the earlier Boston-based cookbooks, there is a certain amount of "product placement" in Benedict's cookbook. She mentions some branded food products, including Daisy flour, Nonpareil oil, and Fleischman's compressed yeast, as well as the Claudine brand of flour sifter. The 1904 edition includes a section consisting of advertisements that is introduced with this statement: "It gives me great pleasure to add to my book (for the benefit of the many who ask of me) the firms from whom you can purchase the VERY best, in their separate lines, to be had in this country. I urge every friend of this book to buy from them" (Benedict 1904, 139).

Benedict's recipes use a variety of fats, including butter, lard, oil, and olive oil. *The Blue Ribbon Cook Book* contains three recipes that call for olive oil: deviled crab, mayonnaise, and a chicken, mushroom, and tomato dish called Spaghetti a la King Humbert. The advertisements for locally sold products include one for Holy Father pure Italian virgin olive oil. Lard tends to be used in her recipes for biscuits, breads, and pastries; otherwise, the fat of choice is butter. Interestingly, the recipe for baking powder biscuits includes both butter and lard. This reflects the beginning of a big change in the fats used for cooking. In the earliest cookbooks, lard and its close cousin bacon drippings were the primary cooking fats, although some butter was used. In parts of Kentucky, rather than making butter, many households sold most of the cream they produced to local cream stations, as they were called. This cream ended up at commercial dairies and was used for butter and ice cream production. Therefore, lard continued to be very important in rural settings, and for many years, the production of lard was the most important goal of hog raising, butchering, and processing. The preferred hog was colossal and as fat as possible—nothing like the lean animals of today. Lard was rendered on the farm and might have a residue of caramelized tissue in it, producing a brownish cast and a characteristic flavor. This worked well for some applications, but for others, a whiter fat with a cleaner, more neutral flavor was preferable. This led to innovations in the industrial production of cooking fats.

Perhaps the most important of these innovations was the development of solid fats made by hydrogenating vegetable oils. The result was called shortening. The originator of this process in the United States was Cincinnati's Procter and Gamble, which first manufactured Crisco in 1910. Other companies introduced seemingly identical products such as Spry and Snowdrift. Prior to the Crisco revolution, other alternatives to lard were developed. Perhaps the most widely used was Cottolene, consisting of about 90 percent cottonseed oil and 10 percent beef tallow. This was marketed with the tagline "Nature's Gift from the Sunny South" and was sold in buckets like lard (Lincoln 1910). As these new fats were developed and marketed, lard was also undergoing change. Today, most of the lard that is sold is highly processed and filtered to make it white and more neutral in flavor. It is also partially hydrogenated to increase its stiffness and stability (Fowler 2008, 44). There is no mention of products such as Crisco in the 1922 edition of Benedict's cookbook, even though it had been on the market for at least a decade. It is interesting that most other cookbooks of this era did not list shortening as an ingredient either (with the exception of Procter and Gamble's Crisco-based cookbooks). Mrs. Peter A. White includes the use of "salad oil" in her instructions for frying fish in her 1885 cookbook (80), and Benedict mentions oil in two recipes in the 1904 edition of her book. Surprisingly, shortening did not become a widely used ingredient until the 1940s, and by the 1950s, lard had virtually disappeared. For example, the community cookbook *Latonia's Favorite Recipes* has no lard-containing recipes (Trinity Methodist Church 1950). Typically, its cake and roll recipes call for shortening or, in some cases, butter or margarine. In contrast, some of the recipes in the 1956 community cookbook *Cabbage Patch: Famous Kentucky Recipes* call for animal fats; the recipe for Kentucky beaten biscuits includes "2 heaping tablespoons hog lard (grainy)" (Cabbage Patch Circle 1956, 106). I assume this description refers to the kind of lard one could produce at home.

An unusual feature of *The Blue Ribbon Cook Book* not found in the other cookbooks is a section entitled "Simple Dishes for the Sick." Recipes for invalids are often found in domestic science–oriented cookbooks. Some examples from *The Blue Ribbon Cook Book* include barley water, flaxseed tea, beef tea, creamed calf brains, and chicken broth; there are also suggested menus for the sick in the menu section. The recipes include items suitable for liquid and bland diets and a discussion of the peptonization of milk and other foods (the process by which the enzyme pepsin breaks down protein). Here is one of Benedict's recipes for the sick.

Creamed Oatmeal (1904)

> Boil oatmeal as for breakfast, rub it through a fine sieve, add a little cream, and cook very slowly in a double boiler for half an hour longer. When perfectly smooth, add a very little salt and rich cream. This is the most delicate preparation of oatmeal that an invalid can take. (Benedict 1904, 118)

As noted earlier, Benedict was closely associated with community efforts to improve health care, especially for the poor and women. There is still an important community service organization in Louisville called the Jennie C. Benedict Circle.

Benedict's recipes often appear in more recent Louisville cookbooks. The short *Kentucky Heritage Recipes* cookbook, published by the Historic Homes Foundation in 1976 to raise money for historic homes in Louisville, includes her recipes for lemon wafers, eggnog, fruitcake, rum punch, and hollandaise sauce.

A number of other cookbooks compiled by Kentucky women deserve attention. One of these women is Nannie Talbot Johnson (aka Mrs. W. A. Johnson),[7] a culinary entrepreneur whose career shared features with Jennie Benedict's. Johnson wrote *What to Cook and How to Cook It*, which was revised and reprinted a number of times. The 1899 edition is usually cited as the first; however, the words "Seventh, Enlarged Edition" appear on the cover, and the book is augmented with an appendix of recipes—evidence of a revision. The last edition seems to be the eighteenth, published in 1923. The cookbook is a blend of old and new elements. The most anachronistic feature is consistent use of the block format. There is little evidence in the text that supports the idea that it was written with wood and coal stoves in mind. Measurements are modern, with some exceptions; in contrast to Benedict's instructions, the measurements are specified as rounded rather than level. There is no mention of actual cooking temperatures and little about cooking times. In contrast, a modern feature is that the recipes provide quite a bit of detail about procedure—not as much as today's cookbooks, but more than earlier cookbooks. She includes an extensive discussion of sweets, especially candy. In 1912 Mrs. Johnson published a companion volume to *What to Cook and How to Cook It* entitled *Cake, Candy, and Culinary Crinkles.* Although this volume contains recipes (including many for icings and candies; see below), it is primarily concerned with the techniques of presentation. As Johnson explains, "Culinary Crinkles consist in shaping, cooking to a nicety, arranging and garnishing, observing always the best way to serve in order to please the eye and invite the appetite" (1912, 3).

Plain White Candy (1912)

> Pour over three pounds of granulated sugar, one pint of water, put on the stove and stir until dissolved; add a pinch of soda, two tablespoons of vinegar and a teaspoon of butter; cook over a quick fire. Have a tumbler of cold water, and when the candy begins to cook in large bubbles, put a teaspoon of it in the water, and if it becomes hard and cracks on the side of tumbler, pour at once on a greased slab or flat china dish. When it begins to harden so that it makes a dent when pressed by the finger, gather it all in a lump and pull until it gets light and creamy; pull the flavoring into it and make it into long, thin strips and cut into one or two inch pieces. By the use of fruit coloring, this candy can be made any desired color by putting in the coloring after the candy has been pulled white. Continue to pull until the coloring has been uniformly mixed through. (Johnson 1912, 196–97)

Apparently, Johnson began writing cookbooks, cooking professionally, and teaching cooking classes when her husband died. She is an interesting figure in the culinary history of Kentucky. An intriguing fact is that Mrs. Johnson is cited as the cooking instructor of Irma Rombauer, the original author of *The Joy of Cooking* (1931).[8] Rombauer took cooking classes from Johnson as part of a summer program sponsored by the Bay View Association Methodist Church near Traverse City, Michigan, sometime around 1915. This was near the Rombauers' summer home. Mrs. Rombauer's daughter notes that "the Johnson School was perhaps

Mother's only exposure to formal culinary training. But it brought out her unusual and at first rather inexplicable flair of decorating cakes" (Becker 1966, 2).[9]

Like Jennie Benedict, Nannie Talbot Johnson was a food-focused entrepreneur. Around 1920 she and her two daughters established the Cherokee Inn in Louisville. The business apparently began as a tearoom and evolved into a boardinghouse with the economic stresses of the Depression. As part of an oral history project focused on preservation of the Cherokee Triangle neighborhood, Frances Hannah Lamason recollected, "I had some Johnson relatives . . . Nannie was from Paris, Kentucky, and she wrote a cookbook called *What to Cook & How to Cook It*. Her cookbook was a step above the older cookbooks because I think she actually had measurements in it. My friends remember my mother taking us there for afternoon tea when we were so big. This was part of our education in etiquette. We would go for tea and cinnamon toast at [the] Cherokee Inn" (Thomas 2003, 199–200). The inn was a landmark on Cherokee Road until it was demolished and replaced by an apartment complex in 1972. Whereas the inn was an attractive (though unadorned) two-story Italianate building, typical of the better neighborhoods of late-nineteenth-century Louisville, the apartment complex was described by one community leader as an aesthetic monstrosity. The community's resistance and reaction to the loss of the inn and other nearby historic buildings led to the establishment of the Cherokee Triangle Preservation District.

Much of *What to Cook* consists of rather straightforward recipes that use basic techniques. Here is a simple recipe for chicken fricassee.

Fricassee Chicken (1899)

Wipe, and cut at the joints in pieces for serving. Cover with boiling water. Cook one hour or until tender, reducing the water to nearly a pint. Remove the chicken from the liquor, dredge with salt, pepper and flour, brown in hot butter or pork scraps. Put the chicken on toast on a hot platter; add to the liquor one cup of cream or milk and heat it again. Melt one large tablespoon of butter in a sauce pan;

> add two tablespoons of flour, and when well mixed pour on slowly the cream and chicken liquor. Add salt and pepper and pour the same over the chicken. Trim a platter with toast, arrange the chicken on toast, pour the cream dressing over it and garnish with parsley. (Johnson 1899, 54–55)

This is a typical Johnson recipe. It is presented in block format, the measures are standardized, and she gives instructions for presentation.

The cookbooks of Jennie Benedict and Nannie Talbot Johnson contrast with the elegant little cookbook written by Mary Harris Frazer and published in 1903 by a Louisville printer. The preface of *The Kentucky Receipt Book* claims that the recipes "have been collected for generations, including Creole and French receipts known only to the wealthy planter families of the far South" (Frazer 1903, 3). This statement, along with the names of some of the recipes, provides a cultural context. Frazer was raised in Louisiana and, through her life experiences, learned about Virginia and Kentucky cooking. Frazer is concerned with how the food tastes, and the recipes are very technique-oriented for 1903, yet they are presented in the older block format.

The *Kentucky Receipt Book* is not presented as a Louisville cookbook, but its River City roots are evident. Its mix of recipes could be considered an early manifestation of Louisville's foodways or culinary traditions. The essential parts of Louisville cuisine are classic Kentucky dishes such as green beans and cured pork seasoning meat, country ham, and biscuits, with a big helping of traditional Gulf coast dishes and highlighted by elements of ethnic cuisine—most prominently, German and other European influences. All this is coupled with an interest in good food, eating out, and new culinary ideas, or a more cosmopolitan view of food.

The recipe selection is quite interesting. Reflecting Frazer's Louisiana roots, she includes a recipe for a southern classic—banana pudding—although it does not contain vanilla wafers. Hers is sometimes cited as the earliest published recipe for banana pudding.

Banana Pudding (1903)

Take ½ dozen bananas, peel and cut into pieces an inch thick, put in baking dish and pour over custard made in the following manner: Custard—One pint of milk, 3 eggs, beat the yolks light, add milk, also 2 tablespoons of granulated sugar. Have the milk boiling, add the eggs and let it cool until it thickens; when cool pour over the bananas. Make a meringue with whites of the eggs and granulated sugar, put on top of custard, set in oven a few minutes to brown. Serve at once. (Frazer 1903, 221)

Frazer includes sixty recipes for oysters, giving them a separate section of their own. This recipe for gumbo, taken from another section, also uses oysters.

Gumbo Fille (1903)

Take 1 large chicken and fry in butter, with 1 onion chopped finely (prepare chicken day before needed). Pour into a covered dish with the gravy and set away until next day. Then to the chicken add 3 quarts of cold water and cook until done. Remove chicken from kettle; have 2 large spoons gumbo fille[10] powder; put in cup with cold water, stir until ropy; then add this to the soup and boil. Take 1 quart of large oysters, plump in their liquor, drain on a sieve; add them to gumbo, also the chicken. Have 1 pint of rice well cooked and serve at the same time. (Frazer 1903, 14)

Kentucky Receipt Book is the source of many of the recipes presented on the Old Louisville Guide website. Old Louisville is a federally designated Historic Preservation Area near the city's downtown. The neighborhood's Victorian architectural treasures and culinary traditions are also conveyed in David Domine's *A Feast for the Eyes: Recipes from America's Grandest Victorian Neighborhood* (2010).

African American–Authored Cookbooks

This era produced the earliest Kentucky cookbook written by an African American. Miss Atholene Peyton's *The Peytonia Cook Book* was published in Louisville in 1906. She had deep roots in the city. Peyton was an 1897 graduate of Louisville's Central Colored High School and then went on to the Colored Normal School, which provided teachers for Louisville's public schools until it closed in 1935. Peyton served on the domestic science faculty of the segregated Central Colored High School and was the faculty sponsor of the Girls' Cooking Club. In one of her applications on file in the Jefferson County Public Schools archives, she noted under "honors": "Wrote the first Negro Cook Book in Kentucky." Her career at Central Colored High School lasted from 1904 until her death in April 1951. Peyton also taught domestic science at the Neighborhood Home and Training School for Colored Boys and Girls, located on Fifteenth Street in Louisville. The Training School was supported by the Neighborhood Circle of the King's Daughters. As mentioned earlier, Jennie Benedict was closely associated with this organization's domestic science training program, so perhaps Peyton and Benedict were colleagues. Peyton also represented the Louisville schools at an event in Frankfort featuring Dr. Booker T. Washington, held to commemorate the construction of a new dormitory at Kentucky State University, from which she earned a degree in 1935.

Peyton also served on the domestic science faculty of the summer Chautauqua of the National Training School for Women and Girls in Washington, D.C. This was organized by the Woman's Convention, an auxiliary of the National Baptist Convention, which was and remains an important African American religious organization. The president of the training school was the well-known African American educator Nannie Helen Burroughs, who advocated for the improvement of African American women's marketable skills. Domestic science training was an important aspect this advocacy.

According to a news item in the *Indianapolis Freeman* (1907), *The Peytonia Cook Book* "has achieved a wonderful degree of popularity among the best authorities on the culinary art." The cookbook itself includes a warm introduction by Nannie Helen Burroughs. Most recipes are presented in the standard format, although a few utilize the block format. The cookbook has a clear domestic science look and feel, and the recipes are described as tested. Although it is accurate to think of *The Peytonia Cook Book* as a general cookbook without a regional mission, there are references to southern and even African American cuisine. In her narrative on cooking greens, Peyton notes, "In fact, in the South jowl is used in preference to bacon with greens" (1906, 52). She also includes a few recipes for game, and the narrative accompanying her recipe for possum states: "Opossum and coon are both strictly Southern dishes, and are both unheard of in the north. These two dishes are generally eaten by the darky, and no one else has the knack of making them so toothsome" (ibid., 66). Her recipe for cobbler observes, "A cobbler is just a deep pie, and I believe they are eaten in no place like Kentucky" (ibid., 98).

In addition to recipes, Peyton provides sections on "kitchen equipment" and "waitress service," as well as a series of sample menus. Certainly, the discussion of waitress service is another manifestation of the vocational thrust of the domestic science movement, and it appears to be oriented toward domestic service or possibly employment in an elegant restaurant. Her description of a properly equipped kitchen includes two types of ranges—gas and coal. Peyton explains, "I believe that bread and cakes are best cooked by coal" (1906, 6). She gives the advice, "Always light the gas or gasoline ovens at least ten minutes before you are ready to bake" (ibid., 19). In the section on cakes, she recommends a Dover eggbeater.

Typical of her book's domestic science orientation, Peyton includes some branded products—Quaker oats, Vissman's bacon and sausage, White Seal ginger ale, Cox's gelatin, Burnett's flavoring extracts, and the ubiquitous Baker's chocolate. In a few cases, Peyton expresses an opinion about the nutritional qualities of some ingredients. These are of interest because they differ so radically from today's thinking. "Fish is not a substitute for meat in nutritive value," she states, "because it has less fat, but it is a pleasant change. Sauces must be served with fish to suply [*sic*] the lacking nutriment" (Peyton 1906, 55). Concerning fruit, she writes, "Cooking changes the character and flavor of fruit, but if sugar is used the nutritive value is increased" (ibid., 111). Here is one of her chicken recipes.

Smothered Chicken (1906)

Cut the chicken up as to fry; wipe dry and salt and pepper. Put in a pan with a slice of bacon and a pint of water; simmer for an hour or more until done. Keep the chicken well covered. Put the chicken on a dish; thicken the liquid and pour on chicken. Serve with rice. (Peyton 1906, 192)

Also authored by an African American is *Kentucky Cookbook: Easy and Simple for Any Cook*, written by Kentucky-born professional cook Mrs. W. T. Hayes (also known as Emma Allen Hayes) and published in 1912. Mrs. Hayes's identity as an African American seems clear, as she describes herself on the title page as a "colored woman." Apparently, she was living in St. Louis with her husband when this fifty-nine-page cookbook was published by printer J. H. Tompkins. John Egerton (1990, 130) cites this as one of the earliest cookbooks written by an African American, along with *The Southern Cookbook* by S. Thomas Bivins (1912); however, the latter does not have roots in Kentucky. Here is Mrs. Hayes's recipe for macaroni croquettes with cheese sauce.

Macaroni Croquettes, Cheese Sauce (1912)

For the croquettes take enough cold boiled macaroni to make 2 cups when cut into small pieces. Add to this 1 teaspoon of lemon juice, ½ teaspoon of onion juice, a little celery salt and seasoning to taste. Mix with 1 cup of white sauce made of 2 tablespoons of butter, 2 tablespoons of flour, seasoning and one cup of boiling milk. Let the mixture cool. Form in cone shaped croquettes, roll in egg and bread crumbs and fry in deep fat till a very light brown. Stick a small spray of parsley in the top of each croquette. Cheese sauce: to 1 cup of white sauce add ½ cup grated cheese and 1 heaping tablespoon of chopped walnut meats. (Hayes 1912, 26)

To help locate these cookbooks in history, it is useful to mention some earlier non-Kentucky cookbooks written by African Americans. A comprehensive chronological bibliography of cookbooks by African Americans, published as an appendix to Doris Witt's *Black Hunger: Food and the Politics of U.S. Identity* (1999), includes Robert Roberts's *The House Servant's Directory, or a Monitor for Private Families: Comprising Hints on the Arrangement and Performance of Servants' Work . . . Upwards of 100 Various and Useful Receipts, Chiefly Compiled for the Use of House Servants* (1827).[11] This is actually a household management manual that includes recipes, rather than a cookbook. According to Jessica B. Harris (2011, 278), the earliest cookbook written by an African American is *A Domestic Cookbook: Containing a Careful Selection of Useful Receipts for the Kitchen by Malinda Russell a Free Woman of Color*, published in Michigan in 1867; it does not have a southern orientation. More clearly southern is Abby Fisher's *What Mrs. Fisher Knows about Old Southern Cooking*, published in San Francisco in 1881. Mrs. Fisher was born enslaved in Alabama; she raised a large family and moved from Mobile to make her mark as a caterer in San Francisco following the Civil War.

The First Kentucky Cookbook Written by a Man

As stated earlier, cookbook writing was largely the domain of women, although through the years, there has been a sprinkling of cookbooks written by men. Based on my research, the earliest Kentucky cookbook written by a man is Tandy Ellis's very interesting short pamphlet titled *Camp Cooking*, published in 1923. James Tandy Ellis, born in Ghent in Carroll County, was known as a poet, short story writer, and newspaper columnist for the *Louisville Times*. The recipe for burgoo included in Marion Flexner's classic *Out of Kentucky Kitchens* (1949) is from Ellis. His recipes for simple country dishes are presented in an old-fashioned block format. The cookbook includes asides, written with humorous intent, that are demeaning to African Americans.

Camp Cooking, Tandy Ellis's 1923 pamphlet.

Baked 'Possum (1923)

> Scald your 'possum the same as you would a hog and scrape him. Do not use skinned 'possum under any circumstances. Soak for half an hour in salt and water, hang out to cool and freeze over night.
>
> When you put him in the baking pan, put some small oak or iron pieces under him to raise him above the grease. A good many people do not like 'possum because they are cooked in so much grease. Elevated about an inch or so above the bottom of the pan, allows grease to drip from him into pan. Baste him occasionally. Boil sweet potatoes until nearly done and about 15 minutes before taking 'possum out of the oven, place them around the 'possum in the pan and bake. (Ellis 1923, 19)

While the Kentucky cookbooks considered here have few possum recipes, it seems like they always involve sweet potatoes.

Cooking with Gas

Church fund-raising cookbooks continued to be published, and the Women's Guild of the Christ Church Cathedral, Lexington, produced *A Book of Recipes* in 1920 and an enlarged and improved edition in 1926.[12] This cookbook is noteworthy because it contains explicit instructions for cooking with gas. The book came out about thirty years after gas was introduced to Kentucky cities. Gas is mentioned in the Benedict cookbooks, but she gives no instructions. The format of *A Book of Recipes* is a combination of the traditional block format and the more modern presentation of a separate list of ingredients followed by a description of the procedure; there are also a few recipes consisting of ingredients only. As was typical of charity cookbooks of the era, editorial control was very light.

The references to cooking with gas suggest that this technique was becoming more widespread, although cooking was still being done by electricity, kerosene, wood, and coal as well. There are no specific instructions for oven temperatures, but the women of Christ Church Cathedral give the following advice on preheating the oven in the introduction to

A 1926 charity cookbook from Lexington.

their cake recipes: "If gas oven is used, light the oven burners and turn low about five minutes before putting in cake. If layer cake, turn up burners so cake will rise slowly as oven heats" (Women's Guild 1926, 71).

The gas range had a number of advantages over wood or coal stoves, including more temperature control, piped-in fuel, and the magic of an "instant on." In addition, gas stoves heated up the kitchen far less and took up less space. Their relative lightness allowed a long-legged design to prevail for a time.

It is surprisingly difficult to determine when the transition from cooking with woodstoves to cooking with gas or electric stoves occurred. Certainly this happened much earlier in the cities than in the countryside. In the case of electricity, there was a gap of about fifty years between the time the first and last places were electrified. Some parts of rural Kentucky did not get electricity until the early 1950s. In both the city and the country, electricity was used first for lights and then for motors; cooking and refrigeration come later. Even long after electrification, wood-fired cookstoves were retained for limited uses, such as canning or heating water for laundry. As mentioned earlier, one of Jennie Benedict's first jobs was to teach classes in cooking with gas in the 1890s.

In Kentucky the transition to gas cooking started with the formation of the Louisville Gas and Water Company in 1838. Originally, this business focused on street lighting, fueled by gas manufactured from coal in the city itself. Louisville had gas street lighting earlier than similar cities, but it was supplanted by electricity in around 1890, as electric lights were brighter. The need to develop an alternative market for the gas supply formerly used for lighting led to the increased use of gas for heating and cooking. In addition, new supplies became available with the construction of natural gas pipelines into Louisville, such as the pipeline from West Virginia built in 1914. What was called natural gas was more reliable, less expensive, and more efficient than manufactured gas.

The function of gas stoves was improved by the invention of the thermostat in around 1915. Even so, it took a long time for cookbooks to specify oven temperatures. Cookbooks from the hearth and woodstove eras used general terms, translated as follows: a very slow oven was equivalent to about 250 degrees; slow, 300 degrees; moderately slow, 325 degrees; moderate, 350 degrees; moderately hot, 375 degrees; hot, 400 degrees; very hot, 450 degrees; and extremely hot, 500 degrees. The transition from this nominal terminology to the use of numbers of degrees started in the mid-1920s and was complete by 1950. The Women's Guild's 1926 cookbook used nominal terms for all recipes for baked goods. About ten years later, another church cookbook included a sprinkling of recipes with degrees specified. For example, a recipe for ice box biscuits states: "Bake 15 minutes at 425 degrees" (South Frankfort Presbyterian Church 1935, 3). Marion Flexner's *Dixie Dishes* (1941) combined the nominal and the digital in each recipe. By the 1950s, nearly all recipes for baked goods specified oven temperatures in degrees.

Socially, these changes in cooking technology played an important role in the redefined expectations associated with both gender and race. Women used their culinary activities—cooking, teaching cooking, and writing cookbooks—to achieve independence and break the constraints of the domestic sphere. Women's traditional domestic roles became the purview of specially trained experts, illustrated by the growing interest in the scientific basis of nutrition, the careful measurement of ingredients, and authoritative instruction through cooking schools. This was part of a much larger, national social movement to increase the rights of women, well described in the writings of Laura Shapiro and others. Less clearly understood is that the emergence of the "expert" cook diminished the value of ordinary individuals' knowledge of food preparation and other things culinary. Traditional cooks and food producers were seen as people who had to be taught rather than respected. Associated with this was an increase in the perceived value of food produced by industry.

Kentucky, especially urban Kentucky, played an important (though regional) role in this transition, as can be seen in the entrepreneurial career strategies of Jennie Benedict, Nannie Talbot Johnson, and Atholene Peyton. In different ways, they each expressed the values underlying the domestic science movement and the gender evolution of which it was a part. At the same time, nostalgic vestiges of the old social order lasted into the 1950s and perhaps beyond.

Chapter Four

Hard Times

The Great Depression and the New Deal

During the 1920s there were real increases in prosperity in Kentucky, especially in cities.[1] These conditions ended with the Great Depression. The conventional beginning of the Depression is the stock market crash of 1929, although there were hard times in rural Kentucky earlier than this, related to the collapse of farm commodity prices after World War I. The Depression touched many Kentuckians early and deeply and had a lasting impact on life in the commonwealth. It created an economic vacuum of joblessness, insolvent banks, and low prices for agricultural commodities. To deal with the Depression, there was massive government spending through various New Deal programs. In this chapter I discuss some of the government programs that changed Kentucky foodways and often led to new cookbooks. Although the Depression era saw fewer cookbooks published, there were some interesting recipe compilations supported by the Work Projects Administration (WPA) through its Pack Horse Libraries, housekeeping aides training programs, and the America Eats program of the Federal Writers' Project.[2] All these national projects had a presence in Kentucky.

The WPA, announced in 1935 by President Franklin D. Roosevelt during one of his Fireside Chat radio broadcasts, was funded by Congress to help overcome the country's impoverishment. It was the largest of the New Deal programs and continued to operate until 1943. The WPA was a "work relief program" whose budget was intended to provide "wages for labor" in localities with high numbers of people on the "relief rolls," rather than to pay for materials and administrative staff (Roosevelt 2012). The core of the program was the construction of roads, sewers, and public buildings in both urban and rural settings, but other activities were funded as well. For example, the WPA was involved in distributing food to the poor, although the primary goal was to enhance farm families' incomes rather than to provide a sound diet to impoverished individuals. The government purchased surpluses—called "surplus relief commodities"—that farmers were unable to sell in the market. The kinds of foods purchased and distributed varied, depending on what was available, but they included flour, dried beans and peas, prunes, oat cereal, onions, butter, corned beef, canned goods such as beans and tomatoes, sugar, apples, and cheese. These foods were distributed twice a month at grocery stores on what came to be called "giveaway days." One government report, describing these events in a rural setting, states, "The relief clients in many cases start gathering at the commodity centers before the merchant has opened his store for the day's business. Some come by wagon, some mule back, but most of them have only their feet for conveyance" (Works Progress Administration 1935). This program introduced some new foods, such as skim milk powder, to people who were eligible for relief.

The WPA program resulted in the writing of a few cookbooks and other materials related to foodways. The first considered here are the recipe books compiled by staff members of the Pack Horse Library project, which was active in thirty eastern Kentucky counties (Appelt and Schmitzer 2001). Whereas most other WPA programs focused on hiring men, the Pack Horse Library project was staffed by women, and the individuals hired had to be otherwise unemployable. They came to be called the "Book Women." From the county seats, where the Pack Horse Library programs were established, the Book Women traveled by horse or mule and delivered library materials to readers without access to public libraries. Their routes, which they rode every two weeks, averaged eighteen miles. Because these programs had no budgets to actually buy books, they had to rely on reading materials created by the Book Women themselves and on discards from other libraries and schools. There was considerable demand for these materials, especially for content focused on homemaking. Borrowers of-

A Pack Horse librarian visiting a reader. (WPA)

ten requested recipes, so cookbooks were very popular, and short compilations of recipes were produced by the Pack Horse Libraries in some counties. I found two of these: one was in a file of WPA materials at the Kentucky Department for Libraries and Archives in Frankfort, which was from the program in McKee, in Jackson County; the other, which I found in the online catalog of the Louisville Free Public Library, was from Whitley County (Whitley Pack Horse Library 1938). Both are quite brief, containing just over thirty recipes.

The volume from McKee is handwritten, and the recipe format is standard. Some of the recipes are attributed to specific women, who were probably program participants. The inside front page states: "This book contains 'Auld Tyme' Cooking and Canning recipes." The manuscript concludes with "household hints." More than half the recipes are for sweets, including pies, cakes, and candy. In addition, there are recipes for biscuits, cornbread, and various vegetable preparations. Although this volume is undated, I assume it is from the late 1930s. The recipe for gingerbread, an important mountain preparation, is shared here.

Old-fashioned Ginger Bread (1930s)

1 cup molasses
½ cup buttermilk
1 egg
¼ cup shortening—butter or lard
1 tablespoon ginger, cinnamon and allspice
1 teaspoon soda
3 teaspoons baking powder

Mix molasses, milk, spices and egg together. Sift dry ingredients, add to first mixture, make dough stiff enough to roll out. Cut and bake in moderate oven. (WPA [1930s?])

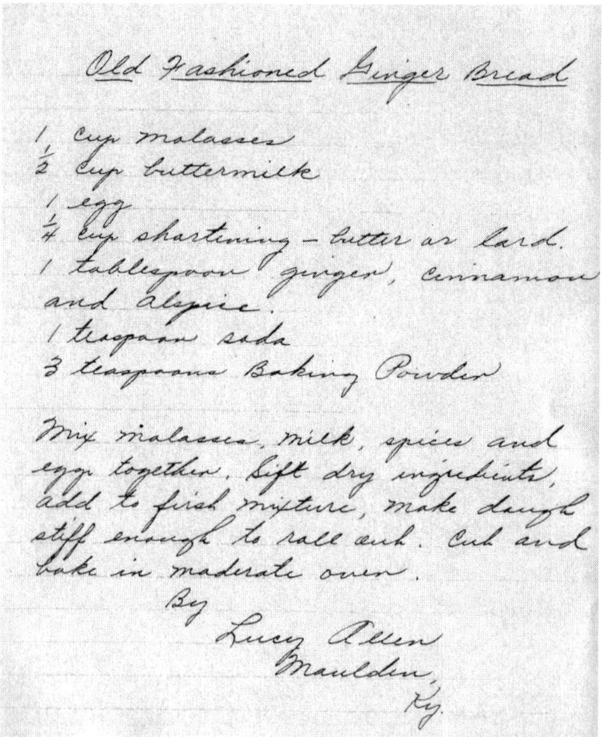

Old Fashioned Ginger Bread

1 cup molasses
1/2 cup buttermilk
1 egg
1/4 cup shortening – butter or lard.
1 tablespoon ginger, cinnamon and alspice.
1 teaspoon soda
3 teaspoons Baking Powder

Mix molasses, milk, spices and egg together. Sift dry ingredients, add to first mixture, make dough stiff enough to roll out. Cut and bake in moderate oven.

By
Lucy Allen
Maulden,
Ky.

A recipe from a Jackson, Kentucky, Pack Horse Library cookbook.

This recipe was contributed by Lucy Allen of Maulden, in Jackson County. Note that the term *molasses* was widely used to refer to sorghum syrup.

Another interesting dessert recipe is the following unsigned one for cold biscuit pudding. It is notable that the condition of the milk is specified—in this case, the recipe calls for sweet milk. This was common practice in an era when refrigeration was limited and milk often soured. In fact, many recipes call for sour milk.

Cold Biscuit Pudding (1930s)

some cold biscuits
½ cup hot water
1½ cups sweet milk
3 egg yolks
1 cup sugar
egg whites

Crumble up cold biscuits and pour ½ cup boiling water over them. Cover and let stand 5 minutes. Add 1½ cups sweet milk, 3 egg yolks and 1 cup sugar. Stir into biscuits and water. Place in oven and let stand until milk and egg yolks are cooked. Flavor if desired. Beat egg whites stiffly and sweeten, spread over pudding and bake brown. (WPA [1930s?])

The other collection of recipes, a typescript entitled *Mountain Receipts*, was compiled by the Whitley Pack Horse Library and published in 1938. It has a more clearly expressed focus than the McKee volume, as its thirty-one recipes were collected from persons 75 to 100 years old living in "isolated hill sections of Whitley County." As the brief preface states, "We have collected, first hand, from these old people a number of recipes which were most commonly used" (Whitley Pack Horse Library 1938, 3). Almost half the recipes are made with cornmeal. Some of the dishes include hoecake, cracklin' bread, gritted bread, cornmeal gingerbread, cornmeal pie crust, hogshead cheese, poke salad, kraut, corn muffins, berry cobbler, dried fruit stack cake, and sassafras tea. The unsigned recipes are in the block format; use mostly imprecise measures, including pinches and handfuls; do not specify times and temperatures; and contain no branded products.

Corn Meal Dumplin's (1938)

> Boil a kettle of greens with a large piece of jowl. When greens and meat are done take them out of the kettle and drop the dumplin's in the broth that is left. To make the dumplin' dough salt the meal you are going to use and then pour enough boiling water over the meal to make it up. Squeeze out the dumplin's while the dough is hot. (Whitley Pack Horse Library 1938, 5)

The second recipe included here is for hogshead cheese, a variation on souse.

Hogshead Cheese (1938)

> Boil Hog's head, liver, tongue, and heart together until tender. Take the meat from bones and cut up fine. Put the cut-up meat all back in the stock where it was cooked and let come to a boil. Stir in enough corn meal to thicken, add black pepper and sage to taste and then pour this mixture out on a pan to cool. It can be sliced for sandwiches or fried in hot fat. (Whitley Pack Horse Library 1938, 7)

In addition to its culinary aspirations, the WPA trained housekeeping aides in most states to provide housekeeping services on a temporary, emergency basis to the sick or elderly. Their duties included cooking, and half of the training manual used in Kentucky consists of recipes or general advice on food preparation.[3] Like the Pack Horse librarians, the aides had to be unemployed and certified as eligible for relief. The recipes in the training manual/cookbook are presented in the standard format, with the ingredients and procedures separate, and oven temperatures are specified. The recipes have a distinct "home economics professional" feel to them. For example, every recipe starts with the same instruction: "Check all materials needed. Use careful *level* measurements." In some cases, lower-cost options are presented, such as how to reduce the number of eggs in a custard recipe. Some of the recipes are "beyond basic," such as the one for peanut butter and jelly sandwiches. Here is the training manual's recipe for summer squash.

Summer Squash and Onions (ca. 1941)

2 quarts summer squash, diced
4 tablespoons butter*
¼ cup minced onion
2 teaspoons salt
¼ teaspoon pepper
1 cup hot water

Method

1. Check all materials needed. Use careful *level* measurements.
2. Wash squash and dice.
3. Melt butter in a saucepan, add onion and cook until light brown.
4. Add squash, salt, pepper and 1 cup of hot water.
5. Cover saucepan [and] cook over a low flame without stirring for 10 minutes.
6. Continue cooking for 30 minutes stirring frequently during this period to keep squash from burning.

*Bacon drippings may be substituted for butter. (Works Progress Administration. 194?. Workbook for Housekeeping Aide Project, Vegetables, 17)

Kentucky and the America Eats Project

The WPA created the Federal Writers' Project to employ out-of-work writers and other professionals. The project is best known for the many state and city travel guides it produced. Another endeavor was the creation of similar guides to America's regional foodways, titled *America Eats*. The project started in 1939 by dividing the country into five geographic regions. The focus was on "American cookery and the part it has played in the national life, as exemplified in the group meals that preserve not only traditional dishes, but also attitudes and customs." Staff writers submitted materials to project headquarters in Washington, D.C., and these materials were assigned to rewriters. Because the purpose of WPA projects was to provide a basic salary to as many Americans as possible, there were few staff writers at the top. As a result, although a lot of material was collected, few reports were published. There is no single archive collection of these documents; those that survive are located in the Library of Congress and in some state archives, and others have been lost.

Materials produced for the America Eats project have been used in some recently published volumes. Nelson Algren's *America Eats* (1992) is based on materials collected in the Midwest. Algren had been hired by the Illinois branch of the Federal Writers' Project to work on the America Eats project. John T. Edge's *A Gracious Plenty: Recipes and Recollections from the American South* (1999) was influenced by the project's concept and includes some excerpts from the materials collected, along with contemporary recipes selected from community cookbooks. The nationally focused *America Eats! On the Road with the WPA* by Pat Willard (2009) and *The Food of a Younger Land* by Mark Kurlansky (2009) are anthologies of project materials, accompanied by the authors' contemporary materials. Willard shares his travels and observations as he revisits the basic WPA strategy of focusing on group events involving food, such as community festivals. He includes one short discussion of burgoo and its history, based on a story originally published in the *Louisville Courier-Journal* in 1932 (the America Eats project also collected newspaper articles and the like). The piece includes familiar stories about the dish's origins in the Civil War and the naming of the 1932 Kentucky Derby winner Burgoo King by the owner of Idlehour Farm in Lexington. The discussion of burgoo is coupled with descriptions of Brunswick stew from North Carolina and the Minnesota-derived Booya, cooked by folks of German ethnicity. Burgoo, Brunswick stew, and Booya share some commonalities, including long cooking times, the use of assorted meats and many vegetables, and a tradition of large batches cooked mostly by men.

The Food of a Younger Land consists of selected America Eats materials, coupled with introductory essays by Kurlansky. The book's organization is based on the project's original geographic structure. It begins with a long but readable essay on the project itself and is illustrated with the author's linocut prints. Kurlansky includes considerably more Kentucky material than Willard's single burgoo recipe. He provides the menu for Christmas dinner at the Brown Hotel in 1940 and recipes for Kentucky ham bone soup, Kentucky burgoo, Kentucky oysters (aka lamb fries), Kentucky wilted lettuce, spoon bread, divinity chocolates, eggnog, the old-fashioned cocktail, and mint juleps. None of these is signed.

I found some America Eats materials at the Kentucky Department for Libraries and Archives, including a copy of a letter dated October 21, 1941, from Marion W. Flexner to the folks working on the project (specifically, to a Mr. Arnold). Her letter contains recipes for ham bone soup, hoppin' John, black-eye peas, and cracklin' cornbread (see below). The ham bone soup recipe is reprinted verbatim in the Kurlansky volume, although it is unsigned. It also appears, signed, in the Cabbage Patch Circle's *Famous Kentucky Recipes* (1952). Flexner's letter says this about cornbread: "The old time Southerner made this with the cracklings or crisp pieces of browned skin, left from rendering the lard after a 'hog killing.' However today in a modern kitchen we can achieve almost the same result by making our cracklings out of ground salt pork, fried crisp. Here is a very satisfactory substitute recipe for the original one."

Cracklin' Corn Bread (1941)

1 cup corn meal, water ground if possible
½ teaspoon soda
1 tablespoon melted fat from salt pork
4 ounces salt pork or enough to make ¼ cup of cracklings
½ cup boiling water
½ cup rich buttermilk
Salt to taste

Wash pork and dry. Put through the fine knife of the meat grinder. Fry until golden brown, then drain until crisp on brown paper. Sift the meal. Add the boiling water, then the buttermilk previously

> mixed with soda. Fold in the crisp cracklings. Heat an 8 inch iron skillet in a hot oven set at 400 degrees. Place 1 tablespoon of the fat from the pork in the pan and grease well. Add more salt to the batter if necessary, but usually the pork will be salty enough to season the batter. Pour the batter into the hot greased skillet and spread the fat over the surface (it will rise to the top). Return the pan to the oven and cook ½ hour or until crust is brown and bread leaves the sides of the pan. Cut into pie shaped wedges and butter while hot. (Letter from M. W. Flexner to Mr. Arnold. October 21, 1941. [KDLA])

The *Louisville Courier-Journal* and Kentucky Foodways

Given the hard times of the Depression, the private sector attempted to improve people's living conditions. Accompanying this effort was a journalistic concern about economical and nutritional food preparation. It was during this era that the *Louisville Courier-Journal* hired its first food editor, dietitian Gladys Marie Wigginton, who wrote under the name Marie Gibson (Finley 1985, 5). In his introduction to *The* Courier-Journal *Kentucky Cookbook,* John Finley notes, "Food editors were needed to sort through the torrent of information newspapers were receiving about new food and kitchen products and to make sense out of it all for the readers" (ibid.). Gibson's byline first appeared in 1936 and continued until 1941. Her columns often included recipes requested by readers, as well as recipes submitted in response to a weekly contest focusing on specific dishes. Aided by her neighbors, Gibson tested the recipes and selected the winners, which were printed in the paper. Her columns were frequently based on the theme of "economizing," such as how to use "second-day" food, or leftovers. One column in the late 1930s was headed: "Suggestions for shortcuts in meat costs, heavy item in budget." The columns also included photographs of the featured dish. Gibson introduced her recipe for "real southern apple dumplings" (see below) as follows: "A simple turn of the wrist makes these apple dumplings different from the common garden variety. After the edges of the dough are brought together over the sliced apple filling, the dumplings are turned over and placed in the baking dish, smooth side up. The results are delicious."

Real Southern Apple Dumplings (1937)

Two cups soft wheat flour
1 teaspoon salt
½ cup shortening
Cold water
4 or 5 tart apples
1 cup sugar
1 teaspoon cinnamon
2 tablespoons butter

Sift the flour and salt together; cut or rub the shortening into the flour with the tips of the fingers or a pastry blender; add water, a little at a time to make a very stiff dough. Do not knead. Roll the dough very thin. Cut in rounds (use a medium-sized saucer). Pare apples and slice thin. Place in the center of each round of pastry. Mix the sugar and cinnamon. Add 1 tablespoon to each dumpling. Moisten edges of pastry, bring together and seal. Place smooth side up in a greased baking dish. Prick tops, dot with butter and sprinkle with remaining sugar and cinnamon mixture. Add ¼ cup water, cover and bake in moderate oven (350 degrees F.) 30 minutes. Remove cover and brown pastry. Serve with whipped cream or lemon sauce. (Gibson 1937)

Marie Gibson was the first in a succession of important *Courier-Journal* food editors and writers that continues today. Collectively, they have influenced Kentucky foodways by introducing new recipes and food trends to their readers, but probably more important, they have served as mirrors, reflecting the innovative culinary practices of central Kentucky cooks back to their community. I discuss this further in later chapters.

Charity Cookbooks

Favorite Recipes (1938), compiled by the Woman's Club of Louisville, is an early example of a cookbook with entertaining and parties in mind. The sales of the cookbook supported the club's important social services program. The Woman's Club of Louisville was established in 1890 and still occupies a large, historically significant building known as Frazier House. A pen-and-ink drawing of the front of Frazier House is included in the 1938 cookbook. A similar photograph dominates the first page of the group's present-day website.

The cookbook includes, on page three, a poem apparently written by one of the members (signed E. B. R.). It reflects women's growing social and economic engagement, yet their continued ties to the domestic sphere and traditional gender roles.

> A woman likes to vote, she likes to make a speech;
> She likes an office job, or else a school to teach;
> She likes to do what men do—go fishing, fly a plane;
> She likes to travel round the world, and come home again;
> She likes to make what men can make, a picture, song, or book;
> But in her very heart of hearts a woman is a cook;
> So in this Club, where many minds compare their differing thought,
> We've done the same for cooking each her specialty has brought.

The recipes, which are signed, list the ingredients first, followed by relatively extensive instructions, similar to what one might find in a contemporary cookbook. The measures used are modern, with a few exceptions such as "wine glasses." Another modern feature is that degree settings for the oven are provided. Some recipes include serving advice in addition to the cooking procedure. For instance, the recipe for salmon croquettes notes that a can of mushroom soup can be used as the sauce.

Some recipes were provided by local eating establishments such as the Pendennis Club, a refined downtown Louisville social club that was established in 1881. Henry Bain sauce, which often appears in Louisville-focused cookbooks, was invented by a Pendennis Club headwaiter. Mrs. Isaac T. Woodson contributed the club's recipe for turtle soup.

Pendennis Turtle Soup (1938)

2 pounds of veal bones
2 carrots
2 onions
1 ounce butter
3 tablespoons flour
2 quarts beef stock or water
1 small can tomatoes
1 small can tomato puree
salt
pepper
whole cloves
½ cup sherry
2 cups boiled fresh turtle meat
2 hard cooked eggs

Roast the bones and vegetables with butter until brown. Add water or beef stock, tomatoes, and tomato puree, salt, black pepper to taste and a few cloves. Boil for two hours. Add sherry wine, strain the soup through cheese cloth. Then add the boiled fresh turtle meat, cut in small squares, and eggs also in small squares. Boil up quickly and serve. (Woman's Club of Louisville 1938, 156–57)

Branded food products are called for relatively frequently. These brands include Philadelphia cream cheese, Fleischman's yeast, Crisco shortening, Baker's chocolate, Dromedary dates, Brer Rabbit molasses, Swans Down cake flour, None-Such mincemeat, Karo syrup, Wesson oil, Knox gelatin, Jell-O gelatin dessert, Kraft mayonnaise, Campbell's tomato soup, and Kraft Velveeta cheese. It is likely that the recipes using these products were originally published in magazines or in company-issued pamphlets.

Mrs. J. G. Minnigerode contributed the following recipe for scalloped oysters.

Scalloped Oysters (1938)

1 pint oysters
4 tablespoons oyster liquor
2 tablespoons milk or cream
½ cup stale bread crumbs
1 cup cracker crumbs
½ cup melted butter
Salt and pepper

Mix bread and cracker crumbs, and stir in butter. Put a thin layer in bottom of a buttered shallow baking dish, cover with oysters, and sprinkle with salt and pepper; add one-half each oyster liquor and cream. Repeat, and cover top with remaining crumbs. Bake thirty minutes in hot oven. Never allow more than two layers of oysters for Scalloped Oysters; if three layers are used, the middle layer will be underdone, while others are properly cooked. A sprinkling of mace or grated nutmeg to each layer is considered by many an improvement. (Woman's Club of Louisville 1938, 90)

The recipes selected for this cookbook no doubt addressed the club members' needs, which apparently included advice on entertaining. This is certainly one of the earliest Kentucky cookbooks with a section on entertainment. In a sense, this cookbook could have served as a prototype for later cookbooks such as the Junior League of Louisville's *The Cooking Book* (1978). By the mid-1950s, there were cookbooks focused entirely on entertainment, such as Marion Flexner's *Cocktail Supper Cookbook* (1955). Later examples include the Younger Woman's Club of Louisville's *Party Cook Book* (1966) and the Queen's Daughters' *Entertaining the Louisville Way* (1969).[4] More recently, Sarah Fritschner, former food editor of the *Courier-Journal*, published two entertainment-focused cookbooks with a Kentucky Derby theme: *Derby 101: A Guide to Food and Menus for Kentucky Derby Week* (2004) and *Sarah Fritschner's Derby: Start to Finish* (2006).

Prohibition Repealed!

The Depression era brought a change in the legal status of alcoholic beverages. The Volstead Act, passed in 1919, had many negative and largely unintended consequences and was repealed with passage of the Twenty-First Amendment in 1933. One response to the repeal of Prohibition was the publication of recipe books for cocktails and other drinks, such as *Irvin S. Cobb's Own Recipe Book* (1936). Cobb, a nationally known humorist from Paducah, wrote newspaper columns, short fiction, and screenplays, and he was the emcee of the 1935 Academy Awards. Cobb died in 1944 and is buried in his native Paducah. The publisher of Cobb's book, Frankfort Distilleries, produced both blended and straight whiskeys under various brands, including Four Roses (still on the market) and Old Oscar Pepper and Kentucky Velvet (no longer available). The recipe book includes a long essay by Cobb on whiskey in general and bourbon in particular, along with seventy-one recipes for cocktails and other drinks, with commentary by Cobb. There is also an essay on the history of Frankfort Distilleries, with considerable emphasis on how it followed the law during the Prohibition era: "During Prohibition, Frankfort sold only though legal channels. So far as is known, no Frankfort whiskey was ever bootlegged" (Cobb 1936, 37). Frankfort Distilleries held a federal distiller's permit, which allowed it to make medicinal whiskey. As the copy states, "In one year, more than 20,000 physicians purchased Frankfort whiskies for office use. One Frankfort brand, Antique, became known as the finest medicinal whiskey made" (ibid., 36).

Cobb includes a recipe for the old-fashioned, and he repeats the myth of its Pendennis Club origins, which has become conventional knowledge but is disputed by some. He asserts, "This cocktail was created at the Pendennis Club in Louisville in honor of a famous old-fashioned Kentucky colonel. I claim it is worthy of him" (Cobb 1936, 41). The legend is that the drink was originally created by a Pendennis Club bartender and promoted by the famous distiller Colonel James E. Pepper. Cocktail guide writer David Wondrich (2007) deflates the story by reporting that the old-fashioned cocktail was mentioned in the *Chicago Tribune* before the Pendennis Club was founded in 1881. In *The Old Fashioned: An Essential Guide to the Original Whiskey Cocktail*, Albert W. A. Schmid (2013) recounts the history of this classic and creates a place for the Pendennis origin legend by referring to the old-fashioned "as we know it today." Schmid's book contains many recipes for the old-fashioned, including a version of Cobb's that includes curaçao, which I don't recall seeing in any other recipes for this classic. The basic strategy, however, is the same: muddle bitters and a cube of sugar, add bourbon and a twist of citrus (most likely lemon), and then garnish with fruit, such as a slice of orange, a maraschino cherry, or perhaps pineapple. Some like to add a splash of club soda or sweet soda.

Chapter Five

New Foods and New Roles

World War II

World War II had an impact on Kentucky cookbooks and recipes. The most important influence was the dramatic increase in women's participation in the labor force, making convenience and efficiency paramount. These issues began to appear in the 1940s and certainly became more common in cookbooks of the 1950s and 1960s. Convenience was also promoted when, after the restrictions of the war years, the nation's robust industrial capacity and pent-up consumer demand led to the widespread use of kitchen appliances such as refrigerators and freezers.

Cookbooks and recipes of the era were shaped, to an extent, by wartime food policies such as rationing. This resulted in the introduction of new foods that were often replacements for rationed items. Also new in the 1940s were Kentucky cookbooks that attempted to tell a story beyond the recipes. In addition, this was the period when Bowling Green's own Duncan Hines published his innovative cookbooks and guides to fine dining.

Cookbooks that Tell a Story

Starting in the early 1940s, some cookbook authors embellished their recipes by including stories about the food, its historical context, the persons who cooked it, and the farmers or artisans who produced it; discussions of the finer technical points of food preparation; and, most of all, recollections about eating the food. The effect of these narratives was to create a web of meaning that enhanced the eating and cooking experience. In a phrase, it made food "good to think," to borrow an idea from anthropologist Marvin Harris (1985). The narrative was built primarily with textual material on various topics but also with the use of creative titles, images and their accompanying captions, and an occasional sidebar. Certainly this increased the pleasure associated with reading cookbooks and encouraged people to collect them. These days, most single-author cookbooks attempt to tell a story in conjunction with each recipe, and some express a consistent theme. Robust narratives appeared much later in the history of community charity cookbooks, but today they are quite common in more elaborately produced examples.

The earliest examples of narrative cookbooks are two by Louisville food writer Marion W. Flexner: *Dixie Dishes* (1941), published in Boston, and *Out of Kentucky Kitchens* (1949), published in New York. *Dixie Dishes* appears to be the first true narrative cookbook among those considered here. Flexner's later volume makes similar use of the narrative style. John Egerton comments about *Out of Kentucky Kitchens*, "In a state noted for its cuisine and its cooks, this little volume holds a place of honor" (1993, 360–61). My mother gave me a copy of this classic cookbook when my family first moved to Kentucky in 1974, and it served as my introduction to Kentucky cuisine. It is still available in the form of a University Press of Kentucky reprint (Flexner 1989). *Dixie Dishes* is very similar but is less well known than the later book. Flexner's other cookbooks include *Food for Children and How to Cook It* (1929; cowritten with Isabel McLennan McMeekin), *Quick Cooking from the Top of the Stove* (1951), and *Cocktail Supper Cookbook* (1955). She started writing with a Louisville women's writing group, which led to the submission of articles to the *Courier-Journal.* Her literary endeavors went beyond cookbooks and included a biography of Queen Victoria for young adults entitled *Drina: England's Young Victoria* (1939) and a book on gardening. Apparently, Flexner's mother also wrote cookbooks.

Marion W. Flexner was born in Montgomery, Alabama, and married Morris Flexner, a Louisville physician. I think *Dixie Dishes* is the first of the southern food cookbooks with clear Kentucky roots, although it

Dixie Dishes, the first narrative Kentucky cookbook.

has a very strong Gulf coast–New Orleans content. Both *Dixie Dishes* and *Out of Kentucky Kitchens* provide detailed recipes for basic Kentucky-style country cooking, among other themes. Flexner's experiences in New Orleans are reflected in recipes for king cake, pralines, and various Creole dishes. In addition to her cookbooks, Flexner combined her interests in food, cooking, and writing by contributing articles to the *New Yorker, Harper's, Vogue, Woman's Day, House and Garden*, and *Gourmet*.

Although Flexner presents her recipes in the modern format found in today's cookbooks, some of the recipes apparently originated from those "cooked by ear" by the African American cooks who worked in Flexner's girlhood homes (Flexner 1941, x). Like Jennie C. Benedict, she learned a great deal from the African Americans that served her family. She recalled, "I suppose it was to keep me employed during the long period after breakfast that 'Aunt Fanny' my grandfather's colored cook, would slip one of her large crisp white aprons over my head and set me to work. As I grew older she taught me many other 'intangibles' of cooking—the 'feel' of different types of dough, the cook and taste method of making sauces, the secret of adding charred onions to gravies for roasts" (ibid., dust cover). When Flexner shares what she learned from these African American cooks, her cookbook becomes biographical. Here and there she re-creates these scenes from her girlhood with a respectful but patronizing tone. For instance, Flexner relates an incident in which the family cook, Molly, gives Flexner's aunt a recipe but leaves out some vital ingredients. Young Marion wondered about this. "'Why did you do it?' I asked. I didn't dare scold Molly—nobody did." Molly responded: "'Lissen chile,' she said seriously, shaking her finger at me, 'dat pie is ma specialty—see? Effen Ah gives my receipts to everybody what axes for 'em, what Ah gwine ter lef' ter surprise 'em wid?' She put her hand kindly on my arm. 'Ah'll give you a piece of advice from an ol' woman—always keep sumpin' in reserve what you kin do better'n ennybody else, and don' share dat secret wid no one'" (ibid., 125–26).

In addition to recipes from the cooks who worked in her household, Flexner provides recipes from her mother, friends, some restaurants, and, in *Out of Kentucky Kitchens*, recipes from hard-to-find Louisville cookbooks. Here, I discuss two of these cookbooks on which Flexner drew:

Random Recipes by Minn-Ell Sherley Mandeville (1940) and *Query Club Recipes* (Allen 1941). Both include recipes for iconic Kentucky foods such as burgoo, fried chicken, greens, country ham, mint juleps, and various pies. Because she was writing for a national audience, Flexner includes recipes for traditional preparations that were taken for granted and rarely included in earlier Kentucky-based cookbooks.

Dixie Dishes and *Out of Kentucky Kitchens* are rooted in the Kentucky-inflected version of southern cooking. Perhaps even more clearly than Mary Harris Frazer's *Kentucky Receipt Book* (1903), Flexner clearly shows the basics of Louisville foodways—a foundation of simple Kentucky foods of rural origin coupled with strong Gulf coast influences and a sprinkling of European (mostly German and some French) tendencies. Given the region's cultural and culinary inclusiveness, recipes representative of various ethnic cuisines often show up in cookbooks rooted in Louisville. This is associated with a good-natured interest in food, dining out, and entertaining, especially at Derby time.

Introducing basic country cooking to her *Dixie Dishes* readership required detailed procedures and a narrative that conveyed the cultural context. It makes sense that this early account of basic Kentucky cuisine came from a person with a cosmopolitan viewpoint writing for a national audience. Included here is Flexner's recipe for a cabbage dish that she describes as the "traditional Southern recipe of preparing cabbage," which "screams for corn pone" to dunk in the pot likker. She notes that a dash of apple cider vinegar can be added at the table.

Cabbage with Salt Pork or Country Bacon (1941)

1 head, hard, white cabbage
1 slice hot red pepper
Salt, pepper to taste
½ pound bacon or salt pork
Water to cover cabbage

Put all ingredients on the stove in a heavy iron pot with a tight fitting lid. Wash the salt pork before using it. Cook 2 hours or until the

> liquor is full flavored and the cabbage tender. If salt pork is used, no extra salt will be necessary. The cabbage is likely to turn brown, but no matter.

Flexner goes on to say, "This is a fine luncheon dish for the laundress or the thorough cleaning men, and for you too, if you like it" (1941, 77–78).

Recipes of this era include more detailed discussions of technique than did previous cookbooks. One might attribute this to a decrease in readers' knowledge of cooking. As more women entered the workforce, they had fewer "apron-string cooking classes," and the amount of time they could devote to cooking decreased. The ingredients-only recipes found in community cookbooks from the turn of the century disappeared, and procedures were described in greater detail. Further, cooks and the people they cooked for were more cosmopolitan and adventuresome in their tastes, and cooks needed more elaborate information to produce authentic versions of new dishes. Certainly, Louisville-based cookbooks contained a number of ethnic dishes. The two Flexner cookbooks were clearly written for a sophisticated national audience that would be unfamiliar with the iconic dishes of southern cuisine, seeing them as exotic rather than commonplace. She assumes her readers have never heard of pot likker and think that cornmeal is always yellow. She therefore provides extensive discussions of technique, and, given Flexner's effective and entertaining prose, this makes for interesting reading.

Flexner draws on the rare and "oh so Louisville" *Random Recipes* by Minn-Ell Sherley (aka Mrs. Fulton) Mandeville (1940). Mandeville was a prominent Louisville club woman, and her *Random Recipes*, published in proper letterpress and hard cover, consists of recipes that "have been used up and down 'The River' for generations" (Mandeville 1940, n.p.). Although it includes a wide range of dishes, they are often placed randomly; for example, the Bluegrass classic beaten biscuits shares a page with the gourmet flambéed dessert crepes suzette (ibid., 3). Like many Louisville cookbooks, there is some evidence of entertaining, including a whole section on hors d'oeuvres. Mandeville's recipe for persimmon pudding appeared in many editions of *Kentucky Heritage Recipes* (Historic Homes

Foundation 1976, 59). Unfortunately, the Mandeville volume contains limited narrative beyond the basics of the recipe. Nevertheless, she makes some comments. For instance, her recipe for corncakes ends with the following advice: "Use only white corn meal and never, never put sugar with it. That is an unpardonable sin in the South" (Mandeville 1940, 1). And in concluding her recipe for boiled calf's head, she writes what seems to be a non sequitur: "The best country hams I have ever tasted come from Cadiz, Kentucky. The late King of England was a regular customer" (ibid., 54). Here is her recipe for bread pudding.

Bread Pudding (1940)

3 slices of bread
1 quart cream
1 scant cup sugar
4 eggs
1 teaspoon vanilla

Let bread soak in cream ½ hour. Add well beaten yolks, sugar and vanilla. Lastly add the stiffly beaten whites. Bake in moderate oven 2 hours or more. Serve with hard sauce flavored with whiskey or sherry. (Mandeville 1940, 23)

Flexner's *Out of Kentucky Kitchens* includes recipes for "Minn-Ell Mandeville's Famous Spinach Farmers' Special" and "Minn-Ell Mandeville's Transparent Pie" (Flexner 1949, 149, 219). Flexner pays tribute to Mandeville, calling her "one of the best cooks Kentucky ever produced" (ibid., 219).

Another cookbook used by Flexner is a pamphlet titled *Query Club Recipes*, a compilation of members' recipes published in 1941. The Query Club, described by Flexner as "a small, select Louisville literary group" (1949, 244), consisted of the wives of some of the most important and wealthiest men in Louisville. Many of the recipes, which are signed, are typical of upper-class Louisville society; however, a few are typically Kentuckian, such as country ham. Some Gulf coast favorites are also included, such as chicken gumbo. The members' international orientation and travel experiences are evident in recipes for crème brûlée, borscht, and "Singapore's Famous Million Dollar Cocktail." The contributor notes that the cocktail recipe was "given me by the brother of the man who makes them there at Raffle's Hotel" (Allen 1941, 19). *Out of Kentucky Kitchens* includes two Query Club recipes, which Flexner titles "Dr. Alice Pickett's Bishop's Bread or Buttermilk Coffee Cake" and "Query Club Sponge Pudding with Wine Sauce." In the Query Club pamphlet, Pickett adds this comment about the recipe's origin: "This Southern type of coffee bread was so often served for Sunday breakfasts—in the Bluegrass, the Carolinas and Virginia—to any visiting 'bishops, priest, deacons and other clergy' that it came to be known as 'Bishop's Bread'" (ibid., 31).

Bishop's Bread (1941)

2½ cups flour
½ cup shortening
2 cups medium-brown sugar
1 teaspoon baking powder
½ teaspoon soda
½ teaspoon salt
1 teaspoon cinnamon
1 egg
¾ cup sour milk

Mix flour, salt, brown sugar and shortening, saving nearly a cup of the mixture for sprinkling on top of bread. To the rest of the mixture add baking powder, egg, sour milk, soda and cinnamon. Beat thoroughly. Put batter into two well-greased cake pans, sprinkling the first mixture over the tops. (Extra cinnamon may be added to the sprinkling mixture.) Bake in a hot oven about 25 minutes. Cut in squares or strips and serve piping hot, with lots of butter. (The second pan of bread may be used the next day, after a reheating in the oven.) (Allen 1941, 31)

On the Road with Duncan Hines

Another important person in the culinary history of Kentucky was Duncan Hines, who later became famous for his cake mixes and other grocery items. Born in Bowling Green, he worked as a traveling salesman for a printing company, and while he was on the road, he ate out a lot and started to compile lists of his favorite restaurants in various parts of the county. In 1935 he prepared a list of several hundred good restaurants and distributed it with his Christmas cards. The response was so positive that he continued the project, and updated editions of his guidebook *Adventures in Good Eating* were published into the early 1960s. In 1939 Hines published the first of his annually updated cookbooks called *Adventures in Good Cooking*. This was followed in 1955 with the *Duncan Hines Dessert Book*. Versions of both cookbooks were republished in 2002 under the

The Duncan Hines cookbook.

editorship of his primary biographer, Louis Hatchett. The recipes came mostly from restaurants throughout the United States and Canada, such as the one for deviled crab from the Tarpon Inn in Port Aransas, Texas. Other recipes came from individuals, including a few from Kentuckians, almost all of them from Bowling Green. A portion of the Kentucky recipes are for iconic dishes such as spoon bread, fried chicken, pot liquor, burgoo, fried apples, chess pie, and fried corn. The following recipe for graham cracker pie (recipe 445 in the 1948 edition) is from the only Kentucky restaurant included in the book: Sanders Café in Corbin. The cookbook uses an idiosyncratic two-column format combined with an action format, reminiscent of *The Joy of Cooking.* I simplified the format here.

Graham Cracker Pie (1948)

Crust

Ingredients

30 graham crackers, crushed	½ cup sugar
2 tablespoons flour	1 cup melted butter
2 tablespoons cinnamon	½ cup lard, melted

Directions (Makes two 8-inch pies)

Mix all ingredients and press in pie pans.

Filling

Ingredients

1 quart milk	½ cup sugar
8 egg yolks, beaten	8 egg whites, beaten
4 tablespoons cornstarch	½ cup sugar
2 teaspoons vanilla	1 pinch of salt
Pinch of salt	1 teaspoon vanilla
2 tablespoons melted butter	

Directions

Heat milk.

> Mix egg yolks, cornstarch, vanilla, salt, butter, and ½ cup sugar; add the heated milk and cook until thick. Then fill the pie shells.
>
> Make a meringue of remaining ingredients and cover pies. Brown in 350° oven. (Hines 1948, 445)

Based on his reputation and name recognition, Duncan Hines started a branded grocery business with businessman Roy Park. This enterprise was bought by Procter and Gamble in 1956, which added cake mixes to the offerings. Although this business has changed ownership through the years, Pinnacle Foods still sells Duncan Hines cake mixes and frostings. The Bowling Green Junior Women's Club is the current sponsor of the annual Duncan Hines Festival, held in July. The program includes a concert and a baking contest using Duncan Hines products, sponsored by Pinnacle Foods.

The War and Rationing

World War II had a considerable impact on foodways. Food rationing and related food shortages had important impacts that led to the creation of new recipes and the substitution of scarce ingredients with others that were more readily available.[1] Further, the war itself led to the appearance of new food products that grew out of the need to feed the troops.

Rationing was administered by the Office of Price Administration (OPA) through a coupon-based system. Starting in early 1942, each person received a series of war ration books filled with little perforated stamps, or coupons, coded for various categories of commodities. When rationed foods were purchased, the buyer paid with both money and ration coupons, which had to be torn off in the presence of the grocer to help prevent fraud. Different items required a different number of ration coupons (or ration points); for instance, a measure of beef roast cost more ration points than the same measure beef organ meats. Initially, no change was given for ration coupons; however, by 1944, small plastic disks were used as change. The coupons had expiration dates, adding to the complexity of household management. Food buyers, in effect, had to juggle two kinds of money. Along with the rationing effort, the OPA administered a system of price controls. Rationing lasted beyond the war, and the OPA was finally abolished in May 1947.

Rationed food items included sugar, coffee, meats, canned fish, cheese, canned milk, processed meats (sausage), dried and canned beans, prepared baby foods, and edible fats (including butter, lard, margarine, shortening, and the various oils). The rationing of sugar started early and lasted the longest (until 1947, well after the war ended). Because sugar was a special concern, there were special sugar coupons. The Japanese conquest of the Philippines early in 1942 was the initial crisis that led to sugar rationing. Beyond this, the problem with sugar was that a large portion of it was produced offshore and had to be imported, taking up space on cargo ships that was better allocated to troops and war materiel. Although rationing had some impact on the few cookbooks published during the war, there were recipes that called for sugar and other rationed foods. Foods that were not rationed included eggs, fresh fish, bread, cereal, pasta, mayonnaise, jams and jellies, fresh milk, and cottage and cream cheeses. Canned goods were rationed because of the need to conserve metal. Nonfood items were also rationed, including gasoline, fuel oil, kerosene, cars, tires, shoes and rubber footwear, and even typewriters.

Farmers and others were able to consume anything they produced themselves, and they also received their full share of ration points. Farmers who raised and slaughtered meat animals had to file for a permit if they intended to sell the meat. And farmers who sold rationed commodities directly to consumers had to collect coupons from them.

Cooks adapted. In *Theatrical Seasonings*, which reprints some recipes from a war-era cookbook, Mrs. E. E. Freeman notes, "It was during the war when so many things were rationed, so we used recipes that were inexpensive, yet delicious" (Winchester Council for the Arts 1994, 6). A contemporary community cookbook, *Preserving the Past for the Future* published by the Hopkins County Genealogical Society (2011), reprints portions of *The Victory Handbook for Health and Home Defense.*[2] Included are some suggestions for saving sugar: "As a first help in keeping within your sugar quota, try using less sugar in puddings, gelatins, ice creams,

Rations coupons distributed by the Office of Price Administration during World War II.

etc. You may find you have been adding more sugar than you need" (Hopkins County Genealogical Society 2011, n.p.).

A number of unrationed ingredients could substitute for sugar, including honey, sweet sorghum syrup, and corn syrup.[3] Corn syrup was not a wartime invention; sweetener from corn was first manufactured in 1866, and the familiar Karo syrups were introduced in 1902. Corn syrup appears in a number of recipes in *Stay for Tea*, one of the most interesting Kentucky fund-raising cookbooks of the 1940s. The University of Kentucky Women's Club published *Stay for Tea* (1948) to raise money for a scholarship fund established to honor Mrs. Frank McVey, whose husband was president of the university. She was very involved in programs that supported the university and did a considerable amount of entertaining on its behalf. Like most community cookbooks of the time, *Stay for Tea* has little narrative accompanying the member-contributed recipes. Although published after the war, *Stay for Tea* includes some recipes that reflect the wartime food situation, new food products, and availability of new technology. (Updated versions of *Stay for Tea* were published in 1975, 1983, and 2010; see chapter 8.)

Stay for Tea has five recipes for brownies, two of which use corn syrup. By the way, one of the brownie recipes was submitted by Esther (Mrs.

"*Stay for Tea*"

FAVORITE RECIPES

COMPILED BY

The
Woman's Club
of the
University of
Kentucky

FOR THE BENEFIT OF

The Frances Jewell McVey
Memorial Scholarship Fund

. . .

Printed by
The Thoroughbred Press
Lexington, Ky.

The first of the *Stay for Tea* cookbooks, published in 1948.

A. F.) Rupp, wife of legendary Kentucky basketball coach Adolph Rupp. A sugarless recipe for brownies was contributed by Mary L. (Mrs. H. H.) Jewett.

Sugarless Brownies (1948)

½ cup shortening
1 cup white corn syrup
2 squares unsweetened chocolate, melted
¾ cup sifted cake flour
1 teaspoon vanilla
¼ teaspoon baking powder
¼ teaspoon salt
2 eggs, well beaten
¾ cup chopped nuts

Cream shortening until fluffy, then add corn syrup gradually, continuing to work with spoon until light. Stir in melted chocolate. Sift together dry ingredients and add ¼ of them while beating mixture. Add well-beaten eggs, then remainder of dry ingredients and nuts. Turn into greased 9×9×3 inch cake pan and bake in 350 degree oven for about 35 minutes. Cut into squares when done. Makes 25. (University of Kentucky Women's Club 1948, 125)

Rationing created an incentive to use prepared mixes rather than baking from scratch. However, under the OPA, manufacturers' sugar supplies were also rationed, based on a percentage of their use levels prior to rationing. Another remedy for sugar rationing was to take advantage of the sugar contained in processed foods. *Selected Recipes from the Blue Grass*, published by the United Christian Missionary Society of the Christian Church of Midway in 1944, includes a recipe for a sweet dessert that calls for no sugar at all. Instead, it makes use of marshmallows and the syrup or juice from canned pineapple.

Pineapple Dessert (1944)

One number 2 can of sliced pineapple. Dip slices from syrup. Heat syrup in double boiler. When hot, but not boiling stir this into a pound of fresh marshmallows. Cut slices of pineapple into small pieces and stir in. Let cool thoroughly, then take a half pint of cream whipped stiff. Stir in gently, chill and serve. Will serve about 8. (Christian Church 1944, 33)

A few recipes always contained corn syrup, even before sugar rationing. One of these is pecan pie—a classic southern dessert. Some even say that the recipe was created by the Karo test kitchens in the 1920s.

Pecan Pie (1944)

3 eggs
1 cup white sugar
1 cup dark Karo syrup
1 cup broken pecans
¼ teaspoon salt
1 teaspoon vinegar

Beat eggs, stir sugar in well, add syrup, salt, vanilla, vinegar, and lastly pecans. Pour in uncooked crust and bake 45 minutes in medium oven. This makes a pie to serve six. (Christian Church 1944, 33)

In addition to ingredient substitutions, such as the corn syrup for sugar swap, *Stay for Tea* introduced a new food product: Spam. The canned chopped pork product was first produced in 1937 by the Hormel Company of Austin, Minnesota, largely to make use of the pork shoulders that were a residue of its ham business. The name Spam was the result of a naming contest, and it is believed to be a contraction of *spiced ham*. Because it does not require refrigeration, Spam became an important item in the diets of U.S. servicemen and Allied troops during World War II. Following the war, sales soared. Hormel has expanded the Spam product line with different flavors and ingredients. Based on the success of Spam, Armour produced a similar product named Treet, which some regard as inauthentic. *Stay for Tea*'s Spam recipe was contributed by Opal Palmer.

Beans 'n Spam (1948)

2 cans baked beans
1 can Spam
6 teaspoons (or more) prepared mustard
¼ cup brown sugar
2 tablespoons New Orleans molasses
2 teaspoons ground allspice

Empty the beans into a glass baking dish, slice Spam in six pieces and arrange on top of beans. Score the Spam two ways with sharp knife. Make a paste of prepared mustard, brown sugar, molasses and allspice and cover Spam slices with it. Bake [at] 350 degrees for 40 minutes. (University of Kentucky Women's Club 1948, 216)

Refrigeration Comes to Kentucky Homes

The post–World War II period saw the widespread adoption of refrigerators to replace iceboxes. Refrigerators were first made in about 1915 and became available for home use in the 1920s, but market penetration was limited. For the most part, these refrigerators were electric, but there were also gas-powered models on the market. Like all technological innovations, there was a long interval between early adopters of mechanical refrigeration and later ones, and it took a while for iceboxes to be replaced completely. Interestingly, rural residents who lived near railroad stops were able to have ice delivered regularly. Many brands of refrigerators were available in the early day, including Kelvinator, Frigidaire, and the widely used General Electric Monitor Top.[4]

With refrigeration came an increase in recipes involving chilling. To illustrate, Marion Flexner has this to say about "Ollie's Ice Box Super Rolls": "Since Ollie, our substitute cook, confided to me the recipe for her ice box rolls, I have practically discarded all other roll recipes. For this is without a doubt the greatest boon to housekeeping I have had in years. The dough will keep for several weeks in the electric refrigerator (provided it is not defrosted in the meantime). It lends itself to all possible variations" (1941, 13).

The 1948 version of *Stay for Tea* has a number of recipes that require refrigeration, including a large section on frozen desserts. Note that the term *icebox* is still used in recipes today.

Icebox Cookies (1948)

1 cup butter
2 cups brown sugar
2 whole eggs
3½ cups flour
1 teaspoon salt
¾ cup pecans

Cream butter and sugar. Add beaten eggs, flour and salt, a little at a time. Add pecans. Shape in roll, wrap in waxed paper and place in ice-box over night. Slice thin and bake in moderate oven. (University of Kentucky Women's Club 1948, 138)

Chapter Six

Convenience and Innovation

The Mid-Twentieth Century

This era witnessed a culinary paradox. By the 1950s, Kentucky cookbook writing seemed to be going in a number of different directions: some cooks were motivated by novelty and complexity, and others wanted to simplify. We had both Julia Child's *Mastering the Art of French Cooking* (Beck, Bertholе, and Child 1961) and Peg Bracken's *I Hate to Cook Book* (1960).

Although there seemed to be more interest in cookbooks, there may have been less interest in cooking, or at least a greater focus on convenience. There was a sizable increase in the number of Kentucky cookbooks published, especially community cookbooks. One of the reasons for this was the creation of numerous firms, mostly in the Midwest, that specialized in the publication of limited-run cookbooks compiled by community groups. Newspapers, especially the *Louisville Courier-Journal*, catered to their increasingly food-interested readership. Their food editors and columnists published recipes that reflected state and regional foodways.

The development of processed foods, which started in the late nineteenth century, accelerated dramatically during this period. Branded processed foods were fully embraced: Ketchup was made by Heinz and came in a bottle; it was not some complex recipe cooked down on the stove. Soup came in a can, and it was best if the can said "Campbell's." Recipes made up of almost entirely canned ingredients frequently popped up in community cookbooks in this era. That said, many cookbooks were also more cosmopolitan and often included both ethnic recipes and more complex ones, labeled *gourmet.* Many cookbooks included recipes from around the world.

Charity Cookbooks

There are a number of noteworthy Louisville-based charity cookbooks from this era. One that continues to have a following is a fund-raising cookbook produced in 1952 by the Cabbage Patch Circle, a Louisville community service organization (various editions and reprints were published at least until 1972). Although it is commonly found in a comb-bound paperback format, a hardcover edition was published in 1956. The original title was *Famous Kentucky Recipes* (Cabbage Patch Circle 1952), but subsequent editions used the more familiar *Cabbage Patch: Famous Kentucky Recipes* (1956). Alton Brown (2010), the "Good Eats" guy, identifies four standards for authenticity in community cookbooks: (1) they must be spiral bound or, he says, "they are not to be trusted"; (2) the recipes must be attributed to members of the community; (3) the cookbooks must be democratic, meaning the role of the editor is muted; and (4) they must convey a strong sense of place. The Cabbage Patch cookbooks meet Brown's criteria.

The Cabbage Patch Circle was organized by a group of women in 1910 to support a settlement house on Ninth Street in Louisville. Early in its history it provided housing for the poor, a community clothing bank, a nursery school, and a cooking school. The name Cabbage Patch came from the fact that the settlement house served an area of Louisville that had once been the site of a field used to grow cabbages. Residents of this area became characters in the novels of Alice Hegan Rice, including *Mrs. Wiggs of the Cabbage Patch* (1902), which was made into a movie three times. Rice, who did volunteer social work, was on the Cabbage Patch Circle's first board of directors. The circle recently celebrated its centenary and continues its good works.

As a community cookbook, *Famous Kentucky Recipes* is based on contributed recipes, most of which are signed. In addition to the women of Louisville, there are recipes from other sources, such as the Pendennis Club and the Brown Hotel in Louisville, the Old Stone Inn in Simpsonville, the Talbott Inn in Bardstown, the Beaumont Inn in Harrodsburg,

A Kentucky fund-raising classic compiled by the Cabbage Patch Circle.

and Gabe's Restaurant in Owensboro. Except for Gabe's, these businesses are still open and worth a visit, although the Pendennis Club is private. Gabe's Restaurant and Motor Inn was an important Owensboro landmark before owner Gabriel Fiorella retired in 1985. In advertising, Fiorella styled his restaurant as "The Steak House of the South." The Cabbage Patch cookbook augments his recipe for french fried onions with a short biography that states, "From hamburger wagon to one of Kentucky's most famous eating places, he has parlayed hard work, keen wits and good humor into prosperity and eminence" (Cabbage Patch Circle 1952, 93).

Famous Kentucky Recipes also presents recipes from food writers such as Louisville's Marion Flexner and Cissy Gregg and Mr. and Mrs. Duncan Hines of Bowling Green. Both Mr. and Mrs. Hines contributed apple pie recipes. There are a number of recipes attributed to Jennie C. Benedict, including the fruitcake recipe that started her career, as well as "Miss Jenny's Bluegrass Chicken" and "Benedictine Spread." The recipe for the latter, included here, was contributed by Mrs. Russell T. Walton.

A Recipe for Benedictine

Recipes for Jennie Benedict's creations continue to appear in contemporary cookbooks. The most popular is Benedictine spread, a filling for tea sandwiches. Interestingly, Benedict never published a recipe for Benedictine spread in any of her own cookbooks. Susan Reigler's introduction to the reprinted *Blue Ribbon Cook Book* (Benedict [1922] 2008) pays homage to Jennie Benedict's eponymous sandwich spread and includes a discussion of a number of contemporary recipes for it. Recipes for Benedictine spread are frequently included in recent cookbooks that focus on Kentucky.

Benedictine Sandwich Filling (1952)

1 cucumber
1 cake of Philadelphia cream cheese
1 small onion

salt to taste
mayonnaise

Grind cucumber and onion together, very fine. Put in strainer or cheese cloth and press out juice. Soften cream cheese, add cucumber and onion juice and salt. Add enough mayonnaise to make a soft spread. A little green vegetable coloring may be added, if desired. A dash of Accent (MSG) also enhances the flavor of this always delightful sandwich spread. If a stronger flavor is desired, add a tablespoon or two of the finely ground pulp—let your taste guide you. (Cabbage Patch Circle 1952, 14)

Some consider the green food coloring a characteristic component of "authentic" Benedictine spread. Contemporary recipes treat it as optional, and one recipe uses spinach as a colorant. It seems to me that using only the juice of the onion and cucumber is more authentic than adding the pulp to the spread. Mrs. Walton's inclusion of MSG is unusual, if not unique.

The selection of recipes reflects the food traditions of Louisville expressed earlier, albeit with some differences, in Mary Harris Frazer's *Kentucky Receipt Book* (1903) and Marion Flexner's *Dixie Dishes* (1941) and *Out of Kentucky Kitchens* (1949). Again, we find recipes for the foods of rural Kentucky, including cornbread, biscuits, and greens with seasoning, merged with Creole and Cajun classics from New Orleans and the Gulf coast. For example, the 1952 Cabbage Patch cookbook includes a recipe for jambalaya contributed by Ohio River Green Line Steamers, a towboat company. Another important element is the inclusion of foods for Kentucky Derby parties and other events. Following the table of contents is a suggested menu for a Derby breakfast: old Kentucky country ham, thinly sliced; hot beaten biscuits; turkey hash, served shortcake style with southern cornbread; green asparagus vinaigrette on Bibb lettuce; tiny chess tarts; and Miss Jenny's party mints.

In addition to Kentucky classics, the 1952 Cabbage Patch cookbook includes ethnic dishes of Italian, German, Indian, and Chinese origin. The Louisville community of cooks was becoming much more cosmopolitan over time, and this was reflected by changes in the ethnic composition of

Louisville and an increase in ethnic foods in cookbooks. Here is a recipe for German potato salad contributed by Mrs. Linton A. Caulfield Jr.

German Potato Salad (1952)

potatoes
1 stalk celery
2 hard cooked eggs
1 tablespoon parsley (chopped)
2 eggs beaten
1 onion, diced
½ tablespoon pepper
6 slices breakfast bacon
½ cup sugar
½ cup vinegar
½ cup water
½ tablespoon salt
¼ tablespoon dry mustard

Boil potatoes, peel, dice; add celery, sliced hard-boiled eggs and onion. Beat eggs and add sugar, spices, vinegar and water. Mix well. Pour mixture into hot bacon fat, stir until mixture thickens. Pour over potatoes, etc. Break crisp bacon into small pieces and mix in salad. (Cabbage Patch Circle 1952, 121)

The trend toward a more cosmopolitan selection of recipes was also evident in Marion W. Flexner's *Cocktail Supper Cookbook* (1955), which took a more sophisticated path than her earlier *Dixie Dishes* (1941) and *Out of Kentucky Kitchens* (1949). Her new cookbook was organized around a number of menus with various themes suitable for a cocktail party. As the dust jacket states, the emphasis was on "planned-ahead and cooked-ahead food that knows how to wait." The recipes include arroz con pollo, cannelloni with cheese sauce, Baltimore crab cakes, chocolate mousse, lasagne, paella Valenciana, Philadelphia pepper pot, veal scaloppine, and zuppa Inglese. I included a recipe here from her 1955 cookbook.

Red Cabbage, Sweet-and-Sour (1955)

¼ cup bacon drippings or butter
1 large onion, peeled and minced
2 tablespoons flour
1 large firm head red cabbage, shredded fine
1 bay leaf
Salt and black pepper
2 whole cloves
2 apples pared and shredded
⅓ cup cider vinegar or more
⅓ cup dark brown sugar or more

Melt fat, add onion and flour, stir until brown. Pour in 1 cup water, stirring to make a smooth sauce. Add cabbage, enough water to barely cover, bay leaf, salt, and pepper. Cover, bring to a hard boil. Reduce heat and simmer 30 to 40 minutes. Add rest of ingredients; cook ½ hour longer. Cabbage should be tender by then and sauce spicy. Correct flavoring to your taste. (Flexner 1955, 168)

This resembles one of my family's heirloom German recipes. The interesting difference is that Flexner uses the classic New Orleans practice of producing a roux as the first step. My version is from my cousin's grandfather, Billy Schubert, who was the cook at a German restaurant in Watertown, Wisconsin. He just added a sprinkling of flour near the end of the process to thicken the sauce. Clearly, Flexner's version is a traditional middle European recipe put through a Gulf coast sieve.

Emergence of the Charity Cookbook Publishing Industry

Starting in the 1950s, there was a substantial increase in the number of fund-raising cookbooks published by companies that specialized in this business. In part, this was attributable to technological advances, with offset printing becoming widely available in around 1950. Offset printing was less expensive than letterpress printing, as it could be done from a clean typescript rather than requiring typesetting and linotypes. In contrast, earlier fund-raisers, such as those created by the Women's Guild of the Christ Church Cathedral in the 1920s and *Housekeeping in the Blue Grass*, first published in 1875, were hardbound books printed with a letterpress, typically by printing companies located in the same town as the group that compiled the book. There were many companies that specialized in publishing charity cookbooks, including Fundcraft Publishers (Collierville, Tennessee); Bev-Ron Publishers (Kansas City, Kansas), which became Cookbook Publishers (Lenexa, Kansas); Walter's Cookbooks (Waseca, Minnesota); Cookbooks by Morris (Kearney, Nebraska); Walsworth Brothers (Marceline, Missouri); Circulation Service (Leawood, Kansas); General Publishing and Printing (Iowa Falls, Iowa); G&R Publishing (Waverly, Iowa); Jumbo Jack's (Audubon, Iowa); Famous Recipe Press (Nashville, Tennessee); and Wimmer Cookbooks (Memphis, Tennessee). There were probably others, and some of these have merged or ceased operations. Fundcraft and Cookbooks by Morris seem to be the most prominent, and Tennessee-based Fundcraft has the greatest presence in Kentucky. Wimmer of Memphis and Famous Recipe Press of Nashville produce cookbooks with high production values.

Many of these companies emerged in the Midwest in the 1930s and 1940s. For example, Fundcraft started as a small eastern Kansas print shop in the early 1940s. According to its corporate history, its first cookbook was a fund-raiser for the local Methodist church. By the early 1950s, Fundcraft had purchased new offset printers to reduce costs and make short print runs more feasible. The company expanded through acquisitions and eventually purchased a new building in Collierville, Tennessee, just outside of Memphis. In the 1990s its cookbook production system became Internet based. Today, Fundcraft, Cookbook Publishers, Cookbooks by Morris, and others offer a wide range of services through their websites, including downloadable guides to cookbook preparation, software programs for recipe data entry, cookbook sales, and apparently even access to recipes.

All this procedural assistance, however useful, has had an impact on the product. Many of the cookbooks published by these firms share certain characteristics. One important feature is that descriptions of cooking procedures are limited. Further, with a few exceptions, there is almost no narrative about local or family history or the stories behind the recipes and their origins. Because the cost of printing cookbooks is based in part on length, there is less incentive to include storytelling. Often these cookbooks and recipes are formulaic in form and content. Their repetitive nature is increased by the availability of online "recipe banks" and the "canned" artwork and kitchen hints used by the firms that produce these cookbooks. Cookbook historian Janice Longone summarizes this situation: "More often, these mass-produced books are poorly produced, with much 'canned' material and little or no uniqueness or regional flavor" (1997, 28). This critique does not extend to all the contemporary charity cookbooks produced—especially those that are not published by these cookbook companies. In some, the voices of the cooks and the community can be heard. Many independently and locally produced charity cookbooks are culturally interesting and include excellent narratives about cooking, local history, and families.

Among the Kentucky cookbooks considered here, the earliest example produced by one of these specialized publishers is dated 1950. There are probably earlier ones, but it is sometimes hard to tell, given that a number of cookbooks are undated. This modest volume, published by Bev-Ron of Kansas City, Missouri, was compiled by Trinity Methodist Church of Latonia in Kenton County and is entitled *Latonia's Favorite Recipes*. There are a few anachronisms: one recipe calls for "butter, the size of a walnut," and another evokes the pre-homogenization era by calling for "top milk" in a recipe for custard filling (Trinity Methodist Church 1950, 49, 50). The following recipe for apple crisp was contributed by Mrs. Wm. Sowder.

Apple Crisp (1950)

6 juicy apples
1 cup sugar
2 teaspoons lemon juice
1 teaspoon cinnamon

½ cup butter
¾ cup flour
¼ teaspoon nutmeg

Peel and core apples and cut into quarters. Arrange in greased Pyrex pie plate or shallow baking dish and pour lemon juice over apples. Blend butter, flour, sugar and spices as for pie crust. Press this mixture over top of apples. Bake, temperature 375 degrees for 1 hour. Serve with whipped cream or nutmeg sauce or hard sauce. (Trinity Methodist Church 1950, 55)

In some cases, a cookbook that began as a community fund-raiser was transformed into something resembling a single-author cookbook. First compiled in 1965 by Irene Hayes, *What's Cooking in Kentucky* started as a fund-raiser for the Hueysville Church of Christ in Floyd County, which needed a new roof. Nearly fifty years and several editions later, it has evolved into a Kentucky classic that has sold more than 200,000 copies. Back in 1965, Mrs. Hayes, then the Hueysville postmaster, contacted other Ken-

The original 1965 version of Irene Hayes's *What's Cooking in Kentucky.*

tucky postmasters to facilitate recipe collection beyond her own community. She even interviewed some cooks to reconstruct recipes that were not written down. The recipes selected are a tribute to skilled Kentucky home cooking, according to John Egerton, who calls Hayes's cookbook "an all-Kentucky favorite" (1993, 361). Although the recipes come from many contributors, Hayes produced a cookbook with a consistent voice. The recipes follow an action format that integrates the process with the ingredients list, very much like *The Joy of Cooking.* Although Mrs. Hayes died recently, her cookbook continues under the guidance of her daughter. The current edition has more than 800 recipes. Here is a recipe from the original 1965 edition contributed by Mrs. Mary Franklin of Salyersville, in Magoffin County.

Fresh Apple Cake (1965)

BEAT WELL TOGETHER:
2 cups white sugar
3 eggs
1½ cups cooking oil

DO NOT use mixer for balance of cake.
SIFT TOGETHER:
½ scant teaspoon cinnamon
1 scant teaspoon salt
½ scant teaspoon nutmeg
1½ scant teaspoon soda
½ scant teaspoon cloves
3 cups sifted flour
ADD to above mixture.

THEN ADD:
3 cups finely chopped, soft apples
1 cup finely chopped pecans

BAKE 1½ hours in 325 degree oven. (Hayes 1965, 35)

Early Restaurant and Chef Cookbooks

The first restaurant-based cookbooks were published in the 1950s. These include a series written by Richard T. Hougen, who managed the Boone Tavern of Berea College from 1940 to 1976. The first, *Look No Further: A Cookbook of Favorite Recipes from Boone Tavern Hotel, Berea College, Kentucky* (1955), has the recipe for the tavern's famous spoon bread, which is linked to the creation of Berea's Spoon Bread Festival, and the recipe for what Hougen calls "Chicken Flakes in Birds Nest" (1955, 16, 132). The other volumes are *Cooking with Hougen* (1960) and *More Hougen Favorites* (1971).

The first of the Hougen's Boone Tavern cookbooks.

Southern Spoon Bread (1955)

3 cups milk
1¼ cups cornmeal
3 eggs
2 tablespoons butter
1¾ teaspoons baking powder
1 teaspoon salt

1. Stir meal into rapidly boiling milk. Cook until very thick, stirring constantly, to prevent scorching.

2. Remove from fire and allow to cool. The mixture will be cold and very stiff.

3. Add well egg, salt, baking powder and melted butter. Beat with electric beater for 15 minutes. If hand beating is used break the hardened cornmeal into the beaten eggs in small amounts until all is well mixed. Then beat thoroughly for 10 minutes using a wooden spoon.

4. Pour into well-greased casserole. Bake for 30 minutes at 375 degrees F. Serve from casserole by spoonfuls. (Hougen 1955, 16)

Hougen tells us, "Be sure to use white cornmeal for the true Southern bread" (ibid.).

Food Journalism

A fascinating aspect of the 1950s and 1960s was the influence of newspaper-based food columnists, especially those of Louisville's *Courier-Journal.* Easily the most influential culinary writer of this era was Mary "Cissy" Gregg, who served as the paper's food editor from 1942 until her retirement in 1963 (Finley 1985, 6). Gregg, a native of Cynthiana in Harrison County, graduated from the University of Kentucky with a degree in agriculture and home economics. Her popular food column had an enthusiastic following, and she also wrote two cookbooks for distribution with the paper: *Cissy Gregg's Cookbook and Guide to Gracious Living* (1953) and *Cissy Gregg's Cookbook* (1959). These were combined and published as *Cissy Gregg's Cook Book* in 1981, with an introduction by Deni Hamilton, another *Courier-Journal* food editor. Gregg's recipes appear in many other Louisville-based cookbooks and in more historically oriented anthologies of recipes, including *The* Courier-Journal *&* Times *Cookbook* (1971) edited by one of her successors, Lillian Marshall. That collection declares on the cover that it contains "91 favorite Cissy Gregg Recipes" (Marshall 1971). Many of Gregg's recipes also appear in *The* Courier-Journal *Kentucky Cookbook* (Finley 1985). In addition, one occasionally finds recipes attributed to her in community cookbooks of the era. Gregg is often mentioned by contemporary Kentucky cookbook authors as an important influence.

Cissy Gregg's style is distinctive. She often places herself very much in the kitchen scene, enhancing her recipes with good-natured chats about the meaning of food, regional differences, variations in recipes, and the sensory delights associated with food. Her informal style, totally lacking in pretense, fosters trust and affection. According to Deni Hamilton, "Reading Cissy was like standing beside her at the stove. She conjured up a good picture of what the cook was getting into in the preparation of the dish, and exactly what to expect when it was prepared, even though she was a bit 'wordy' by today's journalistic standards" (quoted in Finley 1985, 6). In a few cases, she presents alternative strategies for preparing the same dish, giving her readers a choice. An excellent example is her classic take on dumplings. She starts with the premise that men prefer dumplings like the ones their mothers used to make. But, as she observes, "All mothers did not make them alike, we have found out." She therefore presents three approaches and tells her readers to "decide for themselves" (Finley 1985, 8). Gregg's discourse on dumplings appears in at least four cookbooks: *Cissy Gregg's Cookbook and Guide to Gracious Living* (1953), John Finley's *The* Courier-Journal *Kentucky Cookbook* (1985), Linda Allison-Lewis's *Kentucky's Best: Fifty Years of Great Recipes* (1998), and Mark F. Sohn's *Appalachian Home Cooking: History, Culture, and Recipes* (2005). Here it is again.

One of the Sunday supplement cookbooks by the much-loved Cissy Gregg.

Chicken 'N' Dumplings

Dumpling No. 1
Make the same kind of pastry you would for pie crust. Use more flour than usual on the board when rolling them out. Roll the dough very-very thin. Cut in strips and drop them into the broth.

Dumpling No. 2
Make a richer-than-average biscuit dough. Go to the half-way place between biscuits and pastry, and at that point you'll find the perfect proportion for a dumpling. Cook the same as dumpling No 1.

Dumpling No. 3
Place in a bowl the amount of flour you want to make up. Two cups of flour, we'll say. Add salt to taste—we used a good teaspoonful. The chicken has been cooked until it is at the place in doneness that, if it had to take one more simmer, it would suffer a complete break-away from the bones.

At this point, tenderly lift it from the stew pot to a serving bowl and keep hot. . . . Dip up a spoonful of the hot liquid and add it to the measured flour in the bowl. Add enough of the chicken broth to make a rather stiff dough. Roll out thin on a well-floured board, cut in strips, I'd say an inch wide, and drop them into the boiling stew. Cover the pot and cook about 10 to 15 minutes. They must be done, though the thickness the dough is rolled will hold the accurate time needed. (Finley 1985, 8)

Cissy Gregg was much loved and had a real following in central Kentucky; her recipes appeared in community cookbooks into the 1960s. Kentucky cookbook author Ronni Lundy includes a story about a Cissy Gregg cookbook in her *Butter Beans to Blackberries: Recipes from the Southern Garden* (1999). When Lundy's mother decided to move from a seven-room house to a smaller condo, she held a big yard sale. As Lundy recounts:

> One of Cissy Gregg's tattered and splattered rotogravure cookbooks ended up in the "Any Book for a Quarter" box. Fortunately for me, my fairy godmother arrived at 7:30 A.M. on the day of the sale, wearing a scarf tied under her chin and cat's-eye glasses. She spotted the Cissy Gregg immediately, pulled it out of the box, snorted with shock, and marched right up to me. "Do you cook?" she barked. "Sure," I said. "Well then why in heaven's name would you let this go?" She shoved the magazine into my hands and pointed square at my nose. "You take this back in the house and don't you sell it for any price. And you'd better thank your lucky stars it was me that found it and not one of those antique dealers." (Lundy 1999, 60–61)

Starting with the work of Marie Gibson in 1936 and continuing with Cissy Gregg, the *Louisville Courier-Journal* has had important food editors and columnists. They include Loyta Higgins, Deni Hamilton, Lillian Marshall, Camille Glenn, Elaine Corn, Sarah Fritschner, Pableaux Johnson, and Ron Mikulak.

Can Opener Cookery and the Quest for Convenience

Although recipes that called for commercial packaged goods first appeared much earlier, the cookbooks of the 1950s included many more brand-name prepared ingredients as cooking became geared toward convenience. This shift relates to changes in the social context of cooking, including whether a household had a kitchen staff, the still strict gender-based division of labor, and the dramatic increase in women's participation in the off-farm labor force. As the primary cook assumed a wider array of responsibilities, convenience became more important, and recipes featured more convenience foods.

According to Laura Shapiro's *Something from the Oven: Reinventing Dinner in 1950s America*, what she calls "package food cuisine" or "can-opener cooking" grew rapidly from the end of World War II until the early 1960s (2004, 6). Cooks used cake mixes, canned soups as noodle binders in casseroles, and Jell-O as a base for various desserts and salads. As more and more women joined the labor force, the need to save time became acute, and the food industry responded by developing products to address that need. Shapiro writes that the "food industry began leaving unmistakable finger prints on the meal and the recipes that characterized home cooking" (ibid., xvii). This change did not happen overnight. The first U.S. patent for manufactured gelatin was issued in 1845, and Jell-O was introduced in 1897 (Wyman 2001). By the 1950s, packaged foods had become mainstream. Some argue that our collective taste adjusted to this change and came to expect the taste of highly processed food (think Heinz ketchup). This kind of cooking continues.

The following recipe from *Famous Kentucky Recipes* was contributed by Mrs. James B. Young and makes use of canned soups and crab meat.

Crab Meat Bisque (1952)

1 can cream of tomato soup
1 can green pea soup
½ cup single cream
1 can crab meat
¼ cup sherry
salt and pepper to taste

Mix tomato and pea soup in a sauce pan until smooth, add cream and mix. Rinse and pick over crab meat. Add to mixture. Heat to a boiling point, add sherry and serve. 1 can of black bean soup can be substituted for the pea soup. Serves four to six. (Cabbage Patch Circle 1952, 24)

The cookbook compiled by the Charity League of Paducah uses the same strategy, known as the soup merger—that is, mixing two different canned soups to create a new soup. In a series of combinations signed by "Petty Larceny," cream of oyster and cream of tomato soups become oyster soup Louisiane, cream of celery and chicken noodle soups make Aunt Ellen's soup, and corn chowder and onion soup result in Indian chowder (Charity League of Paducah 1967, 17).

The following recipe, contributed by Velma Smith, comes from *Kentucky Cooking New and Old*, compiled by the Colonelettes—wives of members of the Louisville Chamber of Commerce. With certain substitutions, it could be what the French's website refers to as an "American Classic." For its rendition of a green bean casserole, French's uses condensed cream of mushroom soup and its own brand of canned french fried onions. According to Jean Anderson's *The American Century Cookbook* (1997, 162), the classic version was developed by Campbell's in 1955.

A Louisville collection with a foreword by Cissy Gregg.

Green Bean–French Fried Onion Bake (1958)

1 can water chestnuts (sliced)
1 4-ounce can mushrooms (sliced)
2 packages French style green beans (frozen)
2 cans French fried onion rings
Buttered crumbs, about ½ cup
2 ounces slivered almonds
About 1½ half cups thick white sauce (4½ tablespoons butter, 4½ tablespoons flour, 1½ cups milk)

Combine above ingredients except onion rings and crumbs. Bake in 350 degree oven and cover with onions and buttered crumbs. Bake additional 10 to 15 minutes. 6–8 servings. Truly a gourmet's delight when served with a standing rib roast. (Colonelettes of Louisville 1958, 41)

By the 1950s, cookbook recipes made it clear that meat, especially chicken, was being marketed much differently, reflecting the quest for convenience. In the distant past, chickens had to be raised, captured, slaughtered, cleaned, and cut into usable pieces before they were cooked (in urban settings, some of these steps would likely be done by butchers). Early cookbooks reflected the fact that people had to deal directly with the process of chicken production—from egg laying to butchering. They exhorted cooks to prepare meat only from freshly killed animals or to take care when butchering to ensure the meat looked good for the table. Further, chicken and egg production had seasons, as did just about everything else. *Housekeeping in the Blue Grass* includes a recipe (lime, salt, and water) for preserving eggs over the winter, when fewer eggs were laid (Presbyterian Church 1888, 165). There was a season for fried chickens and a season for chicken and dumplings—the age-related label "spring chicken" is in our vocabulary for a reason. Because folks had to deal with chickens at the far end of the age spectrum, we have lots of recipes for chicken cooked a long time in water and then cut up or ground—there was a big commitment to chicken and dumplings, chicken salad, and chicken croquettes. By the mid-1950s, recipes that called for specific parts of the chicken, such as breasts and occasionally thighs, started to appear. Whereas earlier recipes consisted, for the most part, of instructions to cut up a chicken and then boil it, bake it, or fry it, the implied first step in today's recipes is "Go to Kroger's and buy a package of boneless, skinless chicken breasts," rather than "Find a chicken, take your ax. . . ." Cooks no longer know where their food originates.

Despite the convenience, recipes that depend on processed food are largely assembly exercises. As Rona Roberts (who read an early version of this manuscript) commented to me, "Ugh, I remember well the twenty-plus years these recipes held sway at the cute little country church [in southeastern Kentucky] where I grew up. [The transition] from completely homegrown, home-butchered, homemade dishes at church to 'assembled' dishes probably happened later [there] than in most places. Now thank goodness homegrown and homemade is making a comeback" (2013).

Historic Preservation at "Shakertown"

A series of significant, historically oriented fund-raising cookbooks are those based on food served at the Trustee's House restaurant at the Shaker Village in Pleasant Hill, in Mercer County. Known as Shakertown to central Kentuckians, Shaker Village is at the center of an important success story for historic preservation. One part of the preservation strategy was to create regional dining destinations to draw people to this collection of restored buildings and farmlands. Elizabeth C. Kremer was a crucial part of the Shakertown restoration and preservation strategy starting in the late 1960s, when she was recruited to manage the Shakertown restaurants. Raised in Cynthiana, Kremer had experience establishing restaurants in Cincinnati, Louisville, and New York. She came to Mercer County after being food manager for Schrafft's, the famous Boston-based chain. Shakertown became one of central Kentucky's fine dining destinations during her tenure.

The publication of cookbooks was an important part of the Shakertown culinary program. Kremer researched Shaker foodways and then adapted the original recipes. Her first Shakertown cookbook was *We*

Make You Kindly Welcome (1970), followed by *Welcome Back to Pleasant Hill* (1977). Here is a classic recipe for Shaker lemon pie.

Shaker Lemon Pie (1970)

2 large lemons
4 eggs, well beaten
2 cups sugar

Slice lemons as thin as paper, rind and all. Combine with sugar; mix well. Let stand 2 hours, or preferably overnight, blending occasionally. Add beaten eggs to lemon mixture; mix well. Turn into nine inch pie shell, arranging lemon slices evenly. Cover with top crust. Cut several slits near center. Bake at 450 degrees for 15 minutes. Reduce heat to 375 degrees and bake for about 20 minutes or until silver knife inserted near edge of pie comes out clean. Cool before serving. (Kremer 1970, 12)

The Kremer volume acknowledges that this recipe comes from *The Shaker Cook Book* by Caroline B. Piercy (1953). The unique "all-in" treatment of lemons no doubt reflects their cost and their value to the Shaker communities. Apparently, the Shakers obtained lemons as a result of their commercial activities, which took them all the way to New Orleans and the Gulf. In 2001 *We Make You Kindly Welcome* was named to the Walter S. McIlhenny Community Cookbook Hall of Fame. This award recognizes community cookbooks that have sold more than 100,000 copies and is sponsored by the McIlhenny Company (the maker of Tabasco sauce), headquartered at Avery Island, Louisiana. It is the only Kentucky cookbook so honored.

Chapter Seven

Iconic Recipes and Kentucky Foodways

The Bicentennials and Beyond

Although social and technological changes have an impact on foodways, food practices and food preferences are somewhat stable and can lag behind other changes. There is a cultural investment in doing things a certain way. This can be seen in the Kentucky cookbooks compiled in observance of the nation's and the state's bicentennials and the many other cookbooks commemorating historic events associated with a particular county, church, or other entity. This chapter focuses less on the social context and more on the recipes for historically iconic foods.

One does not actually eat tradition; one eats food. In the framework of interpretive rhetoric, it is very easy to forget that food tastes great and makes one feel good. The Kentucky food practices shaped by the historical and environmental circumstances of early settlement led to certain taste preferences. These preferences meant that certain foods became especially important and dominant in the diet. In turn, some of these foods took on a special status and became cultural icons that, in a sense, represent foodways in people's thinking. A few of these foods are unique to Kentucky, but most are also important in the larger region.

It seems to me that if you asked Kentuckians which foods are representative of Kentucky and have an iconic status, they would tend to mention certain foods (Sohn [2005] did this for Appalachian foods using a focus group technique). Recipes based on meat might include fried chicken, chicken and dumplings, country ham, bacon, sausage, and various small-game animals, such as squirrel and turtle. In the realm of vegetables, we can include anything fresh from the garden, starting with sliced tomatoes and moving on to green beans seasoned with ham or bacon, shuck or soup beans, various greens (both wild and garden varieties), fried apples, and corn pudding. Quick breads are part of the story, from the cornbreads, including cracklin' bread, to spoon bread and biscuits—some beaten, some not. And we cannot forget desserts, such as jam cake, stack cake, fruit cobbler, gingerbread, and chess pie and its myriad cousins.

Some foods are associated with specific parts of the state. The contrast between the Bluegrass and the mountains is clearest to me and probably to most people. If I lived in Bowling Green or Paducah, my perspective would be different. There are especially clear contrasts in baked goods in the Bluegrass versus the mountains. For instance, wheat flour biscuits are more important in central Kentucky, whereas cornbreads are more important in the mountains. It is not a matter of either-or; it requires counting and comparing. The distribution of beaten biscuits is clearer than that of biscuits in general. I think of beaten biscuits as a Bluegrass food. There are also differences in iconic cake recipes. Although stack cake is clearly a mountain recipe and jam cake is more or less a Bluegrass food, the stack cake–jam cake boundaries are anything but absolute. That said, there are probably many more jam cakes made in the mountains than stack cakes made in the Bluegrass.

When people discuss western Kentucky foodways, barbecued mutton and burgoo are mentioned early in the conversation. There is a longstanding western Kentucky practice of slow-cooking mutton over smoky hardwood fires and basting the meat with a thin, vinegar-based, chili- and pepper-flavored sauce, usually called *dip.* This contrasts with the Monroe County (southern Kentucky) style of cooking pork shoulder. Although these are important food icons, pulled or chopped pork and chicken slow-cooked over smoke are served in barbecue restaurants all over the state, east and west. And there are many barbecue restaurants in western Kentucky that do not serve mutton. Burgoo—a thick, long-cooked meat and vegetable soup—is part of the western Kentucky barbecue tradition that has spread across the state. Anderson County in the heart of the Bluegrass region has an annual Burgoo Festival.

Other Kentucky foods, such as goetta and rolled oysters, are more narrowly distributed. Goetta, like scrapple, is very much a northern Kentucky food. It was contributed to Kentucky foodways by German immigrants. There are published recipes for goetta, but it is generally something one buys prepared in a store or restaurant. Rolled oysters, something like oyster croquettes, originated as Louisville bar food and are not widely available. I have had them on four occasions, three of them in Louisville restaurants. Among the numerous Kentucky cookbooks I have examined, I found only one recipe for rolled oysters.

Some regional preparations have been the subject of heated disputes. For example, there are two opposing stories about the origin of beer cheese, a cracker spread made of yellow cheese (often Cheddar), beer, and spices. It was created either as Louisville bar food or at Allman's, a prominent Clark County catfish restaurant on the banks of Howard's Creek, a tributary of the Kentucky River. The matter was settled legislatively in 2013 when Governor Beshear signed House Bill 54, which contained an amendment giving an imprimatur to Clark County as the birthplace of beer cheese. I am glad that was settled, as Winchester in Clark County has an annual Beer Cheese Festival. The dispute over beer cheese was nothing compared with the "Pie Wars." There has even been litigation over "Derby Pie," which, through the aggressive application of copyright laws, can be made and sold only by Kern's Bakery of Louisville. The recipe was devised at the Melrose Inn in Prospect, Kentucky, by members of the Kern family. As a result, if a pie recipe that approximates Derby Pie is included in a Kentucky cookbook, it is always called something else, such as Run for the Roses Pie, Pegasus Pie, First Saturday in May Pie, or even Not Derby Pie.

Many of the recipes in this chapter are for iconic dishes and from cookbooks with a focus on history, culture, or community. These include selections from cookbooks compiled to observe the nation's bicentennial (1976) and Kentucky's statehood bicentennial (1992), as well as those commemorating the anniversaries of other entities such as counties or churches.

Bicentennial Cookbooks

A landmark among Kentucky-based bicentennial cookbooks is *Kentucky Hospitality: A 200-Year Tradition*, compiled by the Kentucky Federation of Women's Clubs. The project's goals included showing "the essence of Kentucky in the essays, the illustrations and the recipes" (Cooper 1976, vii). The book's well-researched, nicely crafted essays describe Kentucky foodways during different periods and in different settings. Some of the topics include early Kentucky food-related folk beliefs, foods and kitchens of the pioneer days, early inns and spas, the Shakers of Pleasant Hill, and elegant dining in the commonwealth. *Kentucky Hospitality* is an excellent source of information about Kentucky's culinary history. Most of the recipes are contributed by members of the women's clubs; others come from historic cookbooks or from restaurants, including Levas' in Lexington, the Lynn Hotel in Hodgenville, and the Old South Inn in Winchester (all closed) and the still open Brown Hotel in Louisville and Talbott Tavern in Bardstown. In addition to the introductory essays, some of the recipes themselves are embellished with discussions of their history and background. This book succeeds as both a regionally focused cookbook and a culinary history.

One of the recipes is for the iconic dish known as wilted lettuce—sometimes called killed lettuce or kilt lettuce. It can also be used for various wild greens, which were traditionally collected in the early spring—the first fresh vegetables people had to eat since the fall. There are many different types of wild greens and substantial local variation in their names, leading to some confusion; they include dandelion, dock, lamb's-quarter, plantain, poke, and wild cabbage. In *Dixie Dishes*, Marion Flexner refers to wild greens as "fence corner greens" (1941, 79). In addition to wild greens, people grew other greens such as spinach, turnips, mustard, kale, and collards in their gardens, tobacco beds, and newly planted cornfields.

Wilted Lettuce (1976)

6 slices bacon
¼ cup vinegar

¼ teaspoon salt
1 teaspoon sugar
⅛ teaspoon pepper
¼ pound leaf lettuce

Warm a large bowl by filling it with very hot water. Fry bacon, remove from pan, and set aside to crispen. Pour water from bowl to dry it. Put cut lettuce into the bowl. Add other ingredients to hot bacon grease and pour over lettuce immediately. Cover bowl and let lettuce wilt for 5 minutes. Uncover and sprinkle with crumbled bacon. Serve at once. Serves 4. (Cooper 1976, 166)

This recipe was contributed by Mrs. Charles Hagan of the Lexington Women's Club. Other versions add chopped green onion to the lettuce and chopped hard-boiled egg to the bacon.

Larue County Kitchens was compiled by a committee of the Hodgenville Woman's Club as a charity project to celebrate the nation's bicentennial. This was a huge project, and the volume contains almost 400 pages of recipes, which are signed and presented in the standard format. Included are a few recipes from landmark restaurants such as the Brown Hotel, the Doe Run Inn, the Old Stone Inn, and the Whistle Stop restaurant in Glen-

A bicentennial compendium from central Kentucky.

dale. Some of the classics are presented in multiple versions—for example, there are six recipes for spoon bread. The book's acknowledgments state, "For months during this Bicentennial year, Larue County Cooks have been flattered, bullied, wheedled and cajoled into divulging their most outstanding culinary secrets" (Hodgenville Woman's Club 1976, iii). Although this is not a narrative cookbook, its historical aspect is conveyed by the photographs that introduce the various sections. The cookbook is still in print. The following recipe, signed by Carol (Mrs. Robert) Haynes, is one of fifteen for jam cake included in this encyclopedic cookbook.

Jam Cake (1976)

3 cups all purpose flour
1 cup butter or margarine
2 cups jam (any kind)
1 cup coarsely chopped black walnuts
1 cup raisins
2 cups brown sugar
1 cup buttermilk
6 eggs
1 teaspoon soda
2 teaspoons cinnamon
2 teaspoons nutmeg
2 teaspoons allspice

Cream butter and sugar thoroughly. Add eggs one at a time, mixing well after each. Put the raisins in a shallow pan, cover and place in 350 degree oven until warm and plumped about 5 to 7 minutes. Measure flour, cinnamon, allspice, nutmeg and soda. Sift together three times. Add flour mixture and buttermilk alternately to creamed mixture, then mix in jam (medium speed on electric mixer). Stir in walnuts and raisins. Turn batter into greased, waxlined 9 inch layer cake pans. Bake at 325 degrees for about 30 to 35 minutes. Do not overbake. Makes 4 layers. (Hodgenville Woman's Club 1976, 314)

Traditionally, jam cake has a caramel frosting. Dolly (Mrs. Jesse) Marcum contributed the following recipe to the Larue County cookbook.

Caramel Frosting (1976)

1 stick butter
1½ cups brown sugar
vanilla
⅓ cup cream
1½ cups confectioner's sugar

Cook first 3 together at a boil for 2 minutes. Have sugar sifted and beat into mixture. (Hodgenville Woman's Club 1976, 315)

Other bicentennial cookbooks include the Kentucky Living *Cookbook: Bicentennial Edition*, edited by Susan Arena (1974); the Mercer County Historical Society's *The Kentucky Bicentennial Cookbook: Famous Historical Kentucky Recipes, 1776–1976*, edited by Ruth Payne of Harrodsburg; the Winchester Mrs. Jaycees' *Mrs. Jaycees Spice Centennial Cook Book* (1975); *Historic Cookbook—1776–1976*, produced by the Woman's Club of Marion; *What's Cooking at Athens: 1976 Bicentennial Edition*, a project of the Athens Christian Church; and the Elsmere Volunteer Fire Department's *The Bicentennial Story of Elsmere, Kentucky, 1776–1976*. Cookbooks have also been published to commemorate the commonwealth's bicentennial in 1992 and various community groups' anniversaries. These include *Kentucky Bicentennial Cookbook*, compiled by the Clay County Homemakers (1992), and *The Springfield Woman's Club Presents a Tasting Tour through Washington County, Kentucky* (1987).

Cookbooks beyond the Bicentennial

Not all the cookbooks of this era were motivated by a desire to commemorate the bicentennial or other anniversaries. One of these is Kathryn M. Fraser's *By the Seasons: Cookery at the Homeplace—1850* (1983). This cookbook was developed to support the educational program of the U.S. Forest Service's Land between the Lakes living history center: The Homeplace—1850. The Land between the Lakes consists of the land remaining after the Cumberland and Tennessee Rivers were impounded. The Homeplace, located on the Tennessee portion of the land, is a re-creation of an 1850s homestead and farm; it maintains some heritage breeds of farm animals, such as Cotswold sheep and Tamworth hogs. Reenactors demonstrate mid-nineteenth-century rural food preparation techniques at the Homeplace. Some of the recipes in Fraser's book are adapted from nineteenth-century cookbooks, some originated from the people who inhabited the Land between the Lakes in the past, and others were developed at the Homeplace. Fraser has modernized the recipes for contemporary use, providing standard measures as well as specific cooking times and temperatures. The book is organized by season; each section begins with a well-informed essay describing the typical farming and cooking processes of the season. Further, many of the recipes are accompanied by short discussions of their historical context.

The brief introduction to the recipe for sauerkraut with apples points out that while we think of sauerkraut as an example of German cooking, during the 1850s, pickling was a common method of food preservation. Sauerkraut may not seem like an iconic Kentucky dish, but pickling vegetables was an important strategy for farm families who had to make the bountiful harvest of their summer and fall gardens last through the winter.

Sauerkraut with Apples (1983)

2 tablespoons bacon drippings or lard
½ cup chopped onion
2 medium-sized apples (about ¾ pound)
2 cups sauerkraut
1 medium-sized potato (about ⅓ pound)
1 cup water
1 tablespoon brown sugar
1 teaspoon salt

> Melt the bacon drippings or lard in a large skillet over medium heat. Add the onions, and cook them gently for about ten minutes, stirring occasionally, or until they are limp and transparent. Meanwhile, peel the apples, quarter them, remove the cores, and slice the quarters about ⅛ inch thick. Add the apples, the potato, the sauerkraut, the water, the brown sugar, and the salt to the onion. Stir together thoroughly. Cover and simmer 15–20 minutes or until the potatoes are tender when pierced with the point of a sharp knife. Transfer to a heated platter and serve at once. Makes six servings. (Fraser 1983, 111)

Appalachian Kentucky cookbooks are another rich source of iconic recipes. These cookbooks can be divided into four types: personal narrative, analytical, family, and community. A good place to start is Sidney Saylor Farr's *More than Moonshine: Appalachian Recipes and Recollections* (1983). It is a classic cookbook organized around the author's personal narrative. Farr incorporates reminiscences about her younger days spent near Stoney Fork, situated alongside Black Mountain in Bell County. This is a narrative cookbook at its most personal, and the rich cultural narrative enhances her presentation of traditional recipes. Farr followed *More than Moonshine* with *Table Talk: Appalachian Meals and Memories* (1995). This volume makes use of oral history interviews with various individuals from North Carolina, Kentucky, and elsewhere, and the recipes were provided by the women and men interviewed. A shorter volume entitled *Spoon Bread Cook Book* was published in 1997. Farr worked as a librarian at Berea College and served as an associate editor of the magazine *Mountain Life and Work* and the editor of *Appalachian Heritage*. Her last book was *My Appalachia: A Memoir* (2007), which won the best book award of the Appalachian Writers' Association.

The greens in the following recipe were the kind gathered by Farr's grandmother: watercress, poke shoots, lamb's-quarter, sheep sorrel, dock, and many others (as noted earlier, there is a great deal of local variation in the names of these greens).

Granny Brock's Greens (1983)

4 cups early greens
4 slices bacon
3 green onions
3 tablespoons vinegar
2 tablespoons sugar
½ teaspoon salt
¼ teaspoon dry mustard
Dash of pepper

Gather greens early in the day if possible. Wash in pure spring water until all grit is removed. Fry bacon and remove from skillet, leaving fat to cool. Mix chopped onions and greens together in large bowl and then put in individual bowls if desired. Crumble bacon over greens. To the fat in skillet, add vinegar, sugar, salt, mustard, and pepper. Heat and pour over greens. Toss until wilted. Serve immediately. (Farr 1983, 86)

More recently, Mark F. Sohn (an avid recipe collector and a skilled cook) produced *Mountain Country Cooking: A Gathering of the Best Recipes from the Smokies to the Blue Ridge* (1996). Although the book addresses all of southern Appalachia, it is clearly based on Sohn's experiences living in Pikeville, in eastern Kentucky, where he is a faculty member at the University of Pikeville. He also wrote a food and cooking column for the Pikeville-based *Appalachian News-Express* for a number of years, which serves as the foundation for this book. The recipes are presented with historical notes, cooking information, and variations, including what Sohn calls "Healthy Choice Alternatives" that feature reduced fat, sugar, or salt. Included here is his recipe for soup beans.

Soup Beans (1996)

1 pound dried pinto beans, washed and picked over for pebbles
7 cups of water
8 ounces salt pork or two ham hocks

> In a glass or ceramic container, soak the beans in the water over night. Do not drain. Place the beans and water in a saucepan and add the pork. Simmer on medium heat, covered, for 4 to 8 hours. Add water as needed to keep the beans covered. When cooked, the beans hold their shape but are soft throughout. Remove the pork, and serve as a side dish. (Sohn 1996, 138)

Sohn offers the following soup-making alternative: "While many serve the broth as pot likker to be sopped up with corn bread, I like it thick, like cream soup. To thicken, boil down the liquid, or use a fork to mash some cooked beans. When I am in a hurry, I take a cup of beans, puree them in a blender, and return them to the soup" (ibid.). He also provides a number of menu ideas, such as soup beans coupled with buttermilk, cornbread, and wilted lettuce. He also suggests serving the beans with fried potatoes and sauerkraut.

A more analytical companion *to Mountain Country Cooking* is Sohn's *Appalachian Home Cooking: History, Culture, and Recipes* (2005). He clarifies some of the interesting links between European and Appalachian cuisines and provides information about regional food festivals and mail-order sources for some foods. He discusses the historical and cultural context of this cuisine and includes a listing of "iconic recipes" based on focus group research. The recipes contained in *Appalachian Home Cooking* are adapted from traditional prototypes and formatted in an innovative way. The following recipe is for a classic Kentucky summertime dish made with white half-runner or pole beans and bacon. These beans are heavily seeded but produce an excellent result with somewhat longer than usual cooking times.

Green Beans with Bacon (2005)

2 strips (2 ounces) bacon, cut into ¼ inch pieces
2 pounds white half-runner beans or pole beans
1 cup (1 medium) onion (optional)
½ cup water
1 teaspoon salt
¼ teaspoon ground black pepper

Procedure
Step 1. Break, string, and remove the ends from fresh beans. If using, dice the onion.

Step 2. Fry the bacon in a large covered saucepan and then remove it to drain on a paper towel. Dump the beans, optional onion, water, salt, and pepper into the saucepan with the bacon grease. Bring to a boil and reduce the heat to a simmer.

Step 3. Braise covered until the beans are tender, about 25 minutes. Add water if necessary, but when the beans are ready, most of the water should have evaporated. Stir and serve. (Sohn 2005, 205–6)

Appalachian Kentucky culinary traditions are also nicely dealt with in some noteworthy community cookbooks. The cookbooks published by the Magoffin County Historical Society are excellent in this regard. The first, *Olde Tyme Cookbook*, was published in 1989; this was followed with *Cooking with Memories: Recipes and Stories of Magoffin County Kentucky Past and Present* (1998), *Circle of Friends Cookbook* (2003), and *Good Times Cookbook: Now Being Served in Magoffin County* (2006). The Magoffin County Historical Society has also published several family-type cookbooks (1997, 2000, 2009) as part of its annual Founders' Day celebration. Community members contributed the recipes, which are accompanied by photographs of their families. In some cases, there are also stories about the person who originated the recipe, historical reflection on the food, or some other interesting bit of information to put the recipe in context.

The earliest Magoffin County cookbook is an especially strong collection of iconic recipes such as fried chicken, fried apples, tomato gravy, gingerbread, gritted bread, jam cake, stack cake, dried apple pies, and blackberry cobbler. Patty Auxier was the editor of this first cookbook and played an important role in the others. The recipe for fried apples was submitted by Sue Hamilton Shackelford, who attributes the recipe to Dora Wisecup Hamilton. In the narrative accompanying the recipe, Shackelford writes: "As I was growing up on the farm on Mash Fork, we always had all the apples we wanted to eat of several varieties from the apple trees

The earliest of the Magoffin County Historical Society cookbooks.

originally planted in the old orchard by the Rev. 'Uncle' Smith Adams from whom my Dad bought the farm many years ago. Later, these old trees were replaced by the ones my Mother set out herself in our yard" (Magoffin County Historical Society 1989, 27).

Fried Apples (1989)

8 apples (any cooking variety) These can be sliced and peeled or unpeeled. Especially good are Golden Grimes—my first choice—or Rome Beauty or Jonathan.
1 tablespoon butter
1 tablespoon vegetable oil or bacon drippings

Cook and fry for about 10 minutes on medium low heat. Then, sprinkle granulated sugar over the top of the apples and cook for a few minutes more. Cook covered. During the last few minutes, remove cover. (ibid.)

Shackelford goes on to say that she normally employs a different method that uses less fat: "The way I normally fry them, is I only add enough vegetable shortening to keep the apples from sticking and sprinkle the sugar over the apples as they first begin to cook. Cover the apples and keep a low medium heat and enough juice will cook out of the apples, so very little oil is needed. By removing the lid near the end of the process, a nice glaze is formed over them, if using Golden Grimes apples. Makes a pretty dish" (ibid.).

Stack cake is another iconic Kentucky dish. As Ronni Lundy describes it, "Stack cake is the ultimate mountaineer's dessert—a not too sweet, but satisfying and complexly flavored dessert made of 4–6 thin layers of molasses tinged, biscuit-like cake covered with a dark, rich dried apple puree" (1991, 310). Even though stack cakes required store-bought spices, "the cake was popular [in the past] because the ingredients (flour, molasses, and eggs) were inexpensive and usually kept on hand" (Magoffin County Historical Society 1998, 147). With the skill of a good cook, these simple ingredients could produce a delicious dessert.

Various stack cake recipes call for four to eight layers—or even more. The layers are thinner than those used in other kinds of cake. Rather than the typical pourable cake batter, the dough is stiff and is rolled out, similar to biscuit making. Because of this, recipes often give indeterminate directions, such as, "Add flour until you have a stiff dough." The dough always contains spices—cinnamon, ginger, nutmeg, and allspice—and it is sweetened with molasses and brown sugar. Some recipes call for sorghum or sorghum molasses, and I expect *molasses* is sometimes used as a synonym for *sorghum*. Because there are multiple layers—usually more layers than the cook has pans—the cake is baked in relays. Although cake pans are generally used today, stack cake was originally baked layer by layer in an iron skillet. The filling, based on dried apples, contains the same spices and sweetening ingredients as the dough. The dried apples are cooked into a thick, robust, dark brown filling. Recipes typically call for the stack cake to set for at least a day (and up to a week), wrapped with a towel, before eating: "cake should be stored in a cake saver for a couple of days before it is eaten" (Magoffin County Historic Society 1989, 149). This "aging" is an important step, as it allows the apple filling flavors to blend with the cake and the layers to soften.

Stack cake was originally more of an everyday item rather than a food for festive occasions—some called them "washday" cakes. However, these cakes have taken on iconic status as a culturally significant Appalachian food (Sohn 2005, 267–70). According to Sidney Saylor Farr, they were used as wedding cakes in the mountains, and relatives of the bride would bring prepared layers to compose the cake. The following Magoffin County recipe is in two parts—the cake and the filling.

Apple Stack Cake (2003)

Cake Ingredients
2 eggs, beaten
1 cup granulated sugar
½ cup molasses
1 cup shortening or margarine
2 teaspoons ginger
1 teaspoon cinnamon
1 teaspoon allspice
¼ teaspoon cloves
6 cups self-rising flour (not to be used all at once)

Preheat oven to 400 degrees. Combine all ingredients but use only 3 cups flour to begin. As you mix the ingredients, gradually add the remaining flour, a cup at a time, until the dough is slightly stiff. Divide the dough into six balls of equal size.

Using an iron skillet, rub a small amount of shortening into skillet and heat in oven. When skillet is hot, sift a small amount of flour into skillet then mash one ball of dough evenly into skillet. Bake for 4 to 6 minutes, being careful not to scorch the bottom. Remove cake from skillet. Coat a paper towel with shortening to wipe excess flour out of skillet. Lightly grease skillet again and repeat the same process with remaining balls of dough. As each layer bakes, assemble the stack cake, coating the top of each layer with the apple filling. Store in a covered container for a couple of days before eating.

Apple Filling Ingredients
3 (8 ounce) bags dried apples
1 cup sugar (or more if apples are tart or if you like sweeter apples)
1 teaspoon cinnamon
½ teaspoon cloves
½ teaspoon allspice

Cook and stir this mixture until it is thick and smooth. After it has cooked, remove from heat. Place filling on top of each layer of stack cake as it comes from the oven. (Magoffin County Historical Society 2003, 101)

Restaurants are another important source of recipes for iconic dishes. *Beaumont Inn: Special Recipes* (Dedman and Dedman 1983), produced by a historic restaurant in central Kentucky, provides excellent examples of traditional Bluegrass cooking. One of the Beaumont Inn's specialties is country ham, and as I understand it, the inn buys one-year-old hams from Meacham's, near Sturgis in western Kentucky, and then ages them for another year in a specially built meat house at its Harrodsburg facility in Mercer County. The result is spectacular. The Beaumont Inn's version of corn pudding (see below) may be the most frequently published restaurant-contributed recipe in Kentucky cookbooks.

Beaumont Inn's Corn Pudding (1983)

2 cups white whole kernel corn, or fresh corn cut off the cob
4 eggs
8 level tablespoons flour
1 quart milk
4 rounded teaspoons sugar
4 tablespoons butter, melted
1 teaspoon salt

Stir into the corn, the flour, salt, sugar and butter. Beat up the eggs well; put them into the milk, then stir into the corn and put into a pan or Pyrex dish. Bake inside of oven at 450 degrees for about 10 minute then 350 degrees for 30–35 minutes.

Stir vigorously with long prong fork three times, approximately 10 minutes apart, while baking, disturbing the top as little as possible. (Dedman and Dedman 1983, 72)

Kentucky Junior League Cookbooks

The Junior League of Louisville published *The Cooking Book* in 1978, the earliest of the Kentucky Junior League cookbooks. This volume was followed by *To Market, To Market* in 1984, compiled by the Junior League of Owensboro; it is still in print. In 1988 the Junior League of Louisville published *Cordon Bluegrass: Blue Ribbon Recipes from Kentucky* and, more recently, *Splendor in the Blue Grass, a Cookbook* (2000) and *Bluegrass Gatherings* (2013). The most recent release from its Owensboro counterpart is *Home Again, Home Again* (2004). The recipes are very sophisticated and oriented toward entertaining rather than everyday family cooking.

These attractive cookbooks are part of a phenomenon started by the Junior League of Augusta (Georgia) in 1940 with the publication of *Reci-*

pes from Southern Kitchens. Junior League cookbooks are big sellers both nationally and in Kentucky. Over time, they evolved into large-format, well-designed, slick publications with sophisticated and complex recipes that emphasize entertaining. Junior League cookbooks sell well and often remain in print for some time. *Charleston Receipts*, published in 1950, is the oldest Junior League cookbook still in print; it has sold nearly 1 million copies. These cookbooks are often sold through bookstores, and a few were actually published by commercial publishers. The Kentucky Junior League cookbooks have been good sellers, but not on the same scale as the Charleston classic. *The Cooking Book* had three print runs, which took it to 25,000 books; it is now out of print.

Although these are fund-raising cookbooks compiled by local groups, they differ in style from most other community cookbooks. Clearly, they are intended to be sold in a much larger region than just the local neighborhood. They are much more elaborately produced, with far better graphics and illustrations, and they are executed with a more consistent editorial voice than a typical community cookbook. The recipes are more complex, which one might associate with entertaining rather than home cooking or "harried housewife" simplicity. Though technically not "Junior League" cookbooks, similar non–Junior League works have the same high production value. Some examples are *Bluegrass Winners: A Cookbook*, compiled by the Garden Club of Lexington (1985); *Creating a Stir in the Bluegrass and Beyond*, produced by the Fayette County Medical Auxiliary (1999); and *Beyond the Fence: A Culinary View of Historic Lexington*, a fund-raising effort of Central Baptist Hospital Foundation's Cancer Program (2010). I selected a recipe for burgoo from *Bluegrass Winners.*

Kentucky Burgoo (1985)

2 pounds beef, cubed
soup bone
½ pound lamb, cubed
1 frying chicken, cut up
4 quarts water
salt and pepper to taste

A comprehensive collection by the Garden Club of Lexington.

red pepper to taste
2 cups diced potatoes
3 cups chopped onions
2 cups lima beans
4 carrots, diced
2 green peppers, diced
3 cups corn (fresh, if possible)
2 cups okra, diced
6 cups tomatoes
½ teaspoon garlic
1 cup minced parsley

Put the beef, soup bone, lamb, chicken, water, salt, pepper, and red pepper in a heavy pot with a tight-fitting lid. Bring to a boil, then simmer, covered, for two hours. Remove the chicken skin and bones and cut meat into bite-sized pieces. Return meat to pot. Add potatoes, onions, lima beans, carrots, green peppers, and corn. Simmer two hours. Mixture will be thick but should not stick. Add water sparingly, if necessary. Add okra, tomatoes, and garlic and simmer 1½ hours longer. Add parsley and remove from stove. This soup will keep in refrigerator for a long time. The flavor improves with standing. Makes 10 servings. (Garden Club of Lexington 1985, 124)

Food Professionals' Cookbooks

During this period, Kentucky's professional food writers continued to produce some fine cookbooks. Camille Glenn wrote two noteworthy Kentucky cookbooks. Raised in the setting of her family's hotel business in Dawson Springs, Glenn was a caterer and a cooking teacher in addition to writing food features and a column for the *Louisville Courier-Journal*. Chef Kathy Cary, the proprietor of Lilley's: A Kentucky Bistro, reported that her mother took cooking lessons from Glenn. The most significant of Glenn's cookbooks is *The Heritage of Southern Cooking* (1986). Although this is a southern rather than a Kentucky cookbook, Glenn's Kentucky roots clearly show in her recipe selection.

The Heritage of Southern Cooking, a collection of regional recipes from Camille Glenn, a respected Louisville food writer and teacher.

Old Kentucky Beer Cheese (1986)

2 pounds sharp Cheddar cheese, at room temperature
2 cloves garlic, mashed
3 tablespoons Worcestershire sauce
1 teaspoon dry mustard
Tabasco sauce to taste
½ bottle beer, or more as necessary
1 teaspoon salt, or to taste

1. Cut the cheese into cubes and place them in a food processor or electric mixer. Process until perfectly smooth. Add the garlic, Worcestershire, mustard, and Tabasco.

2. Add the beer, a little at a time, while continuing to beat the cheese, until the mixture is a good, firm spreading consistency. (Too much beer will make the cheese too fluffy.) Stir in the salt, and refrigerate. (This is a superb keeper.)

3. Serve on small slices of rye or pumpernickel bread, or on crackers. Delicious with cold, cold beer. (Glenn 1986, 27)

Another noteworthy single-author Kentucky cookbook is *Charles Patteson's Kentucky Cooking* (1988). Drawing on his Kentucky background and his experience running a New York–based catering business, Patteson provides a number of iconic recipes, coupled with a rich narrative about them. In addition to his own early experiences in Kentucky, Patteson's recipes come from other noteworthy Kentucky cookbook authors, such as Marion Flexner, and a distinguished list of Kentucky restaurants and ham curers. Many iconic recipes are included: burgoo, beaten biscuits, chess pie, Benedictine spread, Hot Brown sandwich, country ham, corn pudding, and caramel-iced jam cake. Patteson's cookbook parallels the narrative style of Flexner's classics of the 1940s—*Dixie Dishes* and *Out of Kentucky Kitchens.* Like Jennie Benedict, Flexner, and others more recent, he credits the role of African American cooks in the development of his culinary skills. The stories about his boyhood and the social context of food in Kentucky, including Derby Day, are written for an audience that is less familiar with Kentucky life. The recipes and narrative are enhanced by attractive pen-and-ink drawings by Shirley Felts. The recipe reproduced here is part of a set for Derby entertaining.

Grits Soufflé Casserole (1988)

6 cups water
1½ cups hominy grits
½ cup (1 stick) butter
1 teaspoon salt
8 ounces sharp Cheddar cheese, grated
1 teaspoon Tabasco sauce
4 eggs, separated

Preheat the oven to 350 degrees. Butter a 2-quart baking dish or bowl. Combine the grits, butter and salt with the water in a saucepan. Cook, stirring constantly, 5 to 10 minutes until thick. Remove from the heat. Stir in the cheese and Tabasco. Beat the eggs yolks until light and lemon colored; fold into the grits mixture. Beat the egg whites until they hold stiff peaks. Gently fold them into the grits. Scrape into the prepared dish.

Bake for 1 hour, until set and browned on top. (Patteson 1988, 33)

Ronni Lundy's cookbooks of the 1990s are gems of the narrative cookbook genre. They celebrate local culinary traditions and discuss local culture in a respectful and informed way. Lundy's cookbooks are very readable and are excellent sources for both historically authentic and contemporary versions of many iconic dishes from rural Kentucky. She provides detailed descriptions of technique in the context of her regionally focused narrative. Although her recipes focus on the South, Lundy draws on her extensive Kentucky experiences. She was born in Corbin and moved to Louisville at age one. A former restaurant reviewer and music

An example of Ronni Lundy's narrative cookbook craftsmanship.

critic for the *Courier-Journal*, Lundy was also the editor of *Louisville Magazine* and one of the founders the Southern Foodways Alliance.

Readers can learn a great deal about Kentucky foodways from Lundy's cookbooks. She is a master at creating a rich narrative flavoring around both iconic dishes and country-themed innovations. Her *Shuck Beans, Stack Cakes, and Honest Fried Chicken: The Heart and Soul of Southern Country Kitchens* (1991) is organized around a country music narrative, and many of the recipes are from well-known performers. *The Festive Table: Recipes and Stories for Creating Your Own Holiday Traditions* (1995) focuses on holiday meals such as Thanksgiving, Kwanzaa, and Easter. Her most recent cookbook is *Butter Beans to Blackberries: Recipes from the Southern Garden* (1999), which has an autobiographical cast. In addition to family recipes, Lundy includes recipes from both well-known chefs and relatively obscure everyday restaurants. The following is from *Shuck Beans, Stack Cakes, and Honest Fried Chicken.*

Green Tomato Casserole (1991)

5 medium green tomatoes, some just starting to ripen
1 medium onion
2 dozen soda crackers
1 tablespoon melted butter
⅛ teaspoon salt
ground black pepper
½ cup buttermilk

Chop tomatoes into pieces about ¼ inch square and put in a large bowl. Chop onion very fine and toss to mix well with tomatoes. With a rolling pin, crush crackers and add to tomatoes. Pour butter, salt, and as much pepper as you want (we like a lot) over the tomatoes and mix. Then add buttermilk and mix well. Pour into a 2-quart buttered casserole and bake at 325 degrees for 45 minutes. If top isn't brown, run under broiler for a few minutes. (Lundy 1991, 187–89)

Following a somewhat similar strategy as Lundy's are the cookbooks of Linda Allison-Lewis. Allison-Lewis wrote the food column for *Kentucky Living*, the membership magazine for the Kentucky Rural Electric Cooperatives, from 1995 until her death in 2011. She compiled two recipe collections based largely on that column and rooted in Kentucky food traditions: *Kentucky's Best: Fifty Years of Great Recipes* (1998) and *Kentucky Cooks: Favorite Recipes from* Kentucky Living (2009). These books also include recipes from Kentucky restaurants, Kentucky bed-and-breakfasts, readers of her column, Kentucky chefs, and her mentor, the much-loved Louisville food columnist Cissy Gregg. Allison-Lewis has a flair for storytelling, which comes across nicely in her cookbooks.

Sausage and Egg Casserole (1998)

1 pound bulk pork sausage
6 eggs
2 cups milk
1 teaspoon salt
1 teaspoon dry mustard
6 slices white bread, cut into ½-inch cubes
4 ounces Cheddar cheese, grated (1 cup)
¼ cup chopped mushrooms (optional)

Brown and crumble sausage in skillet; drain and set aside. In a large bowl, beat eggs; add milk, salt, and mustard. Stir in bread pieces, Cheddar cheese, sausage, and mushrooms, if desired. Pour into greased 13×9×2 baking dish. Cover and refrigerate overnight, if desired (remove 30 minutes before baking), or bake immediately. Preheat oven to 350 degrees. Bake uncovered for 40 minutes, or until knife inserted comes out clean. (Allison-Lewis 1998, 102)

Allison-Lewis suggests that whole wheat or sourdough bread can be substituted for the white bread.

African American Cookbook Writers

Some accomplished African American cooks produced cookbooks that present their share of recipes for iconic foods. This includes *Thelma's Treasures: The Secret Recipes of the Best Cook in Harrodsburg* (Thomas, Evans, Curry, and Linton 1992). Thelma Clay Linton of Harrodsburg was a respected caterer and an important leader in the business, social services, and religious communities. Susanna Thomas's introductory essay states, "In our town of Harrodsburg in Mercer County, Kentucky, Thelma Clay Linton is an institution, revered for her outstanding country cuisine and her remarkable character" (ibid., 10). The recipes are presented in the standard format, with detailed and often nuanced discussions of the process, accompanied by Linton's commentary. Here is what she has to say about cooking green beans:

> Half Runners are my favorite bean, but Kentucky Wonders will do, too. I use a pepper pod from the garden to season. . . . There's a girl in town who brings her cooked beans by so I can season 'em, but she says they still don't taste like mine. Then I found out what she done. She was stirring 'em and addin' more water. You are not supposed to stir green beans. When I put mine on, I let them cook about three hours. Well, after they've cooked about two hours, you might take a fork or spoon and just kinda turn 'em over from the bottom lightly. (Ibid., 62)

Here is Linton's approach to frying chicken.

Fried Chicken (1992)

chicken
salt
flour
pepper
paprika
Puritan oil

Put the chicken pieces in a big pot of water. Add two tablespoons of salt for every one chicken that you use. Soak the chicken in the salty water overnight in the refrigerator. The next day, drain off the water, pat the chicken pieces dry.

Mix the flour (enough to coat all of the chicken) with the pepper and the paprika and a little bit of salt to taste. Coat each piece of chicken with this mixture.

In an iron skillet, add the Puritan oil and cook it until it sizzles. The grease should be even up with the chicken. Then add a few pieces of chicken and turn down the heat to medium. Cook the chicken a half hour or so on one side and flip it and cook it a half hour on the other side until it is evenly browned.

Remove the pieces from the pan as they are done and drain them on a paper towel. (Thomas et al. 1992, 45)

Cookin' up a Storm: The Life and Recipes of Annie Johnson, published in 2003 (this is the second edition; the first was published in 1998), is also based on a collaboration—this one between Annie Johnson, the cook, and Jane Lee Rankin, the author. Annie Johnson was born to sharecropping parents in the Deep South and died in 2001, when she was in her early eighties. She moved with her husband to Louisville and eventually went to work for Rankin's family when Jane Lee was six years old. She performed various duties, including being the family's cook. The two became quite close. Rankin eventually graduated from culinary school, and while she was testing Johnson's recipes, they were written down (apparently, until then, they had existed to some extent only in her memory). The recipes in the book are accompanied by both aphorisms about living one's life and cooking advice from Johnson. She says this about her recipe for hummingbird cake: "I leave the butter out at night if I'm gonna bake a cake the next day. I leave it out so it be soft. See, 'causin' you not supposed to melt butter to make a cake. It makes it tough" (Rankin 2003, 112). Here is Johnson's recipe for macaroni and cheese—it is the one I use.

Macaroni and Cheese (2003)

2½ tablespoons salt
4 cups uncooked macaroni (1 pound)

A collaborative effort from Annie Johnson and Jane Lee Rankin.

¼ cup vegetable oil
¼ cup all-purpose flour
3 cups milk
½ teaspoon salt
1 pound (3 cups plus one cup) sharp Cheddar cheese, grated

Butter a 2-quart casserole dish.

In a large pot, bring 6 quarts of water and 2½ tablespoons of salt to a boil.

Add the macaroni and cook until almost tender. It should be a little chewy.

Drain the macaroni and rinse with cold water. Pour into buttered casserole dish and set aside.

To make the sauce, heat the oil in a skillet and add the flour, stirring and cooking over medium heat until all the lumps are gone. Slowly add in the milk, stirring all the time. Bring to a boil and simmer for 10 minutes.

Add ½ teaspoon of salt and 3 cups of the cheese to the sauce and stir until melted. Pour over the macaroni and stir to combine.

Sprinkle the remaining 1 cup of cheese on top of the dish.

Bake in a 350 degree oven for 30–40 minutes, or until the cheese topping is golden brown. (Rankin 2003, 64)

The African-American Heritage Center of Simpson County, located in Franklin, has compiled an excellent community cookbook. The center, which includes a museum focused on African American life, is housed in the bungalow home of African American business leader George W. Mahin and his wife, Gertrude. *Heritage Cookbook: A Collection of Traditional and Favorite Recipes* (1998) contains recipes contributed by residents of this southern Kentucky community. It is described as "a collection of African American recipes. . . . Most of them are real heirlooms handed down through generations with a few alterations. We treasure the generosity of those who have given them to us and have made it possible for us to pass them on to others" (African-American Heritage Center 1998, 1). The recipes are presented in the standard format. As in many community cookbooks, there are sometimes a number of different recipes for the same dish, such as five versions of

A fund-raiser with an African American focus.

chess pie. The center's monthly e-mail newsletter often includes a recipe from the cookbook. The following recipe was contributed by Mary B. Moss.

Peach Cobbler (1998)

Crust
1⅓ cups all-purpose flour
8 tablespoons butter, cut into at least 8 pieces
½ teaspoon salt
4 tablespoons sugar
1 egg
1½ tablespoons cold water

Filling
6 cups sliced, peeled peaches (or a combination of peaches and blueberries)
3 tablespoons flour
1 cup sugar
2 tablespoons butter

Combine flour, sugar, butter, and salt in a medium-size bowl. Use a pastry cutter or 2 knives to cut the butter into the flour until the mixture resembles coarse meal. In a small bowl, beat egg and water together. Stir into flour mixture until well combined, then press the mixture together with your hands to form a ball. Flatten the ball into a 1-inch disk; wrap in plastic and refrigerate. Slice peaches into a 10-inch deep dish pie plate. Combine flour and sugar in a bowl and stir to disperse flour. Sprinkle mixture over peaches. Cut butter into small nuggets and sprinkle over peaches.

Heat oven to 450 degrees. Roll pastry into a circle to fit the top of the pan, leaving about ½-inch space around the rim. Cut 3 slits in the center. Put the cobbler into the oven and reduce heat to 425 degrees. Bake 40 minutes or until interior is bubbly. Yield: 8 servings. (African-American Heritage Center 1998, 54)

Chapter Eight

Eating Locally and Sustainably

Contemporary Kentucky Cookbooks

One theme that dominates many of today's Kentucky cookbooks is the local sourcing of foods. In this way, Kentucky cookbooks reflect a movement that is national and perhaps even worldwide. The local food movement advocates more direct relationships between food consumers and producers, with the goal of obtaining cleaner and higher-quality food in a way that is economically, environmentally, and socially sustainable. Kentucky poet, essayist, and novelist Wendell Berry (1981, 2009) and novelist-essayist Barbara Kingsolver (2008) have made important contributions to this discussion locally, nationally, and internationally. Other writers whose works resonate with this idea are food writer Michael Pollan (2006, 2009), journalist and cookbook author Mark Bittman (2009), and restaurateur Alice Waters (2007). There are many others.

The motivation to "eat local" relates to a number of concerns about the sustainability of the contemporary food system as it has evolved. One concern is the cost of transporting food from faraway places to local tables. These costs are diverse and include the expenditure of fossil fuel to ship foods, the breeding of plants and animals that are suitable for industrial food production at a distance, and the demise of local family farms. The archetypal food that demonstrates the eat-local philosophy is the tomato. Just compare the durable, uniform, mealy, tasteless tomatoes produced on industrially scaled farms with the succulent but vulnerable tomatoes raised in one's own garden or bought at local farmers' markets.

Historically, the Kentucky food system started out as more or less highly local and was then radically delocalized, largely through market forces and state and national policies (van Willigen and van Willigen 2006). Today, with some exceptions, the food systems that operate in Kentucky have become largely dependent on the national and international systems. As Jim Embry, director of the Sustainable Communities Network of Lexington, wrote in a 2012 op-ed piece for the *Lexington Herald-Leader*, local food systems "have been steadily dismantled in favor of a centralized model that requires large scale monocultures, massive chemical inputs, fewer farmers and ever more transport." Fayette County farmer Todd Clark, who produces for the local market, notes how the food system has changed: "Our ancestors a century ago would laugh at some of the conversations we're having now. They would be confused about how we got to where we are. What do you mean you're going to do local food? Where else does it come from?" (Spence 2012, 1).

Prior to World War II, for many rural families, eating local meant producing food on their own farms. In the oral history interviews conducted for my earlier book *Food and Everyday Life on Kentucky Family Farms 1920–1950* (van Willigen and van Willigen 2006), the men and women interviewed stressed that they bought little more than salt, sugar, coffee, kerosene, and matches; they produced and preserved most of their own food. Although it was a different story in the cities, for many urban Kentuckians, eating locally was still the norm. To do this now would require the development of many new practices. This chapter discusses some of those practices and how they are reflected in cookbooks.

Sources for Eating Locally

Farmers' markets are an important source for locally grown and produced foods. The Kentucky Department of Agriculture maintains a roster of about 150 farmers' markets throughout the state, many of which have existed for a long time. Although they vary considerably in size and complexity, most are locally organized, maintain a set of rules about what is marketed, and have a stable relationship with the community. Farmers' markets have many advantages, including allowing consumers to buy food

The Lexington farmers' market on a Sunday in the early fall. (John van Willigen)

directly from the growers. The food is far fresher than that found in stores; it has usually been harvested that morning or no later than the day before, rather than being picked and shipped days earlier from who knows where. Supermarkets generally carry only one or two unidentified types of each produce item, whereas farmers' markets offer many different varieties, with the selection changing from time to time. For example, at the peak of the green bean season, one can choose from a range of pod-dominant varieties such as tenderettes, jade, or blue lake or bean-dominant varieties such as Kentucky Wonder pole beans, white half-runners, cornfield beans, and various heritage types. One can also get more information about the use of pesticides, since in many cases the growers are available to answer questions about their practices. Also, recipes are often available either directly from the growers or on the market's website.

CSA Box Contents—Mid-July

blackberries	tomatoes
garlic	tomatillos
green bell peppers	stringless green beans
yellow squash/zucchini	eggplants
rainbow Swiss chard	

A similar direct relationship between producer and consumer is found in CSAs (an acronym derived from the concept of community-supported agriculture). With CSAs, participants buy shares of a farm's produce for the season and receive a weekly portion of the vegetables produced on the farm. The term *share* is important: as a participant, one is sharing both the payoff and, to some extent, the risk of operating a farm. For example, when growing conditions are good, there is more produce of a higher quality. Some farms also offer egg and meat CSAs. The CSA I belong to, Elmwood Stock Farm of Scott County (elmwoodstockfarm.com), supplies almost all organic produce. I generally participate in the spring and summer season, although this past year, I also participated in the fall. I make a single payment prior to the first delivery; then, during the season, I collect my box of vegetables at a local pickup point every Wednesday. The vegetables included in my share change from week to week, ensuring that I eat seasonally. I wait impatiently for the first tomatoes and try to come up with strategies to prepare the large amount of greens in the first few boxes. Sometimes the allocation includes vegetables I would otherwise eat infrequently. Occasionally I get something that causes me to blurt out, "What's that?" Think purple kohlrabi. Anyway, it's fun to figure out how to cook these new items. Elmwood Stock Farm includes a number of recipes, often from shareholders, in its weekly newsletter.

In addition to farmers' markets there are also farm markets. Whereas farmers' markets involve producers who gather temporarily on a regular seasonal schedule, farm markets are typically located at a permanent site with a single proprietor. There are many different kinds. Marksbury Farm Market, established in 2009 in Garrard County, provides affordable slaughtering to local farmers, allowing local livestock producers to market their products to local consumers while following all the government rules. In addition, Marksbury has a retail store that sells the beef, pork, chicken, and other products produced in the region. Information about this and other farm markets can be obtained from the directory compiled by the Kentucky Farm Bureau's certified roadside farm markets program. It includes information about fruit and vegetable producers, greenhouses, landscape nurseries, Christmas tree farms, vineyards and wineries, dairy producers, meat markets, and cheese makers. The Farm Bureau program also provides marketing assistance.

Kentucky Proud

A related program that goes beyond farmers' markets and farm stores is the Kentucky Proud program, which certifies Kentucky-origin farm produce and food products. Kentucky Proud is administered by the Kentucky Department of Agriculture to increase farm incomes by promoting food products grown, raised, or manufactured in Kentucky through programs directed at consumers, distributors, and producers. The Kentucky Proud logo is familiar to anybody who visits farmers' markets, farm markets, or participating restaurants. The current advertising slogan is "Nothing Else Is Close." The program provides cost sharing for advertising, support from marketing specialists, free Web pages, and direct sales through the

The Kentucky Proud logo. (Commonwealth of Kentucky)

Kentucky Department of Agriculture website (www.Kyproud.com).The University of Kentucky's School of Human Environmental Sciences, the Family and Consumer Sciences Program in the Cooperative Extension Service, and the Kentucky Department of Agriculture have established a Kentucky Proud Recipe Database Project. Some large corporations such as Kroger's, Walmart, Whole Foods, and Meijer also participate in the program.

Farm-to-Fork Restaurants

The value of eating locally is also expressed by restaurants that feature local produce—sometimes called "farm to fork" or "farm to table" restaurants. These include chef Jim Gerhardt's Limestone, chef Cathy Carey's Lilly's: A Kentucky Bistro, and chef Edward Lee's 610 Magnolia in Louisville; chef Ouita Michel's Holly Hill Inn in Midway; and chef Jonathan Lundy's Jonathan at Gratz Park in Lexington. These restaurants follow the advocacy of Alice Waters, who in 1971 organized the Chez Panisse Restaurant in Berkeley, California; it featured organic local produce and became an icon in the local food movement. Her *Chez Panisse Menu Cookbook* (1982) has been recognized as an influential contribution to the cookbook genre. An important part of Waters's strategy is that she developed ongoing relationships with producers. This idea has been adopted by a number of Kentucky restaurants that feature the names of local producers on their menus and websites.

Many restaurants that are not in the "fine dining" category also have a strong commitment to local food sources. Some examples are Ouita Michel's sandwich shop, Wallace Station of Midway; the Windy Corner Market in rural Fayette County; and the downtown Lexington institutions Alfalfa and Stella's Deli. There are many others around the state.

Kentucky Cookbooks that Support Local Eating

The importance of eating local is expressed in various ways in contemporary Kentucky cookbooks. Generally, they exhibit an increased commitment to placing foods in their local cultural, social, and historical context.

This is expressed most directly by the inclusion of much more information about local foods and producers and the inevitable emphasis on seasonality. Also, respectful descriptions of local food practices and traditions, as well as more robust depictions of local history and culture, communicate an eating local orientation. These concerns are reflected by expanded narratives in cookbooks. As a result, contemporary cookbooks are often very interesting to read. In concrete terms, the expanded narratives often include information about and advocacy for local food sources such as farmers' markets, farm markets, community-supported agriculture, and state and local programs that support local producers.

One manifestation of the eat local movement is the strategy used by the Kentucky Extension Association of Family and Consumer Sciences in its 2003 compilation titled *Pride of Kentucky: Great Recipes with Food, Farm, and Family Traditions* (supported by the University of Kentucky Cooperative Extension Service and the Kentucky Department of Agriculture). Its distinguishing feature is the extensive participation of state-level commodity groups, including beef, soybean, poultry, pork, egg, and sorghum producers. This is reflected in the choice of recipes. The involvement of the Kentucky Soybean Association and Promotion Board is represented by a number of recipes that use tofu and other soy-based products, for example. The recipes for catfish and freshwater shrimp reflect the participation of the Kentucky Aquaculture Association. Other participating organizations included the Farm Bureau, the Kentucky Association of Electric Cooperatives, and the Kentucky Extension Homemakers Association. *Pride of Kentucky* also contains recipes from restaurants and from celebrity chefs with Kentucky ties. This volume was the official cookbook of the 2003 Kentucky State Fair.

Montgomery County Lemon Shrimp (2003)

1 pound freshwater shrimp, peeled and deveined
5 ounces fresh mushrooms, sliced (2 cups)
1 medium green bell pepper, cut into strips
1½ cup bias-sliced celery
¼ cup sliced green onions

2 tablespoons vegetable oil
1 (6-ounce) package frozen pea pods
2 tablespoons cornstarch
1 teaspoon sugar
1 teaspoon salt
1 teaspoon chicken bouillon granules
⅛ teaspoon pepper
1 cup water
½ teaspoon grated lemon zest
3 tablespoons lemon juice

Sauté the shrimp, mushrooms, bell pepper, celery and green onions in the hot oil in a large skillet for 5 to 6 minutes. Add the pea pods. Sauté for 1 to 2 minutes. Combine the cornstarch, sugar, salt, bouillon and pepper in a bowl. Stir in the water, lemon zest and lemon juice. Stir in the shrimp mixture. Cook until thickened, stirring constantly. Serve over hot cooked rice. (Kentucky Extension Association 2003, 81)

A recently published Kentucky cookbook with a focus on healthier and local eating is Maggie Green's *The Kentucky Fresh Cookbook* (2011). She has a strong commitment to eating locally, and the recipes make use of seasonally available Kentucky-produced ingredients. The cookbook is organized as a seasonal calendar of menus, with special attention paid to holidays such as Thanksgiving, Christmas, and Derby Day. Traditional Kentucky foodways are part of the *Kentucky Fresh Cookbook* story, and many of Green's recipes are fresh takes on traditional favorites.

Maggie Green is from Lexington, and her knowledge of and interest in food grew out of her family's kitchens, her study of food and nutrition at the University of Kentucky, her culinary arts studies at Sullivan University, and her work as a registered dietitian. The book's focus is cooking meals at home using fresh ingredients, which ties in to another important concept: seasonality. Consistent with this, Green provides the tools to build menus and prepare dishes based on the seasonal availability of food and herbs in Kentucky. Further, she discusses a strategy for incorporating local and fresh food into one's cooking, makes suggestions for

Maggie Green's cookbook advocates preparing seasonal, locally sourced foods.

Kentucky-sourced foods, includes references to many growers and suppliers, and provides a "Kentucky Produce Availability Chart" organized by month. Some of her recipes are adapted from other Kentucky cookbooks such as *Pride of Kentucky.*

Stove Top Bourbon Barbecue Chicken (2011)

One 3½- to 4-pound chicken, cut into 8 pieces
Salt and pepper for seasoning
1 sweet onion, finely diced
1 cup ketchup
2 tablespoons apple cider vinegar
2 tablespoons honey or Kentucky sorghum or molasses
1 tablespoon Kentucky bourbon
1 tablespoon Worcestershire sauce
¼ teaspoon freshly ground black pepper

Season the chicken pieces with salt and pepper. In a Dutch oven or skillet with a lid, brown the chicken on both sides over medium heat. Set the chicken aside. Drain out all but 1 teaspoon of the fat. Add the onion and cook until soft, about 5 minutes. Stir in the ketchup, scraping brown bits off the bottom of the Dutch oven. Stir in the vinegar, honey or sorghum, bourbon, Worcestershire sauce, and pepper, and bring to a boil. Add the chicken and turn to coat with the sauce. Reduce heat to low. Cover and simmer for 30 minutes. Uncover and cook 15 more minutes to cook the chicken thoroughly and thicken the sauce. Serve hot. (Green 2011, 246)

Local food traditions are clearly the basis of the Kentucky cookbooks distributed by McClanahan Publishing House in Kuttawa, near Land between the Lakes in western Kentucky. McClanahan was established in 1983 by Paula Cunningham to publish a book on local history written by her husband, William Cunningham (Egerton 1990, 180). Although McClanahan has published books on a range of topics, it specializes in cookbooks. The business was recently sold, but current owner Michelle Stone continues its emphasis on Kentucky cookbooks, and there is no question that McClanahan still leads the way in the publishing of attractive Kentucky cookbooks. I found a number them to be especially interesting. For instance, Elizabeth Ross's *Kentucky Keepsakes: Classic Southern Recipes* (1996) and *Cornmeal Country:*

Sharon Thompson's collection of iconic Kentucky recipes.

An American Tradition (2004) include many variations for standard preparations. In *Kentucky Keepsakes* she includes thirteen recipes for the Hot Brown sandwich and eleven recipes for hush puppies. Ross cites her sources, and the list of cookbooks she consulted is extensive. *Cornmeal Country* has more of a southern than Kentucky orientation, but it is an excellent source for scoping out the wonderful world of cornbread.

Another noteworthy McClanahan cookbook is Sharon Thompson's *Flavors of Kentucky* (2006). It contains contemporary versions of many iconic Kentucky recipes and could be used as a primer on Kentucky cuisine. She includes Kentucky classics such as the Hot Brown sandwich, beaten biscuits, blackberry cobbler, burgoo, and beer cheese. Many of the recipes are from Kentucky's professional chefs. Thompson, currently the food editor for the *Lexington Herald-Leader*, has a blog and a website based on *Flavors of Kentucky*. The following recipe is from Thompson's sister-in-law.

Margaret's Blackberry Cobbler (2006)

2 cups fresh blackberries
1 cup all-purpose flour
1½ cups sugar, divided
1 teaspoon baking powder
1 stick butter, melted
½ cup milk
½ teaspoon vanilla extract
½ cup hot water

Place the blackberries in the bottom of a 9-inch square baking pan. Combine the flour, ½ cup sugar, baking powder, butter, milk and vanilla extract in a bowl and pour over the blackberries. Combine the remaining 1 cup sugar and hot water in a small bowl and stir to dissolve the sugar. Pour over the flour mixture. Bake at 350 degrees for about 45 minutes. (Thompson 2006, 136)

There are a number of Kentucky restaurants that combine iconic Kentucky cuisine, a commitment to locally sourced ingredients, and world-class culinary innovation. As mentioned earlier, one of these restaurants with a farm-to-fork orientation is Jonathan at Gratz Park, and chef Jonathan Lundy has documented his approach in a cookbook: *Jonathan's Bluegrass Table: Redefining Kentucky Cuisine* (2009). Lundy, who was raised in Midway, has deep roots in Kentucky and a strong commitment to the use of locally produced ingredients. His culinary training involved serving as an apprentice to chef Emeril Lagasse and completing the program at the College of Culinary Arts at Johnson and Wales University. Lundy's restaurant is organized around the concept of blending "the traditional flavors of the Bluegrass with modern world cuisine" (Lundy 2009, 9). His cookbook includes a number of iconic Kentucky dishes, including burgoo, macaroni and cheese, pimento cheese, beer cheese, cheese grits, corn pudding, deviled eggs, wilted lettuce, country ham, and the Hot Brown sandwich. There are also many Gulf coast dishes that have become a part of Kentucky cuisine, such as bananas Foster, oysters Rockefeller, and shrimp and grits. That said, Lundy puts a significant twist on virtually everything, which indeed redefines these basic dishes. Cheese grits is one example. The cookbook version is called "Pimento Cheese Grit Fries." The grits are cooked in a red pepper puree, heavy cream, and water to which white Cheddar cheese, salt, white pepper, and cayenne are added. This is then spread on a greased cookie sheet, refrigerated until stiff, cut into bars, and frozen. The frozen bars are then fried in oil. The final result is dressed with green tomato piccalilli relish and plated with fire-roasted banana pepper mayonnaise. Sounds great! Local ingredients are also the basis of Colonel Newsom's country ham pot stickers. Lundy adds the Winchester-produced soft drink Ale-8-One to cocktails, and he uses Spaulding's doughnuts to make New Orleans bread pudding, attesting to his whimsical approach.

In larger cities, there are community groups that advocate for the creation of local food policies, especially to address school lunch programs and food for low-income families. In 2009 the organization Sustainable Berea published a cookbook containing recipes contributed by participants in its annual 100-Mile Potluck (a meal based on ingredients grown within 100 miles of Berea). The following recipe was contributed by Kent Gilbert.

Oven Braised Pork Shoulder Roast with Garlic and Rosemary (2009)

Pork shoulder roast
10 cloves of garlic, peeled into slivers
2 cloves elephant garlic, peeled into slivers

onions, chopped
1–2 cups water or water/wine mix
rosemary sprigs
oil
salt to taste
pepper to taste
Optional: potatoes

Make cuts in pork (especially the fat) and insert all garlic slivers. Stuff fresh rosemary sprigs into slits as well. Sprinkle onions over meat. Add potatoes to pot if desired. Add water or water/wine mix to bottom of heavy roaster or ovenproof crock and roast at 325–350 degrees for about 35 minutes per pound of meat. Add salt, pepper and oil to taste. Cover the dish. (Sustainable Berea 2009, 40)

Another important theme in contemporary cookbooks is ensuring a healthy diet. Eating healthy is part of the eating local movement—in particular, eating fewer processed foods and more organic foods. This has been a concern for many decades, in fact. There are numerous examples of how recipes have changed over time to make them healthier. A clear example can be found in the series of fund-raising cookbooks produced by the University of Kentucky Women's Club, starting with *Stay for Tea* in 1948. To celebrate the club's centennial in 2009, it published *Stay for Tea, the Centennial Edition* (2010), which presents new, healthier versions of recipes from earlier editions. This project involved collaboration with the university's program in nutrition sciences and extensive taste testing. Faculty and students in the nutrition program apparently prepared both the original and the new alternatives and organized taste tests, which often revealed that the tasting panels preferred the new version over the original. The modified recipes employed various strategies, including reducing the amount of fat by using fat substitutes such as applesauce, replacing fattier meats with ground turkey, reducing the number of egg yolks (or whole eggs), using skim milk and fat-free dairy products, substituting whole grain flour for white flour, reducing the amount of refined sugar or using noncaloric sweeteners (e.g., Splenda), and adding less salt.

The following recipe for gingerbread was modified by Alicia Arnett of Dietetics. The original recipe from the 1948 cookbook was contributed by Frances Jewell McVey, wife of university president Frank McVey (to whom that first cookbook was dedicated). Mrs. McVey did some food writing in addition to her duties as campus hostess and recipe writer. The use of applesauce as a moisture-providing fat substitute had a large impact of the number of calories. The original 1948 recipe called for a cup of shortening (half butter and half lard). The revised version retains the word "shortening" in the description of the process.

Gingerbread (2010)

1 cup applesauce
½ cup sugar
1 well-beaten egg
2½ cups sifted all purpose flour
1½ teaspoon baking soda
½ teaspoon salt
1 teaspoon ground ginger
1 teaspoon ground cinnamon
½ teaspoon ground cloves
1 cup sorghum
1 cup buttermilk

Preheat oven to 350 degrees. Cream together applesauce, sugar, and egg in a large bowl. Sift together dry ingredients. Add sorghum and buttermilk alternately with dry ingredients to shortening, sugar and egg mixture. Beat well and bake for 25–30 minutes or until toothpick comes out clean. (University of Kentucky Women's Club 2010, 177)

Coda

This book reflects changes in the social and economic context of cooking and meal preparation, different degrees of cooking knowledge on the part of cookbook users, new technology related to cooking and preservation, the appearance of new ingredients, changing views on diet and health, and evolving styles in the format of the recipes themselves, among other topics.

How have the users of cookbooks changed? The earliest Kentucky cookbook, *The Kentucky Housewife*, was apparently written for mistresses of large households employing staffs that might include enslaved people. With the Civil War and emancipation, these circumstances changed dramatically. Some argue that the surge in cookbooks published toward the end of the nineteenth century was related to the decreased availability of household staff and the loss of their food preparation expertise.

Another difference in cookbook users was their level of knowledge of cooking, which seemed to be connected to the changes brought about by World War II. Often mentioned is the decline in cooking information conveyed through "apprenticing" to one's mother or auntie. If Mom was off working, she didn't have as much time to cook and pass on her knowledge. As a result, cookbooks became more detailed, and people learned to cook by reading text rather than by watching older, more experienced cooks and modeling their techniques. In addition, there was greater experimentation in cuisine. The American diet started to become much more multicultural in the 1950s. Pizza, tacos, lasagna, mousse, and chop suey have now been thoroughly integrated into the American diet. These dishes have become Americanized—adapted to American tastes, available food items, and modern cooking technology. For those who are interested, new foods and new recipes appear more or less continually, transforming their cooking through new cookbooks, magazine and newspaper articles, and the Internet.

The changing technology of cooking is evident in some of the recipes. Cooking meats on the hearth was hard work and involved the risk of physical injury. This slowly changed with the advent of the wood-fired cookstove and then the availability of gas and electric cooking. This transition is difficult to factor out, as there was great variation in when and where these changes occurred. Middle-class Louisvillians abandoned their woodstoves in the nineteenth century, whereas this occurred almost fifty years later in some rural counties.

The template for recipes also changed over time: ingredients were listed separately from procedures, precise measurements were specified, and far more detailed instructions were included (some early recipes did not mention procedure at all). In the middle of the twentieth century, many cookbooks began to couple recipes with elaborate narratives on a variety of topics. Cookbook writers provided far more contextualizing information, and readers were taken beyond what was needed to re-create the recipe. Authors told stories about how they obtained a recipe, provided word pictures describing the context for cooking or eating the food, and revealed details about the originator of the recipe. In the domain of Kentucky cookbooks, this started with Marion Flexner's *Dixie Dishes* (1941) or perhaps even earlier, with Tandy Ellis's *Camp Cooking* (1923). These books include the historical background or cultural meaning of food preparation; the personally oriented social context of the recipe, including experiences cooking or eating the dish; and how the food relates to community or regional history, among other topics. These narratives reflected the fact that more and more cookbook users were interested in reading about food in addition to actually preparing it. With some exceptions, the amount of narrative in cookbooks produced by the specialized fund-raiser cookbook publishers was somewhat limited, whereas cookbooks produced independently by community groups were often rich sources of narratives about cooking, social life, and history.

The concern for health started in the 1950s and became more emphatic over time. In some cases, cookbooks provided healthier options, such as reduced fat and sugar or increased fiber. (Very early in the twentieth century, improved nutrition sometimes meant *adding* calories.) One significant change involved the kinds of fat used in cooking. Lard more or less disappeared, and there was a slow ascendance in the use of hydrogenated vegetable oil products such as Crisco and Spry, followed by a reduction in their popularity. Likewise, margarine seemed to replace butter and then declined in importance. Over the twentieth century there was a steady increase in the use of vegetable oils (often called salad oils, indicating their original purpose).

The most recent trend in cookbooks is concern about the environment. This can be seen in cookbooks that focus on eating locally. Accompanying this trend is greater appreciation of regional cooking traditions and greater concern about the sources of ingredients and seasonality.

Acknowledgments

I would like to thank thc people who assisted in the preparation of this book. I benefited from the help of the following readers of the manuscript as it developed: Anne van Willigen, Julie Maruskin, Rona Roberts, and chef Bob Perry. Their comments were very useful.

Of course, having access to cookbooks was important. Esther Edwards, Rona Roberts, Betty Abdmishani, Lonnie Williams Jr., and Anne van Willigen gave or lent cookbooks from their collections. Library collections were important sources. Julie Maruskin, director of the Clark County Public Library, made both her personal cookbook collection and the library's holdings available for study. Joe Hardesty of the Louisville Free Public Library assisted with obtaining an early Work Projects Administration cookbook. Jonathan Jeffery of the Western Kentucky University Library's Special Collections helped get a copy of an early and rare Kentucky cookbook. Sharyn J. Mitchell helped find historical materials at the Hutchins Library at Berea College. The collections of the Kentucky Department for Libraries and Archives, the Kentucky Room of the Lexington Public Library, the Special Collections of the University of Kentucky Library, and the Special Collections of Eastern Kentucky University, as well as many public libraries throughout the state, were invaluable in the process of finding cookbooks. A number of community organizations also provided cookbooks. These included the African American Heritage Center of Franklin, the Hart County Historical Society of Munfordville, the Magoffin County Historical Society of Salyersville, and the Hopkins County Genealogical Society of Madisonville.

My visit to Riverside at Farnsley–Moremen Landing, part of the Jefferson County park system, was facilitated by Patti Linn, historic site manager, and Jay Stottman of the Kentucky Archaeological Survey. I was also able to look at early manuscript cookbooks at Liberty Hall in Frankfort with the help of Kate Hesseldenz, the curator of collections. At Liberty Hall during special events it is possible to see hearth cooking demonstrations. Lucy Cooper and Lyn Layton of Paris, Kentucky, helped me better understand cookbook author Nannie Talbot Johnson. Mary Margaret Bell, of the Jefferson County Public Schools Archives, provided information about Atholene Mary Peyton, an African American cookbook author who was on the domestic science faculty of Louisville's Central Colored High School.

Juliana van Willigen compiled the index. Angela Hensley of South Hill Gallery in Lexington scanned many of the images used in the book.

As always, I thank my wife, Jacqueline van Willigen, for assisting and for tolerating the clutter of piles of cookbooks.

Notes

Introduction

1. The recipes have not been tested. Although I have maintained as much of the original format as possible, I spell out abbreviations that might cause confusion (e.g., tablespoon is not written as T).

2. This paragraph draws on the foreword from Scaggs and McGraw (2013).

1. The First Kentucky Cookbook

1. What is now Boyle County was part of Lincoln County in 1805.

2. The information about Mrs. Bryan was found on Ancestry.com, a genealogy website. The basic information comes from Kentucky marriage records. In addition, a woman who was researching her ancestors identified Lettice Bryan as her great-great-great-grandmother and as the author of *The Kentucky Housewife*, based on personal family knowledge and references to Mrs. Bryan in her grand mother's personal papers. The dates that appear in the records support this view.

3. Ultimately, the college merged with the University of Cincinnati.

4. A year later Shepard and Stearns published 2,000 copies of the third edition of *The Book of Mormon*. This version is historically important because it includes the corrections provided by Joseph Smith and was the penultimate edition published during Smith's lifetime.

5. All the cookbooks mentioned so far are readily available in inexpensive facsimile editions or free downloadable versions.

6. *Spaddle* is an archaic word that means "small spade." It was apparently used like a rubber (or vinyl) spatula. Sometimes, Mrs. Bryan refers to a wooden spoon.

7. Cheeses are also made with coagulants other than rennet, some of which are nonanimal.

8. Unslaked lime is calcium oxide. Calcium oxide is chemically unstable and transforms into calcium carbonate.

9. According to the *Dictionary of Regional American English*, a feelark is a meadowlark (Cassidy and Hall 1991, 381).

10. These include Liberty Hall (1796) and Orlando Brown House (1835) in Frankfort, Farmington (1810) in Louisville, Ashland (1809–1811) in Lexington, and the Brown-Pusey House (1825) in Elizabethtown, among others.

11. A trammel is an iron hook that attaches the cooking pot to the hearth crane. They can be simple-shaped hooks or more complex, adjustable devices.

12. Culinary historian Alice Ross describes the convoluted history of the term *spider* in "There's History in Your Frying Pan," *Journal of Antiques and Collectibles* (January 2001).

13. A drachm is ⅛ of an ounce and is the same as a dram.

14. Kentucky did not vote to ratify the Thirteenth Amendment until 1976.

2. The Needs of the "New Regime"

1. This should not be confused with Mrs. Bryan's *The Kentucky Housewife*. The books are quite different, and the title of Mrs. White's book was changed in later editions.

2. Although Moss's cookbook is widely held to be the first charity cookbook, there are alternative views in the culinary history literature. Sanitary fairs were held in large cities in the North to mobilize civilian support for the medical care of soldiers. These events included exhibits and commercial sales. President Lincoln gave a speech at the Philadelphia Sanitary Fair, which raised over $1 million. The situation was desperate, as there were few government provisions for the mass casualties resulting from the Civil War. There was almost no funding on either side for ambulances or medical care or for registering and burying the dead. The U.S. Sanitary Commission was formed in the private sector to address some of these issues on the Union side (Faust 2008, 87–88). Sanitary fairs were one way to raise money for the Sanitary Commission.

3. *Yelk* is an archaic spelling of *yolk* and appears in some other cookbooks from this era.

4. This information is from the website of Janet Jarvits, an antiquarian cookbook dealer. It identifies Mrs. Peter A. White's maiden name as Miss Mag Woolley and states that she was "trained in household duties."

5. Much of the description of woodstoves presented here is from the article "The Kitchen Stove" by George D. Slade (2004), based on his experiences growing up in Harrison County. Although he was quite old when he wrote this, he was recalling experiences more recent than the late nineteenth century.

3. A Turning Point

1. *The Blue Ribbon Cook Book* is based on Benedict's 1897 cookbook titled *A Choice Collection of Tested Receipts*. Both the Fox and the Benedict cookbooks have been republished by the University Press of Kentucky with informative introductory essays.

2. Auvergne was originally established by the Clay family in the eighteenth century. Berle Clay still owns and farms Auvergne. At the time Fox's book was

written, the estate was the property of Brutus J. Clay. Mount Airy was the estate of William Sims, a U.S. congressman and, during the Civil War era, a Confederate senator and member of Jefferson Davis's cabinet.

3. King's Daughters is an interdenominational Christian service organization founded in New York in 1886. It has a Protestant orientation.

4. The majority of land-grant universities were established by the Morrill Act of 1862. These universities usually had home economics departments. Today, these departments are almost always called something else, reflecting the complex changes in both agriculture and gender roles.

5. Laura Shapiro's *Perfection Salad: Women and Cooking at the Turn of the Century* (2001) provides a well-researched and highly readable account of the culinary, institutional, and gender aspects of the domestic science movement. Much of my discussion of the national perspectives on this movement is based on that book.

6. After the death of her husband, she used the name Mary Lincoln.

7. That is, Mrs. William Alexander Johnson, after she married Johnson at age eighteen.

8. The first edition was published in 1931 at Mrs. Rombauer's expense.

9. Nannie Talbot Johnson is called Mrs. Ray Johnson of Paris, Kentucky, in Becker's volume. There is a copy of Johnson's specialty cookbook *Cake, Candy, and Culinary Crinkles* (1912) in the Irma S. Rombauer Papers archived at the Schlesinger Library at Harvard University.

10. This is usually spelled *filé* or *file*. It serves to thicken and flavor the mixture.

11. The bibliography, compiled by Doris Witt with David Lupton, is prefaced by an essay entitled "African American Cookbooks" by Witt. The only Kentucky cookbook listed is Hayes's *Kentucky Cookbook* (1912); the earlier work of Atholene Peyton is not included.

12. The Women of Christ Church Cathedral also published *Christ Church Classics: 200 Years of Favorite Recipes* in 1996, which is supplemented by recipes from both the 1920 and 1926 volumes.

4. Hard Times

1. A culinary metaphor for prosperity was an iconic Kentucky dish called the Hot Brown sandwich. Its ubiquitous presence on Kentucky menus started in 1926, when it was created at Louisville's newly built Brown Hotel by chef Fred K. Schmidt to feed hungry partygoers and recharge their energy after an evening of dancing. Decades later, this dish appears with many variations in numerous Kentucky cookbooks. Although the sandwich continued, the prosperity did not.

2. The WPA was originally named the Works Progress Administration; this was changed to Work Projects Administration in 1939.

3. The manual is undated. I use the estimated publication date of 1941 supplied by the Special Collections Department at the Hitchens Library at Berea College.

4. Queen's Daughters is a women's social services organization active in Louisville. It is associated with Catholic Church membership and was founded in St. Louis.

5. New Foods and New Roles

1. An interesting account of wartime rationing is "Meat Rationing during World War II" by Wilbur Bush, published by the Daviess County Historical Society and available on its website.

2. *The Victory Handbook for Health and Home Defense* seems to be a charity publication project that was instituted during the war in a number of different communities around the country. It contains both standardized and local content, including recipes, local ads, and lists of persons who served during the war. The publication dates range from 1942 to 1945. The issue reprinted by the Hopkins County group has credits from local businesses in Earlington and Madisonville.

3. Corn syrup is produced from cornstarch through the action of certain enzymes. It is different from high-fructose corn syrup, which represents an evolution of the original corn syrup technology and is sweeter than corn syrup.

4. Some say this GE model was called the Monitor Top because the cylindrical fitting on top of the cabinet resembled the turret on the Civil War–era ironclad USS *Monitor.*

References

African-American Heritage Center (Franklin). 1998. *Heritage Cookbook: A Collection of Traditional and Favorite Recipes*. Franklin, KY: African-American Heritage Center of Simpson County.

Algren, Nelson. 1992. *America Eats*. Iowa City: University of Iowa Press.

Allen, Emma Powell. 1941. *Query Club Recipes*. Louisville, KY: John P. Morton.

Allison-Lewis, Linda. 1998. *Kentucky's Best: Fifty Years of Great Recipes*. Lexington: University Press of Kentucky.

———. 2009. *Kentucky Cooks: Favorite Recipes from* Kentucky Living. Lexington: University Press of Kentucky.

Anderson, Jean. 1997. *The American Century Cookbook*. New York: Clarkson Potter/Publishers.

Appelt, Kathi, and Jeanne C. Schmitzer. 2001. *Down Cut Shin Creek: The Pack Horse Librarians of Kentucky*. New York: HarperCollins.

Arena, Susan P., ed. 1974. Kentucky Living *Cookbook: Bicentennial Edition*. Shelbyville, KY: Landmark Community Newspapers.

Astor, Aaron. 2012. *Rebels on the Border: Civil War, Emancipation, and the Reconstruction of Kentucky and Missouri*. Baton Rouge: Louisiana State University Press.

Athens Christian Church, Dorcas Circle. 1976. *What's Cooking at Athens: 1976 Bicentennial Edition*. Iowa Falls, IA: General Publishing and Binding.

Bardstown Woman's Club. 1913. *Bardstown Cook Book*. Bardstown, KY: Department of Home Economics of the Woman's Club.

Barton, Keith C. 1997. "Good Cooks and Washers: Slave Hiring, Domestic Labor, and the Market in Bourbon County, Kentucky." *Journal of American History* 84 (2): 436–60.

Beck, Simone, Louisette Berthole, and Julia Child. 1961. *Mastering the Art of French Cooking*. New York: Alfred A. Knopf.

Becker, Marion Rombauer. 1966. *Little Acorn: The Story behind* The Joy of Cooking *1931–1966*. Indianapolis: Bobbs-Merrill.

Benedict, Jennie C. 1897. *A Choice Collection of Tested Receipts*. Louisville, KY: J. P. Morton.

———. 1904. *The Blue Ribbon Cook Book*. Louisville, KY: Standard Printing.

———. (1922) 2008. *The Blue Ribbon Cook Book*. 4th ed. Reprint, Lexington: University Press of Kentucky.

———. 1928. *The Road to Dream Acre*. Louisville, KY: Standard Printing.

Berry, Wendell. 1981. *The Gift of Good Land: Further Essays Cultural and Agricultural*. San Francisco: Northpoint.

———. 2009. *Bringing It to the Table: On Farming and Food*. Berkeley, CA: Counterpoint.

Bishop, E. C. 1906. *Nebraska Corn Book*. Lincoln, NE: University Publishing.

Bittman, Mark. 2009. *Food Matters: A Guide to Conscious Eating with More than 75 Recipes*. New York: Simon and Schuster.

Bivins, S. Thomas. 1912. *The Southern Cookbook: A Manual of Cooking and a List of Menus, Including Recipes Used by Noted Colored Cooks and Prominent Caterers*. Hampton, VA: Press of the Hampton Institute.

Bosley, Patrick. 2005. *Family Favorites from Moonlite: Recipes that Founded a Kentucky Tradition*. Owensboro, KY: Moonlite Bar-B-Q Inn.

Bracken, Peg. 1960. *The I Hate to Cook Book*. New York: Harcourt Brace.

Brewer, Priscilla J. 1990. "'We Have Got a Very Good Cooking Stove': Advertising, Design, and Consumer Response to the Cookstove, 1815–1880." *Winterthur Portfolio* 25 (1): 35–54.

———. 2000. *From Fireplace to Cookstove: Technology and the Domestic Ideal in America*. Syracuse, NY: Syracuse University Press.

Brooksville Methodist Church, Ladies. 1912. *Brooksville Cook Book*. Brooksville, KY: Ladies of the Methodist Church.

Brown, Alton. 2010. Foreword to *The Southern Foodways Alliance Community Cookbook*, edited by Sara Roahen and John T. Edge, xi. Athens: University of Georgia Press.

Bryan, Lettice. 1839. *The Kentucky Housewife*. Cincinnati, OH: Shepard and Stearns.

———. (1839) 1991. *The Kentucky Housewife*, with an introduction by Bill Neal. Reprint, Columbia: University Press of South Carolina.

Cabbage Patch Circle. 1952. *Famous Kentucky Recipes*. Louisville, KY: Cabbage Patch Circle.

———. 1956. *Cabbage Patch: Famous Kentucky Recipes*. Louisville, KY: Cabbage Patch Circle.

Carlisle, Mrs. John G., et al. 1893. *Mrs. John G. Carlisle's Kentucky Cook Book: Containing Original Recipes Never before Published*. Chicago: F. Tennyson Neely.

Cassidy, Frederic G., and Joan Huston Hall. 1991. *Dictionary of Regional American English*. Vol. 2. Cambridge, MA: Belknap Press of Harvard University Press.

Cebulska, Marcia. 1976. "The Pioneer Kitchen." In *Kentucky Hospitality: A 200-Year Tradition*, edited by Dorothea C. Cooper, 29–35. Louisville: Kentucky Federation of Women's Clubs.

Central Baptist Hospital. 2010. *Beyond the Fence: A Culinary View of Historic Lexington*. Lexington, KY: Central Baptist Hospital Foundation Cancer Program.

Charity League of Paducah. 1967. *A Collection of Recipes from the Charity League*. Paducah, KY: Charity League.

———. 1978. *Seasons of Thyme*. Paducah, KY: Charity League.

Christian Church, United Christian Missionary Society (Midway). 1944. *Selected Recipes from the Blue Grass*. Midway, KY: Christian Church.

Ciullo, Peter A. 2006. *Baking Soda Bonanza*. 2nd ed. New York: HarperCollins.

Clay County Homemakers. 1992. *Kentucky Bicentennial Cookbook*. Leawood, KS: Circulation Service.

Cobb, Irvin S. 1936. *Irvin S. Cobb's Own Recipe Book*. Louisville, KY: Frankfort Distilleries.

Colonelettes of Louisville, Kentucky. 1958. *Kentucky Cooking New and Old: A Collection of Mouth Watering Dishes in the Fine Food Tradition of the South*. 2nd ed. Louisville, KY: Junior Chamber of Commerce.

Cook, Margaret. 1971. *America's Charitable Cooks: A Bibliography of Fund-raising Cookbooks Published in the United States*. Kent, OH: Author.

Coombs, Mary Rochester. 1894. *Kentucky Cook Book*. Bowling Green, KY: C. M. Coombs.

Cooper, Dorothea C., ed. 1976. *Kentucky Hospitality: A 200-Year Tradition*. Louisville: Kentucky Federation of Women's Clubs.

Crittenden County Extension Homemakers Association. 1992. *Heritage Cooking Crittenden County 1792–1992*. Leawood, KS: Circulation Service.

Dedman, Mary Elizabeth, and Thomas Curry Dedman Jr. 1983. *Beaumont Inn: Special Recipes*. 2nd ed. Harrodsburg, KY: Beaumont Inn.

Divina, Fernando, and Marlene Divina. 2010. *Foods of the Americas: Native Recipes and Traditions*. Berkeley, CA: Ten Speed Press.

Domine, David. 2010. *A Feast for the Eyes: Recipes from America's Grandest Victorian Neighborhood*. Kuttawa, KY: McClanahan Publishing House.

Drake, Daniel. 1870. *Pioneer Life in Kentucky*. Cincinnati, OH: Robert Clarke.

Edge, John T. 1999. *A Gracious Plenty: Recipes and Recollections from the American South*. New York: G. P. Putnam's Sons.

Egerton, John. 1990. *Side Orders: Small Helpings of Southern Cookery and Culture*. Atlanta: Peachtree Publishers.

———. 1993. *Southern Food: At Home, on the Road, in History*. Chapel Hill: University of North Carolina Press.

Ellis, Tandy. 1923. *Camp Cooking.* N.p.: n.p.
Elsmere Volunteer Fire Department Ladies Auxiliary. 1976. *The Bicentennial Story of Elsmere, Kentucky, 1776–1976.* Elsmere, KY: National Consumers Research.
Embry, Jim. 2012. "Good Food Revolution Has to Start at Home." *Lexington Herald-Leader,* April 20.
Embry Family. 2004. *Recipes and Remembrances: A Collection by the Embry Family, 314 Overland Drive, Richmond, KY 40475.* Kearney, NE: Morris Press Cookbooks.
Epworth United Methodist Church. 1990. *1890–1990 Epworth United Methodist.* Olathe, KS: Cookbook Publishers.
Estill County Historical and Genealogical Society. 2004. *Recipes Old and New: A Collection of Recipes.* Kearney, NE: Morris Press Cookbooks.
Farmer, Fannie Merritt. 1896. *Fannie Farmer Cookbook.* Boston: Little, Brown.
Farr, Sidney Saylor. 1983. *More than Moonshine: Appalachian Recipes and Recollections.* Pittsburgh, PA: University of Pittsburgh Press.
———. 1995. *Table Talk: Appalachian Meals and Memories.* Pittsburgh, PA: University of Pittsburgh Press.
———. 1997. *Spoon Bread Cook Book.* Berea, KY: Saylor-Farr Publishing.
———. 2007. *My Appalachia: A Memoir.* Lexington: University Press of Kentucky.
Faust, Drew Gilpin. 2008. *This Republic of Suffering: Death and the American Civil War.* New York: Alfred A. Knopf.
Fayette County Medical Auxiliary. 1999. *Creating a Stir in the Bluegrass and Beyond.* Memphis, TN: Wimmer.
Finley, John, ed. 1985. *The* Courier-Journal *Kentucky Cookbook.* Louisville, KY: Courier-Journal and Louisville Times Company.
First Christian Church, Young Ladies' Missionary Society. 1890. *The Louisville Cookbook, Containing over Five Hundred Receipts, Some of Them Original, Many New, and All Thoroughly Tested.* Louisville, KY: Guide Printing and Publishing Company.
First Presbyterian Church, Ladies' Society, Owensboro. 1890. *Women's Wisdom: A Collection of Choice Recipes.* Owensboro, KY: O. T. Kendall.
First Presbyterian Church, Paris, Kentucky. 2009. *Feeding the Flock: A Collection of Recipes.* Kearney, NE: Morris Press Cookbooks.
Fisher, Abby. 1881. *What Mrs. Fisher Knows about Old Southern Cooking.* San Francisco: Women's Co-op Printing Office.
Fisher, Carol. 2006. *The American Cookbook: A History.* Jefferson, NC: McFarland.
Fisher, M. F. K. 1968. *With Bold Knife and Fork.* Berkeley, CA: Counterpoint.
Flexner, Marion W. 1939. *Drina: England's Young Victoria.* New York: Coward-McCann.
———. 1941. *Dixie Dishes.* Boston: Hale, Cushman and Flint.

———. 1949. *Out of Kentucky Kitchens*. New York: Bramhall Press.

———. 1951. *Quick Cooking from the Top of the Stove*. Greenwich, CT: Fawcett Publications.

———. 1955. *Cocktail Supper Cookbook*. New York: Bramhall House.

———. 1989. *Out of Kentucky Kitchens*. Lexington: University Press of Kentucky.

Flexner, Marion W., and Isabel McLennan McMeekin. 1929. *Food for Children and How to Cook It: With an Article on Inducing Them to Eat It*. New York: Henry Holt.

Fowler, Damon Lee. 2008. *Classical Southern Cooking*. Salt Lake City, UT: Gibbs Smith.

Fox, John, Jr. 1903. *The Little Shepherd of Kingdom Come*. New York: Charles Scribner and Sons.

———. 1908. *Trail of the Lonesome Pine*. New York: Charles Scribner and Sons.

Fox, Minnie C. 1904. *The Blue Grass Cook Book*. New York: Fox, Duffield.

———. (1904) 2005. *The Blue Grass Cook Book*. Lexington: University Press of Kentucky.

Fraser, Kathryn M. 1983. *By the Seasons: Cookery at the Homeplace—1850*. Golden Pond, KY: Tennessee Valley Authority.

Frazer, Mary Harris. 1903. *Kentucky Receipt Book*. Louisville, KY: Bradley and Gilbert.

Fritschner, Sarah. 2004. *Derby 101: A Guide to Food and Menus for Kentucky Derby Week*. Louisville, KY: Butler Books.

———. 2006. *Sarah Fritschner's Derby: Start to Finish*. Louisville, KY: Butler Books.

Garden Club of Lexington. 1985. *Bluegrass Winners: A Cookbook*. Lexington, KY: Garden Club of Lexington.

Gibson, Marie. 1937. "Careful Following of Recipes Will Insure Good Piecrust." *Louisville Courier-Journal*, January 4.

Glasse, Hannah. 1747. *The Art of Cookery Made Plain and Easy*. London. (There are various facsimile versions as well as PDF versions online.)

Glenn, Camille. 1986. *The Heritage of Southern Cooking*. New York: Workman Publishing.

Green, Maggie. 2011. *The Kentucky Fresh Cookbook*. Lexington: University Press of Kentucky.

Gregg, Cissy. 1953. *Cissy Gregg's Cookbook and Guide to Gracious Living*. Vol. 1. Louisville, KY: Louisville Courier-Journal.

———. 1959. *Cissy Gregg's Cookbook*. Vol. 2. Louisville, KY: Louisville Courier-Journal.

———. 1981. *Cissy Gregg's Cook Book*, with an introduction by Deni Hamilton. 2 vols. Louisville, KY: Foodwork.

Groft, Tammis Kane. 2005. "Cast with Style: Nineteenth-Century Cast-Iron Stoves." *Gastronomica* 5 (1): 19–24.

Harris, Jessica B. 2011. *High on the Hog: A Culinary Journey from Africa to America*. New York: Bloomsbury.

Harris, Marvin. 1985. *Good to Eat: Riddles of Food and Culture*. New York: Simon and Schuster.

Hayes, Irene. 1965. *What's Cooking in Kentucky*. Hueysville, KY: T. I. Hayes Publishing.

Hayes, Mrs. W. T. 1912. *Kentucky Cookbook: Easy and Simple for Any Cook*. St. Louis, MO: J. H. Tomkins Printing Company.

Hess, John L., and Karen Hess. 2000. *The Taste of America*. Urbana: University of Illinois Press.

Hess, Karen. 1981. *Martha Washington's Book of Cookery*. New York: Columbia University Press.

———. 1992. *The Carolina Rice Kitchen: The African Connection*. Columbia: University of South Carolina Press.

———. 1995. "What We Know about Mrs. Abby Fisher and Her Cooking." Afterword to *What Mrs. Fisher Knows about Old Southern Cooking, Soups, Pickles, Preserves, etc.* by Abby Fisher, 75–94. Bedford, MA: Applewood Books.

———. 1996. *Martha Washington's Booke of Cookery and Booke of Sweetmeats*. New York: Columbia University Press.

Hill, Annabella P. 1867. *Mrs. Hill's New Cookbook*. New York: James O'Kane.

Hines, Duncan. 1935. *Adventures in Good Eating*. Bowling Green, KY: Author.

———. 1948. *Adventures in Good Cooking and the Art of Carving in the Home*. New York: Duncan Hines.

———. 1953. *Adventures in Good Cooking (Famous Recipes) and the Art of Carving in the Home*. Bowling Green, KY: Adventures in Good Eating.

———. 1955. *Duncan Hines Dessert Book*. New York: Pocket Books.

Historic Homes Foundation. 1976. *Kentucky Heritage Recipes*. Louisville, KY: Historic Homes Foundation.

Hodgenville Woman's Club. 1976. *Larue County Kitchens: A Larue County Bicentennial Cookbook*. Elizabethtown, KY: Hub City Printing.

Hopkins County Genealogical Society. 2011. *Preserving the Past for the Future: Recipes, Family Photos and Historical Tidbits*. Madisonville, KY: Hopkins County Genealogical Society.

Hougen, Richard T. 1955. *Look No Further: A Cookbook of Favorite Recipes from Boone Tavern Hotel, Berea College, Kentucky*. Nashville, TN: Abingdon Press.

———. 1960. *Cooking with Hougen*. Nashville, TN: Abingdon Press.

———. 1971. *More Hougen Favorites*. Nashville, TN: Abingdon Press.

Indianapolis Freeman. 2007. "Facts from Falls City." By Special Correspondent, February 23.

Johnson, Nannie Talbot. 1899. *What to Cook and How to Cook It*. Louisville, KY: Pentecostal Herald Press.

———. 1912. *Cake, Candy, and Culinary Crinkles: A Companion to* What to Cook and How to Cook It. Louisville, KY: Pentecostal Publishing.

Johnston, Annie Fellows. 1906. *The Little Colonel, Maid of Honor*. Boston: L. C. Page.

Judd, Naomi. 1997. *Naomi's Home Companion: A Treasury of Favorite Recipes, Food for Thought, and Kitchen Wit and Wisdom*. New York: GT Publishing.

Junior League of Augusta. 1940. *Recipes from Southern Kitchens*. Augusta, GA: Junior League of Augusta.

Junior League of Charleston. 1950. *Charleston Receipts*. Charleston, SC: Junior League of Charleston.

Junior League of Louisville. 1978. *The Cooking Book*. Louisville, KY: Junior League of Louisville.

———. 1988. *Cordon Bluegrass: Blue Ribbon Recipes from Kentucky*. Memphis, TN: Wimmer Brothers.

———. 2000. *Splendor in the Bluegrass, a Cookbook*. Louisville, KY: Junior League of Louisville.

———. 2013. *Bluegrass Gatherings*. Louisville, KY: Junior League of Louisville.

Junior League of Owensboro. 1984. *To Market, to Market*. Owensboro, KY: Junior League of Owensboro.

———. 2004. *Home Again, Home Again*. Owensboro, KY: Junior League of Owensboro.

Kentucky Extension Association of Family and Consumer Sciences. 2003. *Pride of Kentucky: Great Recipes with Food, Farm, and Family Traditions*. Franklin: Kentucky Extension Association of Family and Consumer Sciences.

Kimball, Chris. 2010. *Fannie's Last Supper: Recreating One Amazing Meal from Fannie Farmer's 1896 Cookbook*. New York: Hyperion.

Kingsolver, Barbara, with Steven L. Hopp and Camille Kingsolver. 2008. *Animal, Vegetable, Miracle: A Year of Food Life*. New York: Harper.

Kitchiner, William. 1830. *The Cook's Oracle*. New York: J. J. Harper.

Kremer, Elizabeth C. 1970. *We Make You Kindly Welcome*. Harrodsburg, KY: Pleasant Hill Press.

———. 1977. *Welcome Back to Pleasant Hill*. Harrodsburg, KY: Pleasant Hill Press.

Kurlansky, Mark. 2009. *The Food of a Younger Land: A Portrait of American Food—Before the National Highway System, before Chain Restaurants, and before Frozen Food, When the Nation's Food Was Seasonal*. New York: Riverhead.

———. 2012. *Birdseye: The Adventures of a Curious Man*. New York: Doubleday.

Ladies' Aid Society, Lawrenceburg Baptist Church. 1906. *The Lawrenceburg Cook Book*. Lawrenceburg, KY: Anderson News.

———. 1913. *The Lawrenceburg Baptist Cook Book*. Rev. ed. Louisville, KY: Pentecostal Publishing.

Lincoln, Mrs. D. A. 1884. *Mrs. Lincoln's Boston Cook Book: What to Do and What Not to Do*. Boston: Roberts Brothers.

Lincoln, Mrs. Mary J. 1910. *Home Helps: A Pure Food Cook Book*. Chicago: N. K. Fairbank.

Linn, Patti, and Donna Neary. 1999. *Riverside Receipts*. Louisville, KY: Jefferson County.

Linn, Patti, and M. Jay Stottman. 2003. *Bringing the Past into the Future: The Reconstruction of the Detached Kitchen at Riverside*. Lexington: Kentucky Archaeological Survey.

Long, Genevieve. 1903. *The Blue Grass Cook Book: A Manual of Useful Information for Housewives*. Chicago: W. B. Conkey.

Longone, Janice Bluestain. 1997. "'Tried Receipts': An Overview of America's Charitable Cookbooks." In *Recipes for Reading: Recipes, Lives, Stories, and Readings*, 17–28. Amherst: University of Massachusetts Press.

Lundy, Jonathan. 2009. *Jonathan's Bluegrass Table: Redefining Kentucky Cuisine*. Louisville, KY: Butler Books.

Lundy, Ronni. 1991. *Shuck Beans, Stack Cakes, and Honest Fried Chicken: The Heart and Soul of Southern Country Kitchens*. New York: Atlantic Monthly Press.

———. 1995. *The Festive Table: Recipes and Stories for Creating Your Own Holiday Traditions*. New York: North Point Press.

———. 1999. *Butter Beans to Blackberries: Recipes from the Southern Garden*. New York: North Point Press.

Lynn, Loretta. 2004. *You're Cookin' It Country: My Favorite Recipes and Memories*. Nashville, TN: Rutledge Hill Press.

Magoffin County Historical Society. 1989. *Olde Tyme Cookbook*. Salyersville, KY: Magoffin County Historical Society.

———. 1997. *A Joyful Cooking Journey with the Jenkins Family and Friends*. Salyersville, KY: Magoffin County Historical Society.

———. 1998. *Cooking with Memories: Recipes and Stories of Magoffin County Kentucky Past and Present*. Salyersville, KY: Magoffin County Historical Society.

———. 2000. *Year 2000 Cook Book: Recipes and Stories of Magoffin County, Kentucky*. Salyersville, KY: Magoffin County Historical Society.

———. 2003. *Circle of Friends Cookbook*. Salyersville, KY: Magoffin County Historical Society.

———. 2006. *Good Times Cookbook: Now Being Served in Magoffin County*. Salyersville, KY: Magoffin County Historical Society.

———. 2009. *The Manns Clan Cook Book*. Salyersville, KY: Magoffin County Historical Society.

Mandeville, Minn-Ell Sherley. 1940. *Random Recipes.* Louisville, KY: John P. Morton.

Marshall, Lillian. 1971. *The* Courier-Journal *&* Times *Cookbook.* Louisville, KY: Courier-Journal and Louisville Times Company.

Mendelson, Anne. 1996. *Stand Facing the Stove: The Story of the Women Who Gave America "The Joy of Cooking."* New York: Henry Holt.

Methodist Episcopal Church South, Maysville, Kentucky, 1884. *The New Kentucky Home Cook Book.* Rev. ed. Nashville, TN: Southern Methodist Publishing House.

Miller, Donna B. 2008. "An Incomplete List of Kentucky Cookbooks." Online.

Montell, William Lynwood, and Michael Lynn Morse. 1976. *Kentucky Folk Architecture.* Lexington: University Press of Kentucky.

Moss, Maria J. 1864. *A Poetical Cookbook.* Philadelphia: Caxton Press of C. Sherman, Sons.

Neal, William F. 1985. *Bill Neal's Southern Cooking.* Chapel Hill: University of North Carolina Press.

Nelson, Lynn. 2008. "A Prattle on Three Cookbooks. Or Is It Two?" *On Food and History.* http://www.onfoodandhistory.com/.

O'Neill, Molly. 2004. "The Viking Invasion." In *Corn Bread Nation 2: The United States of Barbecue,* edited by Lolis Eric Elie. Chapel Hill: University of North Carolina Press.

Parloa, Maria. 1880. *Miss Parloa's New Cookbook and Marketing Guide.* Boston: Estes and Lauriat.

Patteson, Charles, with Craig Emerson. 1988. *Charles Patteson's Kentucky Cooking.* New York: Harper and Row.

Payne, Ruth, ed. 1976. *The Kentucky Bicentennial Cookbook: Famous Historical Kentucky Recipes, 1776–1976.* Harrodsburg, KY: Roberts Printing.

Petrini, Carlo. 2004. *Slow Food: The Case for Taste.* New York: Columbia University Press.

Peyton, Atholene. 1906. *The Peytonia Cook Book.* Louisville, KY: Marshall Publishing.

Piercy, Caroline B. 1953. *The Shaker Cook Book.* New York: Crown Publishers.

Pollan, Michael. 2006. *The Omnivore's Dilemma: A Natural History of Four Meals.* New York: Penguin Press.

———. 2009. *Food Rules: An Eater's Manual.* New York: Penguin Press.

Presbyterian Church, Paris, Kentucky, Ladies. 1875. *Housekeeping in the Blue Grass.* Cincinnati, OH: Robert Clark.

———. 1888. *Housekeeping in the Blue Grass.* Cincinnati, OH: Robert Clark.

Queen's Daughters (Louisville). 1969. *Entertaining the Louisville Way.* Louisville, KY: Queen's Daughters.

Randolph, Mary. (1860) 1993. *The Virginia Housewife or Methodical Cook*. Reprint, New York: Dover Publications.

Rankin, Jane Lee. 2003. *Cookin' up a Storm: The Life and Recipes of Annie Johnson*. Updated 2nd ed. Louisville, KY: Grace Publishers.

Rannells, Molly, with Rob Baker and E. Corbin Crutcher. 1996. *The John Jacob Niles Cookbook: With Special Recipes by Mary Tippy Mullins*. Lexington, KY: Watersign Press.

Reigler, Susan. 2008. Introduction to *The Blue Ribbon Cook Book*, 4th ed., by Jennie C. Benedict. Reprint, Lexington: University Press of Kentucky.

Rice, Alice Caldwell Hegan. 1902. *Mrs. Wiggs of the Cabbage Patch*. New York: Century Company.

Roahen, Sara, and John T. Edge, eds. 2010. *The Southern Foodways Alliance Community Cookbook*. Athens: University of Georgia Press.

Roberts, Robert. 1827. *The House Servant's Directory*. Boston: Munroe and Francis.

Roberts, Rona. 2011. *Sweet, Sweet Sorghum: Kentucky's Golden Wonder*. Lexington, KY: Hot Cakes Press.

———. 2013. Personal communication.

Rombauer, Irma S. 1931. *The Joy of Cooking*. St. Louis, MO: Published by the author at A. C. Clayton Printing.

———. 1936. *The Joy of Cooking*. Indianapolis: Bobbs-Merrill.

Roosevelt, Franklin Delano. 2012. *Address of the President Delivered by Radio from the White House 28 April 1935*. Lexington: King Library Press, University of Kentucky.

Ross, Alice, 2001. "There's History in Your Frying Pan." *Journal of Antiques and Collectibles* (January). http://www.journalofantiques.com/hearthjan01.htm.

Ross, Elizabeth. 1996. *Kentucky Keepsakes: Classic Southern Recipes*. Kuttawa, KY: McClanahan Publishing House.

———. 2004. *Cornmeal Country: An American Tradition*. Kuttawa, KY: McClanahan Publishing House.

Russell, Malinda. 1866. *A Domestic Cookbook: Containing a Careful Selection of Useful Receipts for the Kitchen by Malinda Russell a Free Woman of Color*. Paw Paw, MI: Author.

Rutledge, Sarah. (1847) 1999. *The Carolina Housewife*. Reprint, Columbia: University of South Carolina Press.

Scaggs, Deirdre A., and Andrew W. McGraw. 2013. *The Historic Kentucky Kitchen: Traditional Recipes for Today's Cook*. Lexington: University Press of Kentucky.

Schmid, Albert W. A. 2010. *The Kentucky Bourbon Cookbook*. Lexington: University Press of Kentucky.

———. 2013. *The Old Fashioned: An Essential Guide to the Original Whiskey Cocktail.* Lexington: University Press of Kentucky.

Shapiro, Laura. 2001. *Perfection Salad: Women and Cooking at the Turn of the Century.* New York: Farrar, Straus, and Giroux.

———. 2004. *Something from the Oven: Reinventing Dinner in 1950s America.* New York: Viking Penguin.

Sharpless, Rebecca. 2010. *Cooking in Other Women's Kitchens: Domestic Workers in the South, 1865–1960.* Chapel Hill: University of North Carolina Press.

Simmons, Amelia. (1796) 1984. *The First American Cookbook: A Facsimile of "American Cookery."* New York: Dover Publications.

Slade, George D. 2004. "The Kitchen Stove." *Harrison Heritage News* 5 (10): 1, 3–4.

Sohn, Mark F. 1996. *Mountain Country Cooking: A Gathering of the Best Recipes from the Smokies to the Blue Ridge*, with a foreword by John Egerton. New York: St. Martin's Press.

———. 2005. *Appalachian Home Cooking: History, Culture, and Recipes.* Lexington: University Press of Kentucky.

South Frankfort Presbyterian Church, Circle No. 3. [1935?]. *My Favorite Recipes.* Frankfort, KY: South Frankfort Presbyterian Church.

Spence, Carol L. 2012. "To Market, to Market." *Ag* magazine, University of Kentucky College of Agriculture, Food, and Environment (Summer). http://www2.ca.uky.edu/agcomm/magazine/2012/SUMMER2012/Articles/To_Market.html.

Springfield Woman's Club. 1987. *The Springfield Woman's Club Presents a Tasting Tour through Washington County, Kentucky.* Olathe, KS: Cookbook Publishers.

St. James' Parish Church, Ladies' Guild (Pewee Valley). 1900. *Favorite Food of Famous Folk.* Louisville, KY: John P. Morton.

St. Peter's Evangelical Church, Ladies (Louisville). 1906. *Old Kentucky Cook Book.* Louisville, KY: C. T. Dearing Printing Co.

Sustainable Berea. 2009. *Local Foods Cookbook: Recipes from Berea, KY and the Region.* Berea, KY: Sustainable Berea.

Sutterlin, Violet C. 1949. *What's Cooking in Frankfort: A Book of Traditional Recipes by Frankfortians Past and Present.* Frankfort, KY: Frankfort Chapter, National Society of the Daughters of the American Revolution.

Thomas, Samuel. 2003. *Cherokee Triangle: A History of the Heart of the Highlands.* Louisville, KY: Cherokee Triangle Association.

Thomas, Susanna, Virginia Evans, Larrie Curry, and Thelma Linton. 1992. *Thelma's Treasures: The Secret Recipes of the Best Cook in Harrodsburg.* Harrodsburg, KY: Little Barter Press.

Thompson, Sharon. 2006. *Flavors of Kentucky.* Kuttawa, KY: McClanahan Publishing House.

Tipton-Martin, Toni. 2005. "Bluegrass and Black Magic, an Introduction to the New Edition." In *The Blue Grass Cook Book* by Minnie C. Fox. Lexington: University Press of Kentucky.

Trinity Methodist Church, Loyal Worker's Class (Latonia). 1950. *Latonia's Favorite Recipes*. Kansas City, MO: Bev-Ron Publishing.

University of Kentucky Women's Club. 1948. *Stay for Tea*. Lexington: University of Kentucky Women's Club.

———. 1975. *Stay for Tea . . . Again*. Lexington: University of Kentucky Women's Club.

———. 1983. *Stay for Tea . . . and More*. Lexington: University of Kentucky Women's Club.

———. 2010. *Stay for Tea, the Centennial Edition*. Lexington: University of Kentucky Women's Club.

U.S. Department of Agriculture. 1915. *Domestic Needs of Farm Women*. Washington, DC: Government Printing Office.

van Willigen, John, and Anne van Willigen. 2006. *Food and Everyday Life on Kentucky Family Farms 1920–1950*. Lexington: University Press of Kentucky.

Vileisis, Ann. 2008. *Kitchen Literacy: How We Lost Knowledge of Where Food Comes from and Why We Need to Get It Back*. Washington, DC: Island Books.

Wallach, Jennifer Jensen. 2013. *How America Eats: A Social History of U.S. Food and Culture*. Lanham, MD: Rowman and Littlefield.

Waters, Alice. 1982. *Chez Panisse Menu Cookbook*. New York: Random House.

———. 2007. *The Art of Simple Food: Notes, Lessons and Recipes from a Delicious Revolution*. New York: Clarkson Potter.

White, Mrs. Peter A. 1885. *The Kentucky Housewife: A Collection of Recipes for Cooking*. Chicago: Belford, Clarke.

———. 1891. *The Kentucky Cookery Book: A Book for Housewives*. Chicago: Belford, Clarke.

Whitley County Public Library Bookmobile Service. 1993. *Recipes from Our House to Yours*. Williamsburg, KY: Whitley County Public Library Bookmobile Service.

Whitley Pack Horse Library. 1938. *Mountain Receipts*. Williamsburg, KY: WPA District No. 3, Pack Horse Library.

Willard, Pat. 2009. *America Eats! On the Road with the WPA—The Fish Fries, Box Supper Socials, and Chitlin Feasts that Define Real American Food*. New York: Bloomsbury.

Wilson, Mary Tolford. 1984. "The First American Cookbook." In *The First American Cookbook* by Amelia Simmons, viii–xxi. New York: Dover Publications.

Winchester Council for the Arts. 1994. *Theatrical Seasonings*. Winchester, KY: Winchester Council for the Arts.

Winchester Mrs. Jaycees. 1975. *Mrs. Jaycees Spice Centennial Cook Book*. Winchester, KY: Winchester Mrs. Jaycees.

Witt, Doris. 1999. *Black Hunger: Food and the Politics of U.S. Identity.* New York: Oxford University Press.

Woman's Club of Louisville. 1938. *Favorite Recipes.* Louisville, KY: Geo. G. Fetter.

Woman's Club of Marion. 1976. *Historic Cookbook—1776–1976.* Marion, KY: Marion Woman's Club.

Women of Christ Church Cathedral, Lexington. 1996. *Christ Church Classics: 200 Years of Favorite Recipes.* Waseca, MN: Walter's Publishing.

Women's Guild of the Christ Church Cathedral, Lexington. 1920. *A Book of Recipes.* Lexington, KY: Women's Guild of the Christ Church Cathedral.

———. 1926. *A Book of Recipes.* 2nd improved ed. Lexington, KY: Women's Guild of the Christ Church Cathedral.

Wondrich, David. 2007. *Imbibe!* New York: Penguin Group.

Works Progress Administration. 1935. Administrative Reports. Goodman-Paxton Papers, University of Kentucky Library Special Collections.

Wyman, Carolyn. 2001. *Jell-O: A Biography.* San Diego, CA: Harcourt.

Younger Woman's Club of Louisville. 1966. *Party Cook Book.* Louisville, KY: Younger Woman's Club of Louisville.

Annotated Bibliography of Kentucky Cookbooks

This bibliography served as a checklist of resources while researching this book. It is subdivided by decades, and many of the entries are annotated. Included are a variety of different kinds of cookbooks. The most prevalent are those prepared for fund-raising purposes by Kentucky organizations such as churches, homemaker groups, hospital auxiliaries, schools, medical associations, parent-teacher groups, community centers, women's clubs, garden clubs, volunteer fire departments, museums, historic homes, and Junior Leagues; there is even one prepared by the staff of a prison. In addition, there are a number of cookbooks written by professional food writers, caterers, chefs, and restaurateurs.

The starting point for this list was my own collection, augmented by the discussion of cookbooks in John Egerton's *Southern Food: At Home, on the Road, in History* (1993, 359–61) and Margaret Cook's *America's Charitable Cooks: A Bibliography of Fund-raising Cook Books Published in the United States* (1971). I also used "An Incomplete List of Kentucky Cookbooks" prepared by Donna B. Miller (2008), which was posted on the Internet. I obtained many of the citations from the online catalogs of university and public libraries. The collegiate libraries included those at the University of Kentucky, University of Louisville, Morehead State University, Murray State University, Western Kentucky University, Eastern Kentucky University, Northern Kentucky University, Kentucky State University, University of Pikeville, Alice Lloyd College, Miami University, Transylvania University, and Berea College. I also searched the online catalogs of the Clements Library at the University of Michigan and the David Walker Lupton African American Cook Book Collection at the University of Alabama. For the public libraries I used the Kentucky Department of Libraries and Archives' directory of public libraries, which provides links to the individual library websites. The public libraries' online catalogs were a valuable source of information, especially for community cookbooks. The Lexington Public Library, the Louisville Free Public Library, and the Clark, Kenton, and Jessamine County Public Libraries have significant collections. Also useful was the Kentucky Historical Society's library. In addition, I consulted the websites of fund-raising cookbook publishers, including

Fundcraft (by far the publisher of the largest number of Kentucky cookbooks), Cookbooks by Morris, Wimmer Cookbooks, and Cookbook Publishers; unfortunately, these sites do not include publication dates. Finally, I looked at the auction and sale listings on Ebay. Ebay sellers usually list the title and publication date and a short description of the content, but little else. I followed up some leads with work at a number of libraries. These included the University of Kentucky, Eastern Kentucky University, Berea College, Clark County Public Library, Lexington Public Library, Louisville Free Public Library, Mason County Public Library, McCracken County Public Library, Jessamine County Public Library, and Paul Sawyier Public Library (Frankfort).

Although I found many cookbooks, I am sure I missed many more. It seems that every time I look, I find new ones. Also, because of my reliance on online catalogs, libraries without this resource were not searched. So, although this list is long, it should not be considered complete. It you have additions or corrections, let me know at ant101@uky.edu.

In most cases, a source for the book is indicated in parentheses at the end of the citation. I did not list all the sources for each book. A useful online tool for checking availability is WorldCat. Some of the earlier cookbooks can be read or downloaded online from sources such as the Internet Archive (www.archive.org), a not-for-profit organization that provides online texts and other media at no cost; it receives support from the Library of Congress and other institutions. The following abbreviations are used to identify sources:

Abdmishani	Private collection of Betty Abdmishani
Clements	Clements Library, University of Michigan
EKU	Eastern Kentucky University
KDL	Kentuckiana Digital Library
KDLA	Kentucky Department of Libraries and Archives
KHS	Kentucky Historical Society
LFPL	Louisville Free Public Library
LoC	Library of Congress
LPL	Lexington Public Library
Maruskin	Private collection of Julie Maruskin
PC	Personal collection of the author
PL	Public Library
UKSC	University of Kentucky Library, Special Collections
UoL	University of Louisville
WKU	Western Kentucky University

Antebellum Period

Bryan, Lettice. 1839. *The Kentucky Housewife*. Cincinnati, OH: Shepard and Stearns. (UKSC). Egerton cites this important cookbook in the bibliography of his classic work *Southern Food*: "it's a gem: nearly 1300 recipes, many of them painstakingly detailed, embrace the heart and soul of Southern cooking in the decades before the Civil War" (1993, 360). The version I have is an undated facsimile edition produced by Applewood Books, probably sometime in the 2000s. This edition can be read online at Google Books. A facsimile of the 1839 edition was also published in 1970 by Collector Books of Paducah, Kentucky.

———. [1839] 1991. *The Kentucky Housewife*. Columbia: University of South Carolina Press. (LPL). A useful introductory essay by Bill Neal is included in this facsimile edition.

———. 1841. *The Kentucky Housewife*. Cincinnati, OH: Shepard and Stearns. (LoC, Clements). I have no information about the differences between the 1839 and 1841 editions.

1870s

Presbyterian Church, Paris, Kentucky, Ladies. 1875. *Housekeeping in the Blue Grass*. Cincinnati, OH: Robert Clark. (PC, Internet Archive). This is the first Kentucky community fund-raising cookbook included in this list. It was produced in a number of later editions, including 1876, 1878, 1881, 1888, 1896, 1898, and 1905 (Cook 1971, 90). The original 1875 edition can be downloaded from the Internet Archive website in various formats, including PDF. This edition was also reissued by Kentucke Imprints of Berea. I have the 1875 and 1888 editions in my collection. This book is included in Egerton's bibliography of Kentucky cookbooks (1993, 359).

1880s

Methodist Episcopal Church, South, Maysville, Kentucky, 1884. *The Kentucky Home Cook Book*. Nashville, TN: Southern Methodist Publishing House. (Cook 1971).

———. 1885. *The Kentucky Home Cook Book*. Rev. ed. Nashville, TN: Southern Methodist Publishing House. (UKSC). Subsequent revised editions were published in 1890, 1899, 1906, and 1911, and there may be more. Cook (1971) lists this title as well as *The New Kentucky Cook Book*.

White, Mrs. Peter A. 1885. *The Kentucky Housewife: A Collection of Recipes for Cooking.* Chicago: Belford, Clarke. (Miami University, EKU, PC). Although it has the same main title as Lettice Bryan's 1839 volume, this is a different cookbook. For later editions, the title was changed to *The Kentucky Cookery Book: A Book for Housewives.* Apparently, it was also republished in 1903 as *The Bluegrass Cook Book,* by Genevieve Long, although the headers still read "The Kentucky Housewife." Egerton points out that the work's Kentucky connections are not clear, but it is definitely southern (1993, 360). It seems that Mrs. White was born in Lexington and lived in Cincinnati when she wrote the book. It may have been republished on microfiche by Lost Cause Press in Louisville.

1890s

Benedict, Jennie C. 1897. *A Choice Collection of Tested Receipts.* Louisville, KY: J. P. Morton. (UKSC). This is the first edition of what eventually became *The Blue Ribbon Cook Book.* It can be downloaded from the Internet Archive in various formats. Benedict was an important Louisville businesswoman, restaurant owner, social activist, and cookbook author.

Carlisle, Mrs. John G., et al. 1893. *Mrs. John G. Carlisle's Kentucky Cook Book: Containing Original Recipes Never before Published.* Chicago: F. Tennyson Neely. (UKSC). This is the first "celebrity" cookbook on the list. Mrs. Carlisle's husband was Speaker of the U.S. House of Representatives (1883–1889) and secretary of the treasury (1893–1897). There is an elementary school in northern Kentucky named for him. Mrs. Carlisle was the former Mary Jane Goodson. This book is included in Egerton's bibliography of Kentucky cookbooks (1993, 360). It can be downloaded for free at Google Books and the Internet Archive.

Coombs, Mary Rochester. 1894. *Kentucky Cook Book.* Bowling Green, KY: C. M. Coombs. (WKU). This rare book includes two signed recipes that could be from African American cooks, which would make them the earliest signed recipes from African American cooks that appear in this list.

First Christian Church (Louisville) Young Ladies' Missionary Society. 1890. *The Louisville Cook Book, Containing over Five Hundred Receipts, Some of Them Original, Many New, and All Thoroughly Tested.* Louisville, KY: Guide Printing and Publishing Company. (UKSC). This book contains advertisements for various products, including Bridgeford and Company woodstoves made in Louisville, and endorsements for the Dr. Price's line of flavoring extracts and baking powder. In addition, the recipes mention a few other brand-name products, including Coleman's mustard, Nelson's gelatin, and Durkee's salad (dressing?). The recipes are signed by their contributors and are presented in block format; some of them use obsolete measures such as the "teacup." The one recipe for mince pie that does not use meat is called "imitation mince" pie. In contemporary cookbooks, the term *mincemeat* is used, even though it generally does not contain meat. This represents a minor turning point.

First Presbyterian Church, Ladies' Society (Owensboro). 1890. *Women's Wisdom: A Collection of Choice Recipes*. Owensboro, KY: O. T. Kendall. (EKU). Some recipes include brand-name products such as Cleveland's Superior baking powder, Chalmer's gelatine, Fleischman's yeast, and Baker's chocolate.

Johnson, Nannie Talbot. 1899. *What to Cook and How to Cook It*. Louisville, KY: Pentecostal Herald Press. (PC). Mrs. Johnson was from Bourbon County. Besides writing cookbooks, she also taught cooking and owned the Cherokee Inn in Louisville. While teaching a cooking course for the Bay View Association Chautauqua near Petoskey, Michigan, one of her students was Irma Rombauer, who wrote *The Joy of Cooking*. Subsequent editions of Johnson's book were published as late as 1923. In the version in my possession, the first few pages are missing, along with the publication date. The cover of the 1899 edition states that it is the seventh enlarged edition, although it is usually described as the first edition. The 1899 edition can be downloaded in various formats from the Internet Archive. Johnson's title has been used more recently for other cookbooks.

Perkins, Mrs. Annie T. 1894. *The Ten's Recipe Book*. Henderson, KY: Henderson Journal Print. (Cook 1971). This book was compiled for the benefit of the First Presbyterian Church in Henderson.

Portland Methodist Church (Louisville). 1898. *The Epworth League Cook Book: Dedicated to the Epworth Leagues of America*. Louisville, KY: Pentecostal Publishing. (University of Chicago Library). The Epworth League is a national organization for Methodist young adults. Many local chapters produced Epworth League cookbooks.

1900s

Benedict, Jennie C. 1904. *The Blue Ribbon Cook Book: Being a Second Publication of "One Hundred Tested Recipes," Together with Many Others which Have Been Tried and Found Valuable*. Louisville, KY: J. P. Morton. (WKU). There may have been two 1904 editions. In addition to the one listed here, a "third publication" was published by Standard Printing. The 1922 edition of this classic was reprinted by the University Press of Kentucky.

The Best Yet Cook Book: An Everyday Guide, for the Millions, to Economical and Practical Cooking: A Large Variety of Domestic Recipes, Selected and Tested by a Committee of Kentucky Women Experienced in the Science of Cooking. 1907. Marietta, OH: S. A. Mullikin. (UKSC). This book was published for the benefit of the Ladies' Aid Society of the Baptist Church of Madison, Georgia. Other than the reference in the long subtitle, the relationship to Kentucky is not clear.

Christian Church (Bowling Green). 1909. *Cook Book Arranged by the Ladies of the Christian Church of Bowling Green, Kentucky.* Bowling Green, KY: Times-Journal Publishing Co. (Miller 2008).

Farnham, Mrs. G. R. 1904. *Evergreen Cook Book.* Louisville, KY: Baptist Book Concern. (Cook 1971).

Fox, Minnie C. 1904. *The Blue Grass Cook Book.* New York: Fox, Duffield. (PC). The University Press of Kentucky reprinted this volume with an interesting introductory essay by Toni Tipton-Martin that explains the role of African American cooks in the development of these recipes. This cookbook is also closely related to *Housekeeping in the Blue Grass*, in that it shares some recipe donors and is based in Paris, Kentucky. Egerton points out that Fox "gathered recipes from about fifty of her friends to augment her own" (1993, 359). A facsimile of the original can be downloaded from the Feeding America website at the Michigan State University library.

Frazer, Mary Harris. 1903. *Kentucky Receipt Book.* Louisville, KY: Bradley and Gilbert. (UKSC). This book includes recipes from Virginia, New Orleans, and France as well as Kentucky. The introduction notes that Frazer lived in Louisiana as a child and then resided in Virginia and Kentucky. This cookbook exhibits the Gulf Coast influences that are apparent in some of today's Louisville cookbooks. This cookbook can be downloaded in various formats from the Internet Archive. A number of the recipes on the Old Louisville website (www.oldlouisville.com) are from this cookbook. Old Louisville is a neighborhood with many stately Victorian-era homes.

Ladies' Aid Society, Lawrenceburg Baptist Church. 1906. *The Lawrenceburg Cook Book.* Lawrenceburg, KY: Anderson News. (UKSC). The recipes, signed by their contributors, are presented in block format. The book contains numerous advertisements from businesses in the region.

Long, Genevieve. 1903. *The Blue Grass Cook Book: A Manual of Useful Information for Housewives.* Chicago: W. B. Conkey. (UKSC). This cookbook is identical to Mrs. Peter A. White's *The Kentucky Housewife*, published in 1885. For a discussion of this oddity, see the note by Lynn Nelson, "A Prattle on Three Cookbooks. Or Is It Two?" in the *On Food and History* blog (http://www.onfoodandhistory.com/). This book should not be confused with Minnie C. Fox's historically important cookbook with the same main title.

Methodist Episcopal Church South, Ladies, Maysville. 1906. *The Kentucky Home*

Cook Book. 2nd ed. Nashville, TN: Publishing House of the M. E. Church, South. (Ebay). The first edition was published in 1884. The recipes are presented in block style, as is typical of cookbooks from this era. It also includes household hints and home remedies.

Methodist Episcopal Church South, Young Ladies' Aid Society (Russellville). 1906. *A Feast of Good Things*. Adairsville, KY: Enterprise Printing. (Cook 1971).

Peyton, Miss Atholene. 1906. *The Peytonia Cook Book*. Louisville, KY: Marshall Publishing. (LFPL). This is the earliest Kentucky cookbook written by an African American. Atholene Mary Peyton was a domestic science teacher at Central Colored High School in Louisville, where she had been a student. She also taught cooking at the Neighborhood Home and Training School for Colored Boys and Girls in Louisville, which was supported by the Neighborhood Circle of the King's Daughters. She lived in Louisville until her death in 1951.

Shelby, Agnes Scott. 1908. *Easy and Practical Cooking*. Lexington, KY: Transylvania Press. (Clements). Transylvania Press produced a number of cookbooks before the First World War.

St. James' Parish Church, Ladies' Guild (Pewee Valley). 1900. *Favorite Food of Famous Folk*. Louisville, KY: John P. Morton. (UKSC, Google Books). This fund-raising cookbook consists of recipes submitted by celebrities of the day, including James Lane Allen, Charles Dana Gibson, and Mrs. Potter Palmer, as well as various church people. Pewee Valley, which is in Greater Louisville, was a rural area at the time of the book's publication. The cookbook can be downloaded from Google Books.

St. Peter's Evangelical Church, Ladies (Louisville). 1906. *Old Kentucky Cook Book*. Louisville, KY: C. T. Dearing Printing Co. (LFPL).

1910s

Bardstown Woman's Club. 1913. *Bardstown Cook Book*. Bardstown, KY: Department of Home Economics of the Woman's Club. (Kenton County PL). This is a microfiche published by Lost Cause Press in 1974.

Bridgeport Public Schools. 1916. *Bridgeport Remadi, School, Home and Community: School and Community United*. Bridgeport, KY: Bridgeport Public Schools. (KHS). School staff compiled this little volume from recipes submitted by parents. The recipes provide limited instructions.

Brooksville Methodist Church, Ladies. 1912. *Brooksville Cook Book*. Brooksville, KY: Ladies of the Methodist Church. (Clements).

Colville, Jessie Henderson. 1912. *A Kentucky Woman's Handy Cook Book*. Cincinnati, OH: Printed for the author by Jennings and Graham. (Kenton County PL). This is the publication information on Google Books; Miller (2008) also lists a Caxton Press publication in 1923.

Dunlap, Lina. 1910. *Candlelight Tea: A Book of Recipes.* Lexington, KY: Press of the Transylvania Printing Company. (Internet Archive).

———. 1910. *Heart of the Wheat: A Book of Recipes.* Lexington, KY: Press of the Transylvania Printing Company. (Internet Archive).

———. 1910. *Out of the Blue Grass: A Book of Recipes.* Lexington, KY: Press of Transylvania Printing Company. (Internet Archive). All three Dunlap volumes are short, little more than hardcover pamphlets, but they have an attractive design. They can be downloaded from the Internet Archive.

Hayes, Mrs. W. T. (Emma Allen). 1912. *Kentucky Cook Book: Easy and Simple for Any Cook.* St. Louis, MO: J. H. Tomkins Printing Company. (PC). African American Emma Allen Hayes was born in Kentucky but lived in Kirkwood, Missouri, when she copyrighted this volume. It is cited in Egerton's bibliography of Kentucky cookbooks (1993, 360) and can be downloaded in various formats from the Internet Archive.

Johnson, Mrs. W. A. (Nannie Talbot Johnson). 1912. *Cake, Candy, and Culinary Crinkles: A Companion of* What to Cook and How to Cook It. Louisville, KY: Pentecostal Publishing. (Internet Archive). This is both a cookbook and a guide to the culinary arts. A copy of this specialty volume can be found in the Irma S. Rombauer Papers at Harvard Library (Rombauer took cooking classes from Johnson), and it can be downloaded in various formats from the Internet Archive.

Junior Hospital Circle. *The Junior Hospital Circle Cook Book.* 1913. Louisville, KY: Standard Printing. (LFPL). This book was produced to benefit the Children's Free Hospital of Louisville.

Ladies' Aid Society, Lawrenceburg Baptist Church. 1913. *The Lawrenceburg Baptist Cook Book.* Rev. ed. Louisville, KY: Pentecostal Publishing. (UKSC).

McCulloch-Williams, Martha. 1913. *Dishes and Beverages of the Old South.* Knoxville: University of Tennessee Press. (PC). The author lived in Clarksville, Tennessee, which is close to the Kentucky border. The recipes are accompanied by a rich narrative. The University of Tennessee Press's 1988 edition includes an introductory essay by Kentucky food writer John Egerton. A PDF of the original book is available at the Feeding America website at Michigan State University.

Mendelsohn, Felix. 1912. *A Cook Book: Containing Recipes of Quality.* Newport, KY: G. Wiedemann Brewing Company. (WKU).

Methodist Episcopal Church, South, Maysville, Kentucky. 1911. *The Kentucky Home Cook Book.* Nashville, TN: Publishing House of the M. E. Church, South. (LFPL).

Paducah Chapter, United Daughters of the Confederacy. [1916?]. *Milady's Own Book*. Paducah, KY: United Daughters of the Confederacy. (Miller 2008). This title was used for numerous books in both the North and the South. It appears to be a fund-raiser, with block-formatted recipes and a number of pages of advertising from local merchants.

Presbyterian Church, Somerset, Kentucky, The Ladies Society. 1912. *The Somerset Cook Book*. 2nd ed. Somerset, KY: Times Printing. (UKSC). This is included in Egerton's list of noteworthy Kentucky cookbooks (1993, 361).

Presbyterian Woman's Missionary Society (Smiths Grove). [1910?]. *Southern Kentucky Cook Book*. Smiths Grove, KY: Times Publishing Co. (WKU). Cook (1971) lists two other editions—1913? and 1915.

Smith, Elizabeth W. 1911. *The Model Housekeeper*. Louisville, KY: Pentecostal Publishing. (UKSC).

Sweeney, Mary E., and Linda B. Purnell. 1918. *War Cook Book*. Louisville, KY: Mayes Print. Co. (LFPL). Sweeney was the head of the Home Economics Department at the University of Kentucky and Purnell was an assistant in food and nutrition at the university.

Wehrley, Mattie Lee. 1916. *Handy Household Hints and Recipes*. Louisville, KY: Breckel Press. (LFPL). The recipes are presented in an interesting narrative style.

1920s

Benedict, Jennie C. 1922 [2008]. *The Blue Ribbon Cook Book*. 4th ed. Lexington: University Press of Kentucky. (PC). The first edition of this cookbook, published in 1897, had a different title, as did the 1904 editions. The University Press of Kentucky's 2008 reprint of the fourth edition is augmented by an interesting introduction by Louisville food writer Susan Reigler. The 1938 version of this book is probably the last, but there may be others. The book can be read online and downloaded in various formats from the Internet Archive. Egerton wrote, "The recipes in this collector's dream of a cookbook are a blend of Southern and cosmopolitan, from spoonbread and sugar pie to lamb chops" (1993, 359).

Benge, Martha Berkeley. 1927. *Home Made Candies: For the Family, for Pin Money, for the Home Made Candy Shop*. Manchester, KY: Southern Cook Book Co. (UKSC).

Calvary Episcopal Church, Woman's Auxiliary (Louisville). 1923. *A Book of Favorite Recipes*. Louisville, KY: Woman's Auxiliary of the Calvary Episcopal Church. (LFPL).

Christian Church, Ladies' Aid Society (Irvine). 1926. *Collection of the Best*

Recipes by the Best Cooks in Estill County. Irvine, KY: Christian Church. (UKSC).

Colville, Jessie Henderson. 1923. *A Kentucky Woman's Handy Cookbook.* N.p.: Caxton Press. (UKSC). First published in 1912 by Jennings and Graham.

Ellis, [James] Tandy. 1923. *Camp Cooking.* N.p.: n.p. (UKSC). This thirty-four-page booklet is the first cookbook listed in this bibliography that was written by a man. Ellis's recipe for burgoo is included in Marion Flexner's *Out of Kentucky Kitchens* (1949). Ellis, who was born in Carroll County, wrote short stories and poetry. He died in 1942.

Flexner, Marion W., and Isabel McLennan McMeekin. 1929. *Food for Children and How to Cook It: With an Article on Inducing Them to Eat It.* New York: Henry Holt. (UKSC). This was apparently the first cookbook by Marion W. Flexner, an important Louisville cookbook author. The *Kentucky Encyclopedia* contains a biographical essay about her.

Nazareth Academy (Nazareth, KY) Alumnae. 1923. *Nazareth Alumnae Cook Book.* Louisville, KY: Slater Printing Co. (KDL). Nazareth Academy was a Catholic girls' boarding school in Nelson County. A PDF of this cookbook can be downloaded from the Kentuckiana Digital Library.

Wednesday Sewing Club. 1923. *Cook Book.* Williamsburg, KY: Republican Printing. (UKSC).

Women's Guild of the Christ Church Cathedral, Lexington. 1920. *A Book of Recipes.* Lexington, KY: James M. Byrnes. (UKSC).

———. 1926. *A Book of Recipes.* 2nd improved ed. Lexington, KY: James M. Byrnes. (UKSC). This was the first vintage cookbook in my collection. It has numerous pasted-in and written-in recipes, including recipes for deviled oysters and Woodford pudding. The formatting of the recipes and the measures are quite modern.

Women's Missionary Society of the Jonesville Methodist Episcopalian Church, South. 1928. *Jonesville Cook-Book.* Jonesville, VA: Jonesville Methodist Episcopalian Church, South. (PC). This may be a Virginia cookbook, but Jonesville is very close to Middlesboro, Kentucky, in Bell County. In fact, the merchant ads in the book include some from Middlesboro.

1930s

Booth Memorial Hospital Auxiliary (Covington). [1930s?]. *Booth Hospital Cook Book.* Covington, KY: William Booth Memorial Hospital, Women's Auxiliary. (Kenton County PL).

Breckenridge, Robert J. 1936. *From Soup to Nuts: Old Time Recipes that Have Made Kentucky and Louisiana Foods and Liquids Famous, Dinner Service, Celebrations, Toasts, and Helpful Hints.* Lexington: Kentucky Cardinal Series. (UKSC). This work includes stories about burgoo, mint julep, and other iconic Kentucky preparations from sources such as Tandy Ellis.

Cobb, Irvin S. 1936. *Irvin S. Cobb's Own Recipe Book*. Louisville, KY: Frankfort Distilleries. (PC). This pamphlet was sold by mail for ten cents. It contains an essay on whiskey accompanied by a number of recipes for cocktails. It was also published in 1934 and 1943 and was intended to promote the sale of whiskies produced by Frankfort Distilleries after repeal of the Volstead Act; these included Four Roses, which at the time was a blended whiskey. Cobb was a well-known humorist from Paducah.

National Council of Jewish Women, Louisville Section, Ways and Means Committee. 1935. *Just a Few Selected Recipes*. Louisville, KY: The Committee. (LFPL).

Old Crow Distillery Company. [1930s?]. *Old Crow Collection of Great Bourbon Drink Recipes*. Frankfort, KY: Old Crow Distillery. (Clements).

Order of Eastern Star, Naomi Chapter No. 14. 1931. *Our Cook Book*. St. Matthews, KY: Masonic Home Printing Office. (PC). This sixty-four-page pamphlet contains both signed recipes and many advertisements from Louisville businesses. Apparently, it was distributed free to Masonic families in Louisville.

South Frankfort Presbyterian Church, Circle No. 3. [1935?]. *My Favorite Recipes*. Frankfort, KY: South Frankfort Presbyterian Church. (PC). Although it is undated, an introductory essay about the history of the church indicates that it was published in 1935.

Wednesday Bridge Club. [ca. 1938–1942]. *Recipes from the Blue Grass: Published by the Wednesday Bridge Club for the Benefit of Charity*. Winchester, KY: Wednesday Bridge Club. (Maruskin). Apparently, this book was intended to benefit the Bundles for Britain program, which raised money to help the British deal with the ravages of war prior to America's official involvement.

Wehrley, Mattie Lee. 1930. *Handy Household Hints and Recipes*. Louisville, KY: Western Recorder. (Clements). This includes information on nutrition and fireless cookery as well as recipes, some of which are described as international. The publication was sponsored by the Asher Business Women's Council of Louisville. Virginia Asher, an evangelist, created these groups in various cities to further her spiritual goals.

Whitley Pack Horse Library. 1938. *Mountain Receipts*. Williamsburg, KY: WPA District No. 3, Pack Horse Library. (LFPL). This brief pamphlet is a typescript.

Woman's Club of Louisville. 1938. *Favorite Recipes*. Louisville, KY: Geo. G. Fetter. (UKSC). This includes an early compilation of recipes for entertaining. I consider it a prototype for the Junior League cookbooks of Kentucky.

WPA [Works Progress Administration] Pack Horse Library–McKee-Jackson Co., Kentucky, District No. 3. [1930s?]. McKee, KY: WPA District No. 3. (KDLA).

This handwritten pamphlet contains "Auld Tyme" cooking and canning recipes. It is not dated but is similar to the Whitley Pack Horse Library's *Mountain Receipts*; both were developed as library materials for distribution by the Pack Horse Library program. This New Deal program provided home delivery of reading materials by librarians who traveled on horse and mule to isolated homes in a number of eastern Kentucky counties.

1940s

Allen, Emma Powell. 1941. *Query Club Recipes*. Louisville, KY: John P. Morton. (EKU). This short pamphlet is composed of recipes from upper-income and socially prominent persons. The recipes are a mixture of Louisville standards and the more exotic. Two of the recipes appear in Marion Flexner's classic *Out of Kentucky Kitchens* (1949). The Query Club described itself as a literary club.

Bethel Evangelical and Reformed Church. 1948. *Bethel Cook Book*. 2nd ed. St. Matthew's, KY: n.p. (PC). This slender volume depicts the important contributions made by classic German recipes to Louisville foodways. There are recipes for kuchen, springerles, anise platzchen, hasenpfeffer, German potato salad, sour sweet cabbage, and spaetzle alongside recipes for cornbread, corn pudding, jam cake, and chicken and dumplings.

Bowman Memorial Methodist Church, Women's Society of Christian Service, Hazard, Kentucky. 1942. *Hazard Cookbook*. Hazard, KY: The Society. (UKSC).

Bundles for Britain, Paducah Chapter. [1941?]. *Bundles for Britain Cook Book, Tested Recipes from Kentucky Homes, Including Signed Recipes from Famous People*. Paducah, KY: Paducah Printing. (UKSC). This small comb-bound cookbook was produced and sold for one dollar to support Bundles for Britain, an organization that raised money for British relief early in World War II. There were chapters throughout the country, including in Paducah and Winchester. The book itself was "dedicated to the brave women of Britain." Some of the famous people contributing recipes included Deanna Durbin, Mary Pickford, Rudy Vallee, Edward G. Robinson, Joan Fontaine, Bud Abbott, and Lou Costello. There were also recipes from Paducah and nearby areas.

Christ Church Cathedral, Woman's Endowment Association (Louisville). 1949. *The Heritage Cook Book of the Woman's Endowment Association: Christ Church Cathedral, Louisville, Kentucky, 1822–1949*. Louisville, KY: Christ Church Cathedral, Woman's Endowment Association. (UKSC).

Christian Church, United Christian Missionary Society (Midway). 1944. *Selected Recipes from the Blue Grass*. Midway, KY: Christian Church. (PC). This slender volume is a revision of a cookbook published in 1923.

Flexner, Marion W. 1941. *Dixie Dishes*. Boston: Hale, Cushman and Flint. (EKU).

This is the earliest narrative-type cookbook in the bibliography. Flexner provides biographical details and cultural content for both southern and Creole recipes.

———. 1949. *Out of Kentucky Kitchens*. New York: Bramhall Press. (UKSC). This is a classic Kentucky cookbook. Egerton notes, "In a state noted for its cuisine and its cooks, this little volume holds a place of honor" (1993, 361). It has been reprinted by the University Press of Kentucky.

Jennie C. Benedict Circle of the International Order of King's Daughters and Sons. 1948. *The Jennie's Cook Book*. Shelbyville, KY: Jennie C. Benedict Circle of the International Order of King's Daughters and Sons. (LFPL).

———. 1949. *A Selection of Favorite Recipes Offered by Members and Friends of the Jennie C. Benedict Circle of the International Order of King's Daughters and Sons, Shelbyville, Kentucky*. Shelbyville, KY: The Circle. (WKU). Today, this group continues the charitable work of Jennie Benedict.

Mandeville, Minn-Ell Sherley. 1940. *Random Recipes*. Louisville, KY: John P. Morton. (PC). The author was a prominent Louisville club woman. Her recipe for persimmon pudding can be found on the Internet and appears in various editions of the *Kentucky Heritage Cook Book*. Marion Flexner also included some of Mrs. Mandeville's recipes in her books.

Methodist Church, Martin, Kentucky. 1940. *Our Favorite Recipes Compiled and Published by Elliot Bible Class Methodist Church, Martin, Kentucky*. Martin, KY: Methodist Church. (Maruskin).

Senior Women's Club and Younger Women's Club. 1948. *Favorite Recipes of the Senior Women's Club and the Younger Women's Club*. Central City, KY: The Clubs. (UKSC).

Sutterlin, Violet C. 1949. *What's Cooking in Frankfort: A Book of Traditional Recipes by Frankfortians Past and Present*. Frankfort, KY: Frankfort Chapter, National Society of the Daughters of the American Revolution. (Lee County PL, EKU). Many of the recipes are signed by the contributors. The cookbook is dedicated to Cissy Gregg.

Temple Adath Israel, Junior Sisterhood. 1947. *Selected Recipes*. Louisville, KY: Junior Sisterhood of Temple Adath Israel. (LFPL).

University of Kentucky Women's Club. 1948. *Stay for Tea*. Lexington: University of Kentucky Women's Club. (UKSC). This is the first in a series compiled and published by the University of Kentucky Women's Club. The first three volumes in this series are included in Egerton's list of noteworthy Kentucky cookbooks (1993, 361). The most recent volume, the fourth, was published in 2010 (after Egerton's list was published).

Weidemann Brewing Company. 1940. *The Weidemann Book of Unusual Recipes*. Newport, KY: George Weidemann Brewing Company. (Ebay).

Younger Woman's Club of Barbourville. 1948. *What's Cookin' in Barbourville?*

Barbourville, KY: Younger Woman's Club of Barbourville. (Filson Historical Society). There is also a more recent edition.

1950s

Annville Institute Senior Class. 1953–1954. *Kentucky Favorites: Cook Book*. Annville, KY: Annville Institute. (Berea College). This cookbook includes a number of classic mountain recipes such as soup beans, apple dumplings, baked possum, hominy, and fried dried apple pies. The text attempts to mimic local speech; for example, the recipe for jam cake calls for "agg yellers." The Annville Institute, which included a high school, was first established as a mission of the Reformed Church in America in 1909. Although the institute closed in 1978, a number of religious activities continue in its name. Its records are housed at the Berea College Library.

Bridwell, Margaret M. 1953. *Kentucky Fare: A Recipe Book of Some of Kentucky's Mouth Watering Specialties*. Louisville, KY: Author. (UKSC). This twenty-eight-page pamphlet, published to be sold in gift shops, contains many classic Kentucky recipes, including one of the few published recipes for "Rolled Oysters, Louisville Style." The author was the art librarian at the University of Louisville from 1957 to 1970; the art library there is now named for her. She also worked on historic preservation, especially in the part of the city called Old Louisville.

Buckeye High School Parent Teachers Association. [ca. 1955]. *Tasty Treats*. Lancaster, KY: Buckeye High School Parent Teachers Association. (PC). Though the cookbook itself is undated, it contains an ad placed by the Lancaster Ford Dealer that states, "See the 1955 Ford with 'Thunderbird' Styling." The book seems to be a letterpress production.

Cabbage Patch Circle. 1952. *Famous Kentucky Recipes*. Louisville, KY: Cabbage Patch Circle. (PC). There are at least three versions of this charity cookbook classic: one (the original) with a dark green cover (1952), one with a black cover (probably 1954), and one with a white cover (1956; see below). There is a hardcover version of the 1952 edition, which is the only one that does not have *Cabbage Patch* as the main title. I have seen copies published with imprints as late as 1972. Egerton describes this book as "a highly regarded collection of recipes and menus" (1993, 359). The Cabbage Patch was a low-income neighborhood of Louisville. The Cabbage Patch Circle supported a settlement house there, for which this cookbook was a fund-raiser. Most of the recipes are from members, but there are also some from well-known restaurants and cookbook authors. The settlement house still functions and makes important contributions to social welfare in Louisville.

———. 1956. *Cabbage Patch: Famous Kentucky Recipes*. Louisville, KY: Cabbage

Patch Circle. (LPL, UKSC, PC). Cabbage Patch cookbooks are consistently available on Ebay.

Calvary Baptist Church, Class Seven. [ca. 1950]. *Class Seven Cook Book*. Lexington, KY: Calvary Baptist Church. (PC). This short cookbook includes ads that feature five-digit telephone numbers, which dates it. The book itself is undated.

Carrollton Methodist Church, Young Adult Circle of the WSCS. 1950. *Cooking around the World and at Home*. Carrollton, KY: Carrollton Methodist Church. (Maruskin).

Centerville Methodist Church. 1952. *Centerville's Treasure of Personal Recipes*. Kansas City, MO: Bev-Ron Publishing. (Clark County PL). This Bourbon County church recently celebrated its centenary.

Colonelettes of Louisville, Kentucky. 1955. *The Colonelettes in the Kitchen*. Louisville, KY: Colonelettes. (UKSC). The Colonelettes were the wives of members of the Louisville Junior Chamber of Commerce. They called themselves Colonelettes because their husbands dressed as Kentucky colonels at the group's national convention.

———. 1955. *Kentucky Cooking New and Old: A Collection of Mouth Watering Dishes in the Fine Food Tradition of the South*. Louisville, KY: Colonelettes. (LFPL).

———. 1958. *Kentucky Cooking New and Old: A Collection of Mouth Watering Dishes in the Fine Food Tradition of the South*. 2nd ed. Louisville, KY: Junior Chamber of Commerce. (UKSC). The second edition includes a brief congratulatory foreword by Cissy Gregg and was offered as a sales premium by General Electric.

Fariston Christian Church (Laurel County). 1955. *Cook Book*. Marceline, MO: Walsworth Brothers. (UKSC).

Flexner, Marion W. 1951. *Quick Cooking from the Top of the Stove*. Greenwich, CT: Fawcett Publications. (LFPL).

———. 1955. *Cocktail Supper Cookbook*. New York: Bramhall House. (PC). This book is organized around menus and offers a 1950s Louisville take on gourmet dining.

———. 1958. *Cooking the Smart Way*. New York: M. Barrows. (LFPL).

Gregg, Cissy. 1953. *Cissy Gregg's Cook Book and Guide to Gracious Living*. Vol. 1. Louisville, KY: Louisville Courier-Journal. (LFPL). Cissy Gregg was the food editor for the *Louisville Courier-Journal*. Unfortunately, this cookbook is hard to find, although Gregg's recipes do appear elsewhere, including in a number of community cookbooks. According to Egerton, "The gospel according to Cissy is still invoked around Kentucky—a tribute not only to her chatty and highly readable style but also her expert touch with the food Kentuckians have loved for generations" (1993, 359). In addition to Gregg's two books from the 1950s, Egerton mentions the 1981 reissue and Lillian Marshall's edited cookbook (1971), which includes many of Gregg's recipes.

———. 1959. *Cissy Gregg's Cook Book*. Vol. 2. Louisville, KY: Louisville Courier-Journal. (UKSC). This cookbook was printed on newsprint and distributed with the Sunday paper. It is hard to find.

The Guild Christian Church, Bardwell, Kentucky. 1952. *Cook Book*. Bardwell, KY: Carlisle County Museum and Library. (WKU).

Harrison County Homemakers Club. 1954. *Harrison County Homemakers Club Recipes*. Cynthiana, KY: Harrison County Homemakers Club. (UKSC). This is the earliest of the homemaker club cookbooks in this bibliography.

Hines, Duncan. 1953. *Adventures in Good Cooking (Famous Recipes) and the Art of Carving in the Home*. Bowling Green, KY: Adventures in Good Eating. (UKSC). This cookbook contains only a few Kentucky recipes. It was apparently first published in 1939, intended as an annually revised series; thus, there are a number of earlier editions, as well as some later ones. This is a companion to Hines's more well known restaurant guide *Adventures in Good Eating*. *Duncan Hines Dessert Book* was published in 1955. Both cookbooks were republished in 2002 in volumes edited by Louis Hatchett, Hines's primary biographer.

Hougen, Richard T. 1955. *Look No Further: A Cookbook of Favorite Recipes from Boone Tavern Hotel, Berea College, Kentucky*. Nashville, TN: Abingdon Press. (PC). This is the first of three cookbooks by Richard Hougen, manager of the Boone Tavern at Berea College.

Nelson County Extension Homemaker Association. [1950s?]. *My Old Kentucky Home Recipes*. Lexington, KY: Thoroughbred Press. (UKSC). There is also a 1960 edition.

Old Yellow Creek Baptist Church, Woman's Missionary Union. [1958?]. *Personal Recipes by W.M.U. Old Yellow Creek Baptist Church*. Middlesboro, KY: Old Yellow Creek Baptist Church. (Maruskin).

Order of Demolay, Mother's Circle, Shawnee Chapter. [1950s?]. *Favorite Recipes of Mother's Circle, Shawnee Chapter, Order of Demolay*. Louisville, KY: The Circle. (LPL).

Order of the Eastern Star. Grand Chapter of Kentucky. 1951. *Kentucky Golden Jubilee Cook Book*. Louisville, KY: Gibbs-Inman. (UKSC). The recipes were contributed by members of the order, with each local chapter having at least one recipe. There are advertisements.

Owingsville Woman's Club. 1954. *Cook Book*. Marceline, MO: Walsworth Brothers. (PC). Included is a recipe for the uncommon Cold Brown sandwich—the companion to the ubiquitous Hot Brown. The contributor of the recipe, Mrs.

D. C. Dotson, noted, "This used to be my favorite food at the old Brown Hotel Pastry Shop. It's a full meal by itself." It is basically sliced chicken or turkey on rye with sliced tomato and Russian dressing. Owingsville is the county seat of Bath County, which is considered an Appalachian county.

Paris Christian Church, June Stanley Missionary Circle. [ca. 1958]. *Cookbook Compiled by June Stanley Missionary Circle of Paris Christian Church*. Paris, KY: Paris Christian Church. (Maruskin).

Queen's Daughters (Louisville). 1957. *The Queen's Daughters' Recipes*. Louisville, KY: Queen's Daughters. (LFPL). The Queen's Daughters is a Catholic social service organization.

Sacred Heart Model School. 1954. *The Model School Cook Book: Over 600 Choice Recipes*. Louisville, KY: Sacred Heart Model School. (LFPL).

Scott County Homemakers Association. 1957. *Let's Cook with the Scott County Homemakers*. Georgetown, KY: The Association. (LFPL).

St. Paul Methodist Church, Woman's Society of Christian Service. 1950. *What's Cookin' at St. Paul*. 1st ed. Louisville, KY: Woman's Society of Christian Service, St. Paul Methodist Church. (LFPL).

———. [1950s?]. *The Tower of St. Paul: Cookery*. Louisville, KY: Woman's Society of Christian Service, St. Paul Methodist Church. (LFPL).

Strathmoor Presbyterian Church. 1953. *Out of Strathmoor Kitchens*. Louisville, KY: Women of the Church, Strathmoor Presbyterian Church. (LFPL).

Trinity Methodist Church, Loyal Worker's Class (Latonia). 1950. *Latonia's Favorite Recipes*. Kansas City, MO: Bev-Ron Publishing. (Kenton County PL). This is the earliest cookbook in this bibliography produced by Bev-Ron, which specialized in fund-raising cookbooks. The company is no longer in business.

Williamsburg Woman's Club. [1950s?]. *Favorite Foods of Williamsburg*. Marceline, MO: Walsworth Brothers. (LFPL).

Woman's Civic Club (Mt. Sterling). 1955. *Cook Book*. Mt. Sterling, KY: Woman's Civic Club. (UKSC).

Woman's Society of Christian Service, Methodist Church, Nepton, Kentucky. 1950. *Tasty Treats from Neighborhood Kitchens*. Nepton, KY: The Society. (LFPL).

Woodford Memorial Hospital Auxiliary (Versailles). 1959. *Woodford Recipes: Women's Hospital Auxiliary*. Louisville, KY: Grimes Press. (Kenton County PL).

Young Women's Christian Association (Owensboro). 1954. *The Y.W.C.A. Presents Personal Recipes of Owensboro, Kentucky*. Kansas City, MO: North American Press. (UKSC).

1960s

Barr, Jo Ann, and Georgina Strickland. 1968. *A Kitchen Affair: Loved Recipes*. Lexington, KY: Unitarian Church. (UKSC).

Charity League of Paducah. 1967. *A Collection of Recipes from the Charity League*. Paducah, KY: Charity League. (McCracken County PL). The Charity League functions much like a Junior League, in that it sponsors an array of community projects based on fund-raising efforts such as seasonal dances, cookbook sales, and other activities. Like Junior League cookbooks, this one contains a fair number of recipes for entertaining, as well as cosmopolitan dishes. This is a revision of a cookbook published in 1954, which was printed from handwritten originals. The 1967 version uses typeface.

Christ Church Guild (Bowling Green). 1967. *Christ Episcopal Church Cook Book*. Kansas City, MO: Bev-Ron Publishing. (Miller 2008).

Demos, Stanley. 1961. *The Stanley Demos Cookbook*. Cincinnati, OH: J. C. Krehbiel. (LPL). Stanley Demos was the owner-operator of the Stanley Demos Restaurant in Lexington, which is now closed. This hardbound volume was reprinted a number of times, until at least 1976. It is possible that one printing had a different title.

Dick, Erma Biesel. 1962. *The Old House Cookbook*. Louisville, KY: House of Donahoe. (UKSC). Erma Dick operated the Old House Restaurant at 432 South Fifth in Louisville from 1946 to 1979. The restaurant continued to operate under various owners until 1995.

———. 1969. *The Old House Holiday and Party Cookbook*. New York: Cowles Book Co. (KDLA). This cookbook has a midcentury gourmet orientation and includes recipes for onion soup au gratin, vichyssoise, béarnaise sauce, coq au vin, and sole Veronique, as well as a few German recipes.

Episcopal Church of St. Michael the Archangel. 1963. *Favorite Recipes*. Lexington, KY: Church of St. Michael the Archangel. (UKSC).

Favorite Recipes of Kentucky-Tennessee; Contains 600 Recipes from Women's Club Leaders in Kentucky, Tennessee. 1966. Louisville, KY: Favorite Recipes Press. (LFPL). The Berea College library lists a 900-recipe version published in 1964.

First Church of God (Mt. Sterling). 1968. *Missionary Society Cook Book*. Lexington, KY: Uldean W. Johnston. (Maruskin). This cookbook was printed at least three times. The recipes are signed. The transitions between sections are often marked by drawings and poetry, both signed and unsigned.

First Methodist Church, Emily Mae Sunday School Class, Corbin. 1962. *Corbin Cookery*. Corbin, KY: First Methodist Church. (Boyle County PL).

Flatwoods Woman's Club. 1966. *Cooking Favorites of Flatwoods*. Flatwoods, KY: Flatwoods Woman's Club. (UKSC). Flatwoods is in Greenup County.

Flemingsburg Evening Homemakers Club of Fleming County. 1962. *What's Cooking in Fleming County.* Kansas City, MO: Circulation Service. The collection starts with a number of recipes contributed by celebrities, including Mrs. John F. Kennedy's recipe for Baked Seafood Casserole and a recipe for Bacon and Egg Pie (looks like quiche to me) contributed by the wife of Senator John Sherman Cooper. The recipe for "our favorite corn pudding" contributed by Mrs. Wilson W. Wyatt (wife of Kentucky's lieutenant governor at the time) includes the traditional instructions to cut and then scrape the corn and to stir, taste, and add sugar or milk when partially cooked.

Frankfort Younger Women's Club. 1961. *Favorite Recipes.* Frankfort, KY: The Club. (UKSC).

———. 1967. *Capital Kitchens.* Frankfort, KY: Hulette Printing. (UKSC).

Harbeson, Nan. 1968. *A Book of Favorite Recipes.* Kansas City, MO: Circulation Service. (UKSC). Nan Harbeson compiled these recipes with the help of members and friends of the Washington Presbyterian Church.

Hayes, Irene. 1965. *What's Cooking in Kentucky.* Hueysville, KY: T. I. Hayes Publishing. What started as a church fund-raiser turned into a Kentucky classic that is still in print. It is based on contributed recipes. There have been a number of other editions, including 1970, 1979, 1982, 1984, and 1994, with different publishers. Egerton notes, "From its roots in eastern Kentucky, this book has grown through reprints and revisions into an all-Kentucky favorite" (1993, 361).

High Street Christian Church, Women's Council, Esther Circle. 1963. *Favorite Recipes from the Bluegrass.* Lexington, KY: High Street Christian Church. (PC). The recipes are signed and are supplemented with household hints and guidance for cooking for large groups of people; many pages are embellished with inspirational or humorous sayings. There are a few recipes from restaurants, including Beaumont Inn and Boone Tavern. The recipe for Three Bean Salad is presented as "Garry Moore's favorite" (Moore was a famous TV personality at the time).

Hougen, Richard T. 1960. *Cooking with Hougen.* Nashville, TN: Abingdon Press. (Miller 2008). This is the second of three cookbooks by Hougen, manager of the Boone Tavern at Berea College.

Kappa Kappa Gamma, Lexington Alumnae Association. 1962. *Key to Kentucky Kitchens.* Lexington, KY: The Association. (UKSC, PC). The contributed recipes are signed and are presented in the typical contemporary format. The cookbook is enhanced by well-executed pen and ink drawings of selected contributors' kitchens. There are a few recipes from Hougen's *Look No Further* cookbook (1955).

Louisville Times. 1962. *Time-Tested, Tried and Tasted Recipes, Compiled from the* Louisville Times. Louisville, KY: Louisville Times. (UKSC).

Menifee Extension Homemakers. 1968. *Family Favorite Recipes*. Vol. 2. Leawood, KS: Circulation Service. (Menifee County PL).

National Society of the Colonial Dames of America in the Commonwealth of Kentucky. 1963. *The Liberty Hall Cook Book: Receipts and Recipes*. Frankfort, KY: National Society of the Colonial Dames of America in the Commonwealth of Kentucky. (UKSC). Liberty Hall is a historic home in Frankfort. Its library includes manuscript cookbooks from the nineteenth century.

Nelson County Homemakers Clubs. 1960. *My Old Kentucky Home Recipes*. Lexington, KY: Thoroughbred Press. (PC). The signed recipes are organized in sections marked by verses and lyrics from selected Stephen Foster songs.

Order of the Eastern Star, Chapter No. 289 (Hickman). 1960. *Robert E. Lee and Natchez on the Mississippi, Hickman, Kentucky*. Hickman, KY: Order of the Eastern Star. This slender volume includes a brief history of Hickman, the county seat of Fulton County in far western Kentucky. The title is simply the caption that appears on the cover along with a reproduction of two riverboats. The recipes, which are signed, include one for Kentucky Barbecue Sauce for basting that fits the western Kentucky pattern of vinegar-based dips with almost no sugar in them.

Queen's Daughters (Louisville). 1960. *The Queen's Daughters' Recipes*. Louisville, KY: Queen's Daughters. (UKSC). The Queen's Daughters is a charity and social service organization of Catholic women. There are similarly named groups around the country.

———. 1969. *Entertaining the Louisville Way*. Louisville, KY: Queen's Daughters. (UKSC). The suggested menus include ones for Derby Breakfast, Easter Brunch, and Sunday Nite Supper, as well as many others.

Russellville–Logan County Chamber of Commerce. 1969. *The Logan County Cook Book*. Kansas City, KS: Cookbook Publishers. This book includes drawings of Logan County sights.

Schweder, Eve M. 1968. *The Best from the Blue Grass: Diamond Jubilee Cookbook*. Louisville, KY: Gibbs-Inman. (EKU). The book was reprinted in 1974 and 1981.

Southern Hills Methodist Church (Lexington) Senior High Methodist Youth Fellowship. [1960s?]. *Good Cooking*. Kansas City, MO: North American Press. (UKSC).

St. Luke's Episcopal Church (Anchorage). 1965. *Anchorage Fare*. Anchorage, KY: St. Luke's Episcopal Church. (UKSC). This cookbook, from a prosperous Louisville suburb, is based on a reproduction of handwritten recipes.

St. Paul's Episcopal Church. 1961. *Open House for Gourmets*. Louisville, KY: St. Paul's Episcopal Church. (LFPL).

Treasure of Personal Recipes: Pineville, Kentucky. 1963. Kansas City, MO: Bev-Ron Publishing. (Harlan County PL).

Trinity Episcopal Church. 1962. *What's Cooking in Danville*. Kansas City, MO: North American Press. (UKSC).

———. 1969. *What's Cookin' in Danville*. Danville, KY: Trinity Episcopal Church. (Montgomery County PL).

Willett Distilling Company (Bardstown). 1967. *Old Bardstown Bourbon Recipes*. Bardstown, KY: Willett Distilling Company. (KHS). This is a pamphlet.

Woman's Club of Louisville. 1968. *Favorite Fare*. Louisville, KY: The Club. (UKSC).

Woodford County Hospital Auxiliary (Versailles). 1967. *Woodford Recipes*. Versailles, KY: Woodford County Hospital Auxiliary. (UKSC). Maruskin has a 1961 edition.

Younger Woman's Club of Barbourville. 1964. *What's Cooking in Barbourville*. Barbourville, KY: Younger Woman's Club of Barbourville. (UKSC).

Younger Woman's Club of Louisville. 1966. *Party Cook Book*. Louisville, KY: Younger Woman's Club of Louisville. (UKSC). The foreword refers to an earlier version, probably published in 1958, and states, "We are convinced that parties thrive on a well prepared hostess and good but not necessarily elaborate food served with a minimum of fuss." This book has a comprehensive selection of recipes, including the most complicated (though charming) recipe for roasting a turkey I have ever seen. It states: "This turkey is work. It demands more attention than the average six-month-old baby" (88).

1970s

Alpha Chi Omega, Louisville Alumnae Club. [1970s?]. *Belles of Louisville*. Louisville, KY: The Club. (LFPL).

Arena, Susan P., ed. 1974. Kentucky Living *Cookbook: Bicentennial Edition*. Shelbyville, KY: Landmark Community Newspapers. (Shelby County PL).

Athens Christian Church, Dorcas Circle. 1976. *What's Cooking at Athens: 1776 Bicentennial Edition 1976*. Iowa Falls, IA: General Publishing and Binding. (PC).

Barnard, Robin, Barbara Hale, Roxanna Jones, Peggy Lewis, and Judy Sackett. 1979. *A Kentucky Sampler: Recipes from the University of Kentucky Library Staff*. Lexington, KY: n.p. (UKSC).

Barnes, Bertha. 1973. *Rebecca Boone Cook Book*. Harlan, KY: Durham Printing. (WKU). The Internet lists a paperback version published in 1980.

———. 1974. *Antique Cook Book: All Recipes over 100 Years Old*. Harlan, KY: Durham Printing. Barnes lived in Winchester when this forty-eight-page pamphlet was published. The recipes are presented in block format and are accompanied by some historical discussion.

———. 1976. *Pioneer Desserts*. Richmond, KY: Author. (Alice Lloyd College).

Beattyville Woman's Club. 1976. *A Book of Favorite Recipes*. Beattyville, KY: Woman's Club. (Lee County PL, UKSC).

Beechwood PTA (Fort Mitchell). 1976. *Fort Mitchell's Finest Recipes*. Fort Mitchell, KY: Beechwood PTA. (Kenton County PL).

Beechwood School (Fort Mitchell). [1979?]. *Beechwood Cooks*. Fort Mitchell, KY: Beechwood School. (Kenton County PL).

Bell County Homemakers. 1977. *Mountain Laurel*. Pineville, KY: Bell County Homemakers. (UKSC).

Beta Sigma Phi. 1979. *Fun in the Kitchen*. Lawrenceburg, KY: Lawrenceburg Printing Co. (UKSC).

Boyle County Extension Homemaker's Association. 1971. *The Best of Recipes from Boyle County Homemakers*. Boyle County, KY: Boyle County Extension Homemaker's Association. (UKSC).

Burgin Get-Together Homemakers. 1971. *Burgin Get-Together Homemakers Presents a Collection of Mercer County's Favorite Recipes*. Kansas City, KS: Bev-Ron Publishing. (UKSC).

Caldwell County Homemakers Organization. 1971. *Favorite Recipes from Caldwell County*. Princeton, KY: Caldwell County Times. (UKSC).

Casey, W. B., and Lucy M. Casey. 1979. *Sermons and Servings*. Lenexa, KS: Cookbook Publishers (PC). This unusual volume is a combination of sermons and recipes by a Baptist minister and his wife. They retired from Boone Creek Baptist Church in Lexington in 1979.

Charity League of Paducah, Kentucky. 1978. *Seasons of Thyme*. Paducah, KY: Charity League. (UKSC).

Cooper, Dorothea C., ed. 1976. *Kentucky Hospitality: A 200-Year Tradition*. Louisville: Kentucky Federation of Women's Clubs. (PC, UKSC). This bicentennial cookbook includes a number of very good essays on Kentucky foodways as well as many noteworthy recipes. Egerton observes, "Few food books are as well conceived as this one—or as well executed" (1993, 360). There is also a follow-up cookbook, published in 2002, with a similar title.

Corbin Woman's Club. 1976. *Historical Cook Book, 1976*. Corbin, KY: Corbin Woman's Club. (LPL). Corbin is the largest town in Whitley County.

Crescent Hill Woman's Club (Louisville). 1971. *Derbytown Winners Cookbook*. Louisville, KY: Crescent Hill Woman's Club. (UKSC).

Daviess County Extension Homemakers. 1975. *Golden Anniversary Cookbook, 1925–1975: Favorite Recipes*. Owensboro, KY: Daviess County Extension Homemakers. (PC). The cookbook is dedicated to Ida Jo Burg, who was the county extension agent for home economics. At that time, there were fifty-three homemaker clubs in Daviess County. In the recipe for tacos entitled "The Wright Family's Mexican Food," the contributor, Linda Wright Barnes, reflects on the tortilla supply situation in the mid-1970s: "Tortillas which come in a can are what we prefer to use, but they are difficult to find at the grocery lately" (78). Old El Paso brand canned tortillas were discontinued in the 1990s. None of the recipes expresses the Owensboro barbecue tradition, although there is a recipe for barbecue beef that seems to be in the sloppy joe genre.

Durham, Glenn. 1978. *Kentucky State Parks Cookbook: Recipes from Kentucky State Parks and Other Sources*. Harlan, KY: Glenn Durham in cooperation with Kentucky Department of Parks. (UKSC).

Elsmere Volunteer Fire Department Ladies Auxiliary. 1976. *The Bicentennial Story of Elsmere, Kentucky, 1776–1976*. Elsmere, KY: National Consumers Research. (Kenton County PL).

Epworth United Methodist Church, Irene Dorsey Circle. 1972. *Epworth United Methodist Church Cookbook*. Iowa Falls, IA: General Publishing and Binding. (UKSC).

Estill County Homemakers. 1977. *Family Menu Favorites from the Estill County Homemakers*. Irvine, KY: Estill County Citizen Voice and Times. The recipes are signed, and the club affiliation is indicated. Reflecting the times, there are two recipes for Water Gate Cake, both of which make use of Duncan Hines white cake mix, pistachio pudding, and club soda.

The Farmington Cookbook: A Cookbook in Two Parts. 3rd ed. 1971. Louisville, KY: Farmington House. (PC, UKSC). Farmington House is a historic home in Louisville. The first version of this cookbook was published in 1968; subsequent editions appeared in 1969, 1971, 1973, and 1979 (there may be others). The cookbook contains much information about cooking technique.

The Farmington Cookbook: A Cookbook in Two Parts. 5th ed. 1979. Louisville, KY: Farmington House. (LPL). This edition claimed to be the Official Hostess and Entertainment Guide of the Kentucky Derby.

Fayette County Homemakers Association. 1974. *Homemakers in the Kitchen*. Lexington, KY: Fayette County Homemakers Association. (UKSC, Maruskin).

Fayette County Public Schools. 1974. *What's Cooking in Fayette County Schools*. Lexington, KY: Fayette County Public Schools. (UKSC).

First Baptist Church (Fisherville). 1977. *Sesquicentennial: Floydsfork Baptist, 1827: First Baptist of Fisherville, 1977*. Fisherville, KY: First Baptist Church. (LFPL).

First Baptist Church (Leitchfield). 1974. *New Cookbook of Fine Old Recipes: Every Recipe Perfected in Our Church Family*. Iowa Falls, IA: General Publishing and Binding. (UKSC).

Fourth Avenue Methodist Church (Louisville). [1970s?]. *Favorite Food from Fourth Avenue Women.* Louisville, KY: Fourth Avenue Methodist Church. (LFPL).

Frankfort Younger Woman's Club. 1974. *Capital Kitchens.* 2nd ed. Frankfort, KY: Kentucky Investors. (Kenton County PL).

Gainesway Homemakers. 1972. *Gainesway Goodies.* Lexington, KY: Gainesway Homemakers. (PC). The recipes are signed and accompanied by drawings. The book was produced "in-house." It includes a recipe for "Kentucky Derby Pie," which resembles the copyright-protected Derby Pie.

George Rogers Clark High School, Academic Boosters. 1977. *Clark County Cooks.* Pleasanton, KS: Fundcraft Publishing. (UKSC).

George Rogers Clark High School, Band Boosters. 1978. *The GRC Company Front Cookbook.* Winchester, KY: George Rogers Clark High School, Band Boosters. (Maruskin).

Grayson County News-Gazette. 1978. *Country Kitchen Cookbook.* Leitchfield, KY: News-Gazette. (UKSC).

Harlan Woman's Club. 1978. *A Book of Favorite Recipes.* Shawnee Mission, KS: Circulation Service. (UKSC).

Hayes, Irene. 1970. *What's Cooking in Kentucky.* Hueysville, KY: Hayes Publishing. (LPL, PC).

Historic Homes Foundation (Louisville). 1976. *Kentucky Heritage Recipes.* Louisville, KY: Historic Homes Foundation. (UKSC). This publication was created to benefit two historic homes: Farmington and Locust Grove. It is a small but valuable collection of traditional Kentucky recipes, some of which were selected from earlier cookbooks, including those of Jennie Benedict, Marion Flexner, and Cissy Gregg. This is the earliest edition, but there were others in 1977, 1978, 1980, and 1988.

Hodgenville Woman's Club. 1976. *Larue County Kitchens: A Larue County Bicentennial Cookbook.* Elizabethtown, KY: Hub City Printing. (UKSC, PC). This massive collection was still in print in 2010.

Hopkins County, Kentucky, PTA. 1973. *A Book of Favorite Recipes: Hopkins County Kentucky PTA Cookbook.* Madisonville, KY: Hopkins County, Kentucky, PTA. (WKU).

Hougen, Richard T. 1971. *More Hougen Favorites.* Nashville, TN: Abingdon Press. This is the third cookbook from the manager of the Boone Tavern.

Hunting Creek Garden Club. 1976. *Hunting Creek Garden Club Cook Book.* Prospect, KY: Hunting Creek Garden Club. (LFPL).

Hustonville Christian Church, Women's Fellowship. 1976. *Favorite Hometown Recipes.* Hustonville, KY: Christian Church. (Maruskin).

Jefferson County Medical Society, Women's Auxiliary. 1979. *Prescriptions for*

Cooks. Louisville, KY: Jefferson County Medical Society. (WKU). This is a reprint, with some additions, of a cookbook originally published in 1962. It was intended to raise funds to renovate the old buildings of the University of Louisville Medical School.

Junior League of Louisville. 1978. *The Cooking Book*. Louisville, KY: Junior League of Louisville. (WKU). This is the first cookbook published by a Kentucky Junior League. It was designated the "Official Kentucky Derby Festival Cookbook." Egerton notes that this volume "blends old recipes and a little history with modern design and contemporary dishes" (1993, 359). It makes extensive use of photographs from the University of Louisville's archives and was reprinted into the 1980s. Since 1978, the Junior League of Louisville has published a number of other cookbooks. Interestingly, there is a website devoted to Junior League cookbooks (http://cookingwiththejuniorleague.wordpress.com).

Kelley, Kathleen. 1976. *Historic Camp Nelson Cookbook*. Lancaster, KY: Kentucky Valley Press. (Pulaski County PL). This collection includes recipes from Marilyn Stefanski.

Kentucky Association of Rural Electric Cooperatives. 1973. *25th Anniversary Cook Book: 250 Best Recipes from the First 25 Years of* Rural Kentuckian *Magazine*. Louisville, KY: Kentucky Association of Rural Electric Cooperatives. (KDLA). The title of *Rural Kentuckian* was later changed to *Kentucky Living*.

Kentucky DAR Cookbook: A Selection of Recipes Chosen from Favorites of the Members of the Kentucky Chapters of the Daughters of the American Revolution. 1970. Lexington, KY: Daughters of the American Revolution. (UKSC, Madison County PL). Second and third editions were published in 1972 and 1975. The sale of the book benefited the DAR's Duncan Tavern site. This volume is included in Egerton's list of Kentucky cookbooks (1993, 360).

Kentucky Pork Producers & Porkettes. [1978?]. *Kentucky Style Pork Cooking*. Shelbyville, KY: Kentucky Pork Producers & Porkettes. (Marion County PL).

Kremer, Elizabeth C. 1970. *We Make You Kindly Welcome*. Harrodsburg, KY: Pleasant Hill Press. (UKSC). This is included in Egerton's list of noteworthy Kentucky cookbooks (1993, 361). Kremer was the executive in charge of the restaurant at the Shaker Village at Pleasant Hill for a number of years. At the time, Shaker Village was derelict and in need of much work. Creating a regional dining destination was an important aspect of the program of restoration and preservation.

——— . 1977. *Welcome Back to Pleasant Hill*. Harrodsburg, KY: Pleasant Hill Press. (UKSC). This is the second and last cookbook written by Kremer.

Lancaster Women's Club. 1973. *A Treasure of Personal Recipes*. Kansas City, KS: Bev-Ron Publishing. (UKSC).

Layton, Pat. 1971. *Kentucky's Capital City Cookbook*. Frankfort, KY: Roberts Printing Company. (UKSC). Egerton lists a 1982 version in his list of Kentucky cookbooks (1993, 360).

Lewisport Woman's Club. 1978. *Lewisport Woman's Club Presents the Court House Cookbook*. Iowa Falls, IA: General Publishing and Binding. (Ebay). The recipes from club members are signed. The cover features a drawing of the Hancock County courthouse.

Lexington School. 1979. *Scrumptious Soups and Salads: A Collection of Favorite Recipes from the Lexington School*. Lexington, KY: Lexington School. (UKSC). This cookbook was part of a series that was presumably annual. It included *Just Desserts* (1975), *With Spirits* (1976), *Casseroles, of Course* (1977), *Supersaladishes* (1978), *Scrumptious Soups and Salads* (1979), *Hey Mom, What's for Supper?* (1980), and *Let's Entertain* (1981). I own a copy of the 1981 volume. They are punched for insertion in a ring binder and were marketed as the Christmas Corner Collection.

Lexington 3rd Ward Relief Society. 1973. *What's Cookin' in Lexington, Kentucky*. Kansas City, KS: Bev-Ron Publishing. (Russell County PL).

Licking Valley Senior Citizens. 1978. *Oldies but Goodies from SNAP*. Lenexa, KS: Cookbook Publishers. (PC). SNAP is a nutritional program for persons older than sixty years in Bracken, Fleming, Lewis, Mason, and Robertson Counties.

Long, Marlys, Grace Schmit, and Janet Taylor. 1978. *Home on the Run*. Louisville, KY: Edward D. Donahoe Publishing. (UKSC).

Louisville Bar Association Auxiliary. 1977. *You Be the Judge*. Kansas City, KS: Cookbook Publishers. (UKSC).

Marshall, Lillian, ed. 1971. *The* Courier Journal *&* Times *Cookbook; Including 91 Favorite Cissy Gregg Recipes and 61 Photographs in Full Color*. Louisville, KY: Pegasus. (UKSC). Lillian Marshall drew on the recipe files of the *Louisville Courier-Journal*, where she was food editor.

McBrayer, Emma Lee, and Ann McBrayer Garrison. 1978. *A Taste of Mama's Cooking: Special Recipes of Emma Lee McBrayer*. Lawrenceburg, KY: A. M. Garrison. (UKSC).

Meadow Heights Woman's Club. 1973. *Daisy Delights: A Delightful Collection of Favorite Recipes*. Louisville, KY: Meadow Heights Woman's Club. (LFPL).

Midway-Pinkerton International Alumnae Association (Midway). 1977. *Our Favorite Recipes*. Pleasanton, KS: Fundcraft Publishing. (UKSC).

Millersburg United Methodist Church. 1977. *Our Favorite Recipes*. Collierville, TN: Fundcraft Publishing. (UKSC).

Mills, Frances Jones. [1979?]. *Festive Cooking with Frances Jones Mills*. Fulton, KY: Citizens for Frances Jones Mills. (WKU, Kenton County PL). France

Jones Mills held various public offices in Kentucky, including three terms as state treasurer. This cookbook was produced as part of her election efforts.

Monroe County Homemakers. 1979. *Monroe County Homemakers Favorite Recipes*. Tompkinsville, KY: Monroe County Homemakers. (Abdmishani). The cookbook includes a section of county extension agents' favorite recipes, as well as recipes from the homemaker clubs. One recipe for barbecue sauce fits the Monroe County style. Its basic ingredients are vinegar, pepper, cayenne, butter, and lard. Because of the fat, the sauce needs to be heated before use. The cookbook also includes a short essay on the history of the clubs.

Montgomery County Homemakers. 1976. *Montgomery County Homemakers Cookbook*. Lenexa, KS: Cookbook Publishers. (Montgomery County PL).

Moore, Matilda B. 1972. *Out of the Kitchen into the House: Receipts of Elizabeth Kinkead Battaile*. Rev. 2nd ed. Lexington, KY, and St. Paul, VA: Clinch Valley Publishing. (EKU, PC). "Bets" Battaile, as she was known, worked as a cook at various Lexington locations, including the Green Tree Shop, described as "a fashionable tearoom located on East Main street, in a little court, between Walnut and the Esplanade." The cookbook, which includes many Green Tree Shop recipes, was compiled by Battaile's granddaughter and was intended as a remembrance for her family. The collection includes one recipe from Nannie Talbot Johnson, from whom Battaile took cooking lessons.

Muhlenberg County 4-H Council. 1977. *A Helping of 4-H Hospitality*. Collierville, TN: Fundcraft Publishing. (Muhlenberg County PL).

Nelson County Extension Homemakers. 1979. *Favorite Recipes*. Bardstown, KY: Nelson County Extension Homemakers. (Ebay).

Northern Kentucky University. 1978. *Favorite Recipes of Faculty/Staff and Students at Northern Kentucky University*. Collierville, TN: Fundcraft Publishing. (Kenton County PL).

Ole Time Cookbook: Recipes of Yesterday for Today's Menu. 1975. Harlan, KY: Durham Printing and Offset Co. (UKSC). This is a facsimile reprint of *The Harlan Cook Book*, published in 1935 (the header reads "HARLAN COOK BOOK"). The recipes are signed and are presented in the "standard" format. Most of the contributors are from "Harlan and surrounding towns." The recipe instructions reflect a transitional period in the use of kitchen appliances. Cooking instructions vary from nominal oven temperatures to actual degrees. A recipe called "Frozen Salad" instructs the cook to put the mixture of mayonnaise, cream cheese, and whipped cream "in a tray and let freeze 3 hours in an electric refrigerator" (35).

O'Neal, Mary, and Paula Mueller. 1973. *From Park's Kitchen Kupboard*. Lexington, KY: Park Methodist Church. (UKSC).

Payne, Ruth. 1976. *The Kentucky Bicentennial Cookbook: Famous Historical Ken-*

tucky Recipes, 1776–1976. Harrodsburg, KY: Roberts Printing. (UKSC). This comprehensive volume was produced in conjunction with the Mercer County Humane Society.

Pikeville Woman's Club. 1973. *Our Heritage Cookbook*. Kansas City, KS: Bev-Ron Publishing. (KDLA). Apparently, the first version of this cookbook was published in 1960.

Pleasant Grove United Methodist Church, United Methodist Women (Philpot). 1978. *Cherished Recipes: A Collection of Recipes*. Collierville, TN: Fundcraft Publishing. (UKSC).

Port Royal Homemakers. 1977. *Port Royal Homemakers Cookbook*. Port Royal, KY: Port Royal Homemakers. (Henry County PL).

Ravenna Christian Church. 1979. *Christian Women's Fellowship Cookbook*. 3rd ed. Ravenna, KY: Ravenna Christian Church. (Estill County PL).

Sawchak, Cathy. [1970s?]. *Appalachian Sampler*. David, KY: St. Vincent's Mission, Home Economics Program. (UKSC).

Scott County Senior Citizens (Georgetown). 1976. *Cookbook*. Georgetown, KY: Georgetown News and Georgetown Times. (UKSC).

Second Baptist Church, Baptist Young Women (Greenville). 1979. *A Book of Favorite Recipes*. Kansas City, MO: Circulation Service. (Muhlenberg County PL).

Settle, Cherry, Tommy Settle, and Edward G. Klemm Jr. 1979. *The Claudia Sanders Dinner House of Shelbyville, Kentucky Cookbook*. Los Angeles, CA: Crescent. (LPL).

St. Elizabeth Hospital, Women's Guild. 1974. *Kentucky Heritage '74*. Covington, KY: St. Elizabeth Hospital, Women's Guild. (PC). St. Elizabeth Hospital was established in Covington in 1861 and is now active throughout northern Kentucky.

St. James United Methodist Church (Bowling Green). 1977. *Sharing Our Best: St. James United Methodist Church, Bowling Green, Kentucky*. Pleasanton, KS: Fundcraft Publishing. (WKU).

St. Matthew's Episcopal Church (Louisville). 1979. *Favorite Recipes*. Louisville, KY: St. Matthew's Episcopal Church. (LFPL).

Stone, Michelle. 1973. *Merry Christmas from Kentucky*. Kuttawa, KY: McClanahan Publishing House. (Kenton County PL).

Sulpher Well Homemakers. 1977. *Homemaker's Delight*. Kansas City, MO: Circulation Service. (Metcalfe County PL).

Tates Creek Pentecostal Church Auxiliary (Richmond). 1978. *A Collection of Recipes*. Collierville, TN: FundCraft Publishing. (UKSC).

Trigg County Homemakers Association. 1978. *Favorite Recipes*. Cadiz, KY: Broadbent B&B Food Products. (UKSC).

United Methodist Temple, Russellville, Kentucky. 1975. *Taste and Tell Cook Book*. Kansas City, KS: Cookbook Publishers. (WKU).

University of Kentucky, Cooperative Extension Service. [ca. 1979]. *Knox County, 4th Annual Extension-Homemaker Cookbook*. Lexington: University of Kentucky, Cooperative Extension Service. In contrast to other homemaker association cookbooks, this one seems to have been printed by the university. The recipes, which are signed, include one for a dump cake companion called pig pickin' cake tired mama pie.

University of Kentucky Women's Club. 1975. *Stay for Tea . . . Again*. Lexington: University of Kentucky Women's Club. (UKSC). This is one of an irregular series that started in 1948; the most recent volume was published in 2010. The 1975 cookbook includes the recipe for Maxwell Place Spiced Tea from Frances Jewell McVey, whose death was observed in the 1948 edition of *Stay for Tea*. Her husband, Frank McVey, was president of the university. There are a number of recipes from Emily Lihani, who was important in developing the University of Kentucky Library's cookbook collection.

Versailles Baptist Church. 1976. *Versailles Baptist Church Cookbook*. Waterloo, IA: G&R Publishing Company. (PC). This project was undertaken by the Youth Council to finance a mission trip. Versailles is in Woodford County, in the heart of the Bluegrass. The book includes two dump cake recipes but none for Woodford pudding.

Wayne County High School, Junior Class. 1972. *Rootin' Tootin' Recipes*. Monticello, KY: Wayne County High School. (Private collection of Rona Roberts). The cookbook contains a recipe for Molasses Crinkles contributed by Mrs. Lisle Roberts. This cookie recipe and some of its history are featured in *Sweet, Sweet Sorghum: Kentucky's Golden Wonder* by Lisle's daughter Rona. Rona Roberts also produces the noteworthy food blog *Savoring Kentucky*.

Winchester Mrs. Jaycees. 1975. *Mrs. Jaycees Spice Centennial Cook Book*. Winchester, KY: Winchester Mrs. Jaycees. (Clark County PL). This bicentennial cookbook includes a recipe from President and Mrs. Gerald Ford.

Woman's Club of Marion. 1976. *Historic Cookbook—1776–1976*. Marion, KY: Marion Woman's Club. (Crittenden County PL).

Women's Guild of the St. Elizabeth Medical Center. 1977. *A Day of Wine and Roses, 1977*. Covington, KY: Women's Guild of the St. Elizabeth Medical Center. (UKSC).

Woodford County Fire Department, Ladies Auxiliary (Versailles). 1976. *Historic Cookbook*. Versailles, KY: Woodford County Fire Department. (UKSC).

Woodland Christian Church (Lexington). 1977. *Treasured Recipes of Woodland Christian Church (Disciples of Christ)*. Lexington, KY: The Church. (UKSC).

Young, Mary Catherine Kirtley. 1975. *The Cherokee Triangle Olde Time Cook-*

book. Louisville, KY: Cherokee Triangle Association. (University of Alabama). The book has illustrations and includes a poem by Mary Young Martin. Cherokee Triangle is a historic preservation district.

Younger Woman's Club of Berea. 1978. *Berea's Best*. Lexington, KY: Grable Printing. (Kenton County PL). The Younger Woman's Club of Berea produced other versions with the same title in 1965 and 1985.

1980s

Allender, Mary. 1989. *The Hamilton Cooks of Kentucky*. Columbus, KY: Creations by Mary Allender. (LPL).

Allender, Mary, and Maxine Walker, eds. 1982. *Southern Kentucky Cook Book: A Selection of Recipes Chosen from Favorites of Those Interested in the Preservation of the Trabue-Russell House*. Columbia, KY: Adair County Heritage Association (South Central Printing). (Harlan County PL).

American Cancer Society, Kentucky Division. 1980. *Kentucky County Fare*. Memphis, TN: Wimmer Brothers Fine Printing and Lithography. (UKSC).

———. 1982. *Partytime in Kentucky*. Memphis, TN: Wimmer. (WKU). This includes a foreword by Anita Madden, a famous Lexington horsewoman and party giver.

———. 1987. *Capital Eating in Kentucky*. Louisville, KY: American Cancer Society, Kentucky Division. (UKSC).

Anderson, Janet Alm. 1986. *A Taste of Kentucky*. Lexington: University Press of Kentucky. (UKSC). This volume contains snippets of Kentucky folklore in addition to a few recipes.

AORN Bluegrass Chapter of Central Kentucky. 1983. *Just a Sampling: A Collection of Favorite Recipes Compiled from the Members of A.O.R.N. Bluegrass Chapter of Central Kentucky*. Lenexa, KS: Cookbook Publishers. (UKSC). AORN is a professional association of operating room nurses.

Arlington Christian Church (Lexington). 1989. *Recipes Compiled by Chi Rho & CYF Arlington Christian Church*. Waseca, MN: Walter's Cookbooks.

Barren County Homemakers. 1980. *From the Kitchens of Barren County Homemakers*. Glasgow, KY: Barren County Progress. (KDLA, PC). This compilation includes signed recipes contributed by members of the twenty-six homemaker clubs of Barren County.

Bath County Homemakers. 1982. *Nature's Bounty*. Owingsville, KY: Bath County Homemakers. (Clark County PL).

Behringer-Crawford Museum. [1980s?]. *Behringer-Crawford Museum Cook Book*. Covington, KY: Behringer-Crawford Museum. (Kenton County PL).

Bell County Extension Homemakers. 1984. *Mountain Laurel Encore: A Collec-*

tion of Recipes. Pineville, KY: Bell County Extension Homemakers. (UKSC, Clark County PL). There was an earlier edition.

Bell County Women's Club. 1980. *Home Town Recipes of Bell County Senior Citizens*. Middlesboro, KY: Women's Club. (Harlan County PL).

Bethel Presbyterian Church Women's Group. 1989. *Bethel's Bicentennial Cooking*. Waseca, MN: Walter's Cookbooks. (UKSC).

Bethlehem Christian Church, Christian Women's Fellowship. 1984. *Give Us Our Daily Bread*. Pleasanton, KS: Fundcraft Publishing. (Bath County PL).

Blue Grass Trust for Historic Preservation. 1989. *Carriage House Cooks at the Bluegrass Trust*. Lexington, KY: Blue Grass Trust. (Miller 2008).

Boone Manor Nursing Home. 1981. *Boone Manor Nursing Home Cookbook: Featuring Time Tested, Ageless, New and Treasured Knox County, Ky. Recipes*. Shawnee Mission, KS: Circulation Service. (Harlan County PL).

Booth Memorial Hospital Auxiliary (Covington). 1988. *Booth Memorial Hospital Auxiliary 50th Anniversary Cookbook, 1938–1988*. Florence, KY: Booth Memorial Hospital Auxiliary. (UKSC).

Bourbon County Extension Homemakers. 1985. *Bourbon County Homemakers: 50 Years of Cooking*. Paris, KY: Bourbon County Extension Homemakers. (Miller 2008).

Calloway County Homemakers. 1981. *In Good Taste: 5th Annual Cookbook*. Murray, KY: Calloway County Homemakers. (PC). This mimeographed publication includes signed recipes representing the many homemaker clubs of Calloway County. There is a recipe for homemade hominy as well as a short section on microwave recipes.

Carroll County Public Library. 1987. *Once upon a Time: A Collection of Carroll County Recipes*. Carrollton, KY: Carroll County Public Library.

Cedar Creek Community School. 1986. *The Monterey Cookbook: Recipes from Monterey, Kentucky*. Owenton, KY: Cedar Creek Community School. (UKSC).

Chittenden, Russ. 1989. *Uncle Russ Chittenden's Good Ole Boys Wild Game Cookbook: Or How to Cook 'Possum and Other Varmints Good*. Paducah, KY: Image Graphics. (UKSC).

Christ Episcopal Church (Bowling Green). 1984. *The Spirit of Cooking: Favorite Recipes from Christ Episcopal Church*. Bowling Green, KY: Christ Episcopal Church. (WKU). The volume includes original artwork.

Church of Jesus Christ of Latter Day Saints. 1982. *Favorite Recipes from Winchester*. Lenexa, KS: Cookbook Publishers. (Clark County PL).

Clark County Homemakers Association. 1989. *Favorite Recipes from Clark County Homemakers*. Winchester, KY: Clark County Homemakers Association. (Clark County PL, UKSC).

Clear Run Baptist Church (Ohio County). 1987. *Clear Run's Cooking.* Collierville, TN: Fundcraft Publishing.

Convent Cookery. 1980. Crescent Springs, KY: St. Walburg Convent. (Kenton County PL).

Country Squares Homemakers Club (Richmond). 1980. *Kissin' Wears out, Cookin' Don't!* Lenexa, KS.: Cookbook Publishers. (UKSC).

Danville Hospital Auxiliary. 1987. *History Making Recipes.* Olathe, KS: Cookbook Publishers. (Boyle County PL).

Davidson, Tupper, Gwen McKee, and Barbara Moseley. 1988. *Best of the Best from Kentucky: Selected Recipes from Kentucky's Favorite Cookbooks.* Brandon, MS: Quail Ridge Press. (UKSC). Quail Ridge Press publishes a series of Best of the Best state cookbooks, as well as some other cookbooks and nonfiction. The enterprise started with a cookbook that had been rejected by the University of Mississippi Press because it did not meet the criteria for publication. Another edition of the Kentucky volume was published in 2005, by the same authors.

Dedman, Mary Elizabeth, and Thomas Curry Dedman Jr. 1983. *Beaumont Inn: Special Recipes.* 2nd ed. Harrodsburg, KY: Beaumont Inn. (PC). The Dedman family founded this important Kentucky restaurant. The recipe for corn pudding may hold the record for being reprinted in the most cookbooks. There may be an earlier, undated version of the Beaumont Inn cookbook.

Echols, Madonna Smith, and Martha Layne Collins. 1986. *The Crowning Recipes of Kentucky.* Louisville, KY: Marathon International Publishing. (UKSC). The *crown* in the title refers to the world of beauty pageants,

Evans, Mrs. Wilson, and Mrs. Peter H. Steenbergen. 1980. *Kentucky DAR Cookbook.* 4th ed. Berea, KY: Order to Mrs. Wilson A. Evans. (UKSC). A 1970 version also exists.

———. 1982. *Kentucky DAR Cookbook.* 5th ed. Berea, KY: Order to Mrs. Wilson A. Evans. (UKSC).

Farr, Sidney Saylor. 1983. *More than Moonshine: Appalachian Recipes and Recollections.* Pittsburgh, PA: University of Pittsburgh Press. (LPL). This narrative cookbook draws on Farr's early life in Bell County, where she was raised at the foot of Black Mountain. She worked for many years as a special collections librarian at Berea College's Hutchins Library and was also the editor of *Appalachian Heritage.* Her life was documented in her memoir *My Appalachia.* Farr died in 2011.

Favorite Southern Recipes. 1981. Danville, KY: n.p. (PO Box 483, Danville, KY 40422). (UKSC).

Fayette County Homemakers Association. 1988. *Food for Friends.* Lexington, KY: Fayette County Homemakers Association. (UKSC).

Finley, John, ed. 1985. *The* Courier-Journal *Kentucky Cook Book.* Louisville, KY: Courier-Journal and Louisville Times Company. (LPL). This includes a selection of Cissy Gregg's recipes, among others. The introduction provides documentation of the *Courier-Journal*'s food editors.

First Baptist Church (Owensboro). 1981. *Pass the Plate with Supper 8.* Owensboro, KY: First Baptist Church. (Daviess County PL).

First Presbyterian Church (Owensboro). 1984. *Favorite Recipes.* Owensboro, KY: First Presbyterian Church. (Daviess County PL).

First Presbyterian Church (Somerset). 1983. *Presbyterian Potluck.* Lenexa, KS: Cookbook Publishers. (PC). The cookbook contains a short essay on the history of the church. The recipes, which are signed, include two for tabouli.

First United Methodist Church (Winchester). 1983. *Butter 'n Love Recipes.* Pleasanton, KS: Fundcraft Publishing. (Clark County PL).

First United Methodist Church, Frankfort Women. 1982. *Cookbook 1982.* Frankfort, KY: First Methodist Church. (UKSC).

First United Methodist Church, Shalom Fellowship (Hopkinsville). 1984. *Methodist Bicentennial Cookbook, 1784–1984.* Waseca, MN: Walter's Publishing.

Fleur de Lis Garden Club. 1982. *Garden of Eatin'.* Owensboro, KY: Fleur de Lis Garden Club. (UKSC).

Flexner, Marion W. 1989. *Out of Kentucky Kitchens.* Lexington: University Press of Kentucky. (LPL). This is a republication of the 1949 edition.

Florence, Elizabeth Vater. 1982. *Kentucky Cooking at Its Best.* Leawood, KS: Circulation Service. This may be from Cold Spring in western Kentucky.

Franklin County Homemakers. 1988. *Favorite Recipes from Franklin County Homemakers.* Franklin County, KY: Franklin County Homemakers. (UKSC).

Fraser, Kathryn. 1983. *By the Seasons: Cookery at the Homeplace—1850.* Golden Pond, KY: Tennessee Valley Authority. (PC). According to the preface, this is a "history book masquerading as a cook book." The recipes, which are arranged in seasonal sections, were prepared at the historic reconstruction of a western Kentucky farm from the 1850s. They are accompanied by essays about 1850s farm life, based on historical research.

Friends of the Withers Memorial Public Library. 1986. *Friends Favorites.* Nicholasville, KY: Withers Memorial Public Library. (Jessamine County PL). The Withers Memorial Public Library was renamed the Jessamine County Public Library in 2001. The cookbook is printed on index cards held together by a single metal ring.

Garden Club of Lexington. 1985. *Bluegrass Winners: A Cookbook.* Lexington, KY: Garden Club of Lexington. (PC, UKSC). This well-presented collection of more than 400 recipes includes color photographs and some horse farm history.

Gay Twenties Homemakers (Lexington). 1983. *Recipes from the Cookin' Twenties.* Lenexa, KS: Cookbook Publishers. (UKSC).

Gill, Donna. [1985?]. *Donna Gill Recommends.* Shelbyville, KY: Science Hill Inn. (UKSC). Donna Gill, chef at the Science Hill Inn in Shelbyville, produced a number of small, undated cookbooks. Based on the brief foreword in one of them, the series apparently started in 1980 with a volume titled *Georgian Room Favorite Recipes.* The restaurant has a tearoom ambience, and when I eat there, I order the shrimp and grits.

Gill, Donna, Ellen Gill, and Terry Gill. [1980s?]. *What I Like Best about Dining with the Gills.* Shelbyville, KY: Science Hill Inn. (PC, Owen County PL). The same title was used for third and fourth editions published (according to WorldCat) in 1990 and 1996.

Glenn, Camille. 1983. *A Special Collection of Salads, Soups, and Stews.* Louisville, KY: Nana Publications. This was published for the benefit of the Louisville Fund for the Arts. Camille Glenn worked as a caterer, wrote about food for the *Courier-Journal*, and taught cooking in Louisville.

———. 1986. *The Heritage of Southern Cooking.* New York: Workman Publishing. (PC). Although very much a southern food writer, Camille Glenn has strong Kentucky roots. She was originally from Dawson Springs, and many of the recipes in this attractive narrative cookbook are Kentucky classics.

Godbey, Marty. 1985. *Dining in Historic Kentucky: A Restaurant Guide with Recipes.* Kuttawa, KY: McClanahan Publishing House. (LPL).

Grace, Curtis. 1985. *Cooking with Curtis Grace: A Collection of Favorite Recipes from Curtis Grace and His Ninth Street House Restaurant.* Kuttawa, KY: McClanahan Publishing House. (UKSC). The Ninth Street House Restaurant (now closed) was near downtown Paducah, in what was called Lower Town. It was known for its zucchini bread and California chicken salad. These dishes are now presented by House of Grace, a restaurant owned by Curtis Grace's son.

———. 1989. *Cook Talk with Curtis Grace and Friends: A Collection of Favorite Recipes from Curtis Grace and His Ninth Street House Restaurant.* Kuttawa, KY: McClanahan Publishing House. (UKSC).

Greenville Volunteer Fire Department Ladies' Auxiliary, Muhlenberg County. 1982. *A Book of Favorite Recipes.* Leawood, KS: Circulation Service. (Muhlenberg County PL).

Greenville Woman's Club. 1986. *Club House Cookbook.* Lenexa, KS: Cookbook Publishers. (Muhlenberg County PL).

Gregg, Cissy. 1981. *Cissy Gregg's Cook Book*, with an introduction by Deni Hamilton. 2 vols. Louisville, KY: Foodwork. (UKSC, LFPL). It states, "These two volumes are reproductions of Cissy Gregg's cookbooks that were published in the 1950's by the *Courier Journal* without the advertisements and photography."

Grove Ridge Baptist Church, Women's Missionary Union. 1988. *Book of Favorite Recipes*. Leawood, KS: Circulation Service. (Casey County PL).

Hamilton, Deni, ed. 1986. *The Official 1985 Kentucky State Fair Cookbook*. Louisville, KY: Foodwork. (UKSC). The cookbook contains hundreds of recipes (listed by food and competitor categories) for prizewinners at the 1985 State Fair. Foods judged only on appearance are not included. Deni Hamilton, a former food editor at the *Louisville Courier-Journal*, wrote an introductory essay that discusses the competition. Also included are essays written by winners of sweepstakes awards.

———. 1988. *The Official 1986/1987 Kentucky State Fair Cookbook*. LaGrange, KY: Foodwork. (LoC).

Harvest Daze Committee. 1989. *Home Town Recipes*. Poole, KY: Women's Club Publishing Company. (Webster County PL).

Hayes, Irene. 1984. *What's Cooking for the Holidays*. Hueysville, KY: T. I. Hayes Publishing. (UKSC). Hayes also compiled *What's Cooking in Kentucky* (1965, 1970, and later editions). A revised edition of the holiday foods cookbook was published in 2000.

Henry County Historic Society. 1987. *Our Favorite Recipes: Good Country Cooking*. Henry County, KY: The Society. (UKSC).

Holy Cross Parish (Latonia). 1982. *From Our Oven to Yours*. Lenexa, KS: Cookbook Publishers. (Kenton County PL).

Hospice of Clark County. 1986. *Winchester's Favorites*. Hartwell, GA: Calico Kitchen Press. (Clark County PL).

Hutchison United Methodist Church. [ca. 1985]. *Book of Favorite Recipes Compiled by United Methodist Women of Hutchison United Methodist Church*. Paris, KY: Hutchison United Methodist Church. (Maruskin).

Ison, Valeria. 1981. *Mountain Recipe Collection*. Hazard, KY: Ison Enterprises. (UKSC). A "Memorial Edition" was published in the same year.

Jarrell, Michael S., and Shirley Robinson. 1982. *Kentucky Cooks at GTE*. Lexington, KY: General Telephone Company of Kentucky, Public Affairs Department. (UKSC).

Junior League of Louisville. 1988. *Cordon Bluegrass: Blue Ribbon Recipes from Kentucky*. Memphis, TN: Wimmer Brothers. (UKSC). Starting in 1968 with *The Cooking Book*, the Junior League of Louisville initiated a series of noteworthy fund-raising cookbooks. The 1988 volume includes a series of menus and recipes organized around the Derby as well as other classic Kentucky foods. One interesting recipe for mint juleps includes how to impart "mintification" and the correct bourbon–simple syrup ratio.

Junior League of Owensboro. 1984. *To Market, to Market.* Owensboro, KY: Junior League of Owensboro. (UKSC). There have been a number of printings. As of the fifth printing in 1993, the Junior League of Owensboro had sold 75,000 copies, and this cookbook was selected as a *Southern Living* Hall of Fame cookbook. It is still available through the Junior League of Owensboro's website. The cookbook includes wonderful pig-themed illustrations by Katie Cox Shively. The most interesting recipe, however, is titled Daviess County Barbecued Mutton. It includes general instructions for constructing a concrete block pit and firing it with hardwood, as well as a recipe for the barbecue sauce used to baste the slow-cooked mutton. The Junior League also has a more recent cookbook entitled *Home Again, Home Again* (2004).

Kentucky Derby Museum. 1986. *The Kentucky Derby Museum Cook Book.* Louisville: Kentucky Derby Museum Corp. (UKSC).

Kentucky Historical Society. 1988. *The Kentucky Historical Society Cookbook.* Frankfort: Kentucky Historical Society. (UKSC).

Kentucky Mountain Club. 1986. *Kentucky Mountain Club Cook Book.* Lexington: Kentucky Mountain Club. (Pike County PL).

Kentucky Rural Letter Carriers Association Auxiliary. 1980. *A Blend of Old and New Cook Book.* Lenexa, KS: Cookbook Publishers. (Ebay).

Kirksville Christian Church, Christian Women's Fellowship. 1989. *Historical Cookbook.* Kirksville, KY: Kirksville Christian Church. (UKSC). Kirksville is located in Madison County. This is a reprint, with additions, of a cookbook originally published in 1929.

K-Wives Association. 1985. *Cats Cuisine.* Olathe, KS: Cookbook Publishers. (UKSC).

Lafayette Band Association (Lexington). 1980. *Lafayette Band Cookbook: Pride of the Bluegrass.* Nashville, TN: Favorite Recipes Press. (UKSC).

Lansdowne Cumberland Presbyterian Sanctuary Choir (Lexington). 1987. *The Chefs of Lansdowne.* Iowa City, IA: General Publishing and Binding. (UKSC).

Latonia Baptist Church (Kenton County). 1987. *A Collection of Recipes.* Collierville, TN: Fundcraft Publishing. (Kenton County PL).

Lewis County Extension Homemakers Association. 1986. *Favorite Recipes of Lewis County Homemakers.* Collierville, TN: Fundcraft Publishing. (PC).

Lexington Herald-Leader. 1981. *What's Cooking in the Blue Grass: A Kentucky Cookbook.* Lexington, KY: Sunday Herald-Leader. (Miller 2008). This Sunday supplement was also published in 1982 and 1989.

Lexington School. 1981. *Let's Entertain: A Collection of Favorite Recipes from the Lexington School.* Lexington, KY: Lexington School. (UKSC). This is part of a series of cookbooks that began in 1975. The recipes are very cosmopolitan and include gazpacho, spanakopita, empanadas, sauerbraten, and spaghetti alla carbonara.

Liles, Glennis Stuart, and Chuck D. Charles. 1989. *The W-Hollow Cookbook.* Ashland, KY: Jesse Stuart Foundation. (UKSC). This cookbook contains recipes collected from family members of noted Kentucky author Jesse Stuart. Most of the contributors are from northeastern Kentucky, including Greenup and Ashland, but there are also contributions from Ohio, West Virginia, and other states. The recipes have a clear Kentucky connection, and the book includes essays about Kentucky foodways. Glennis Stuart Liles is Jesse Stuart's sister, and W-Hollow is Stuart's residence.

Louisa Elementary Parent Teacher Organization. [1983?]. *The Art of Cooking in Louisa.* Louisa, KY: Louisa Elementary PTO. (Clark County PL).

Lyons, Benita McCoy. [1980s?]. *Scratch Cooking.* Lexington, KY: Real McCoy. (UKSC).

Lyons, Rex, and Rose Lyons. 1988. *The Holly Hill Inn Cookbook.* Lexington, KY: Cider Press. (UKSC). The authors were the original owners of the Holly Hill Inn, which is now owned by Ouita and Chris Michel.

Macedonia Christian Church. 1988. *A Recipe Sampler from the Macedonia Christian Church.* Olathe, KS: Cookbook Publishers. (UKSC).

Magoffin County Historical Society. 1989. *Olde Tyme Cookbook.* Salyersville, KY: Magoffin County Historical Society. The Magoffin County Historical Society cookbooks are notable examples of community-based recipe collections coupled with rich historical and family narratives. This was reprinted in 1999, 2003, and 2007.

Manchester Younger Woman's Club. 1986. *Berry-Good Recipes from the Manchester Younger Woman's Study Club.* Collierville, TN: Fundcraft Publishing. (UKSC).

Marshall, Lillian Bertram. 1980. *Cooking across the South: A Collection and Recollection of Favorite Regional Recipes.* Birmingham, AL: Oxmoor House. (PC). Lillian Marshall was the *Louisville Courier-Journal* food editor following Cissy Gregg. Although this is a southern cookbook, it includes many Kentucky recipes.

Maysville Younger Woman's Club. 1985. *A Taste of Maysville.* Maysville, KY: Standard Quick Print. (UKSC). The Maysville Younger Woman's Club also published *A Taste of Maysville II* in 1994.

McHugh, Frances, and Carol Ann Georges. 1985. *Through the Iron Gate to Kentucky Cooking.* Maysville, KY: Standard Quick Print. (UKSC). The Iron Gate is a gift shop in Washington, Kentucky, in Mason County. This was prepared with a young audience in mind.

McIntosh, Lou Delle. 1980. *My Old Kentucky Homes Cookbook.* St. Paul, MN: Cartwheel Publishing. (UKSC, EKU). This is a pamphlet.

McNamara, Marsha, and Martha Moore. 1986. *Holy Chow.* Frankfort, KY: Church of the Ascension. (UKSC).

Mengel, Frances Harding, and Barbara Harding Mengel. 1984. *Fillies Flavours: A Fantastic Celebration of the Sumptuous Flavours Surrounding the Kentucky Derby Festival*. Louisville, KY: The Fillies. (UKSC).

Middletown Woman's Club. 1987. *Second Helpings with Middletown Woman's Club*. Middletown, KY: Middletown Woman's Club. (LFPL).

Moonlite Bar-B-Q Inn (Owensboro). 1988. *Moonlite Bar-B-Q Inn Collection of Recipes*. Rev. ed. Owensboro, KY: Moonlite Bar-B-Q Inn. (Daviess County PL).

Morris, Myrle. 1980. *Down Home Cookin'*. Booneville, KY: Author. (Berea College). This is located in the library's Mountain Collection.

———. 1986. *Down Home Cookin': Book 2*. Booneville, KY: Author. (UKSC).

Mount St. Joseph Academy, West Louisville. [1980s?]. *From Watermelon and Buttermilk: Mount Saint Joseph Ursuline Family Recipes*. Adamsville, TN: Keepsake Cookbooks. (Daviess County PL).

Mt. Carmel Christian Church (Winchester). 1983. *Yesterday's Treasures, Today's Memories*. Pleasanton, KS: Fundcraft Publishing. (Clark County PL).

Murray Woman's Club. 1982. *Favorite Recipes from the Murray Woman's Club*. 6th ed. Atlanta: Jan Clopton Composition. (Kansas State University).

Nelson County Extension Homemaker Association. 1988. *My Old Kentucky Home Recipes*. 50th Anniversary ed. Leawood, KS: Circulation Service. (UKSC). This is dated as 1938 and 1988 in the Nelson County Public Library online catalog.

Nelson County Extension Homemakers. 1985. *Favorite Recipes from Nelson County, Kentucky: 1785–1985*. Bardstown, KY: Nelson County Extension Homemakers. (Maruskin).

Nickell, Estelle B. 1981. *My Favorite Molasses Recipes*. Shawnee Mission, KS: Circulation Service. (Morehead State University). Estelle Nickell is from West Liberty, Kentucky.

Noel's Chapel First Church of God (Liberty). 1987. *Feed My Sheep*. Collierville, TN: Fundcraft Publishing. (Casey County PL).

Northfield Garden Club. 1985. *Our Favorite Recipes*. Leawood, KS: Circulation Service. (Ebay).

Okolona Woman's Club. 1982. *Okolona's Wilderness Road Cook Book*. Louisville, KY: Okolona Woman's Club. (LFPL).

Order of the Eastern Star, Rose of Sharon Chapter No. 570 (Hindman). [1984?]. *A Book of Favorite Recipes: Knott County Centennial, 1884–1984*. Shawnee Mission, KS: Circulation Service. (Berea College).

Order of the Eastern Star Cookbook. 1983. Lenexa, KS: Cookbook Publishers. (Mercer County PL).

Owen County Extension Homemakers. 1986. *Favorite Recipes of the Owen Co. Homemakers*. Olathe, KS: Cookbook Publishers. (Kenton County PL).

Pack, Mary Frances. 1982. *Lunch-upon-a-Time: Simple Favorites Requested from the Strawberry Patch*. 2nd ed. Middletown, KY: n.p. (UKSC). Strawberry Patch was a tearoom in Middletown, located in Jefferson County.

Paintsville Lions Club. 1987. *Kentucky Apple Festival of Johnson County Silver Anniversary Apple Cook Book*. Paintsville, KY: The Club. (UKSC).

Parker Seal Company (Berea). 1984. *A Collection of Recipes*. Collierville, TN: Fundcraft Publishing. (Berea College). The recipes were compiled by a committee of employees, chaired by Pauline Lakes. The cover title is *What's Cookin' in Berea Kentucky*.

Patteson, Charles, with Craig Emerson. 1988. *Charles Patteson's Kentucky Cooking*. New York: Harper and Row. (Pike County PL). The recipes are accompanied by a historical narrative focused on foodways. The book is illustrated with attractive drawings.

Perryville Homemakers. 1987. *Out of Perryville Kitchens: Old and New*. Perryville, KY: Perryville Homemakers. (Maruskin).

Primrose Volunteer Fire Department, Ladies Auxiliary, Beattyville, Kentucky. [1980s?]. *Burnt Offerings*. Collierville, TN: Fundcraft Publishing. (Clark County PL).

Red Bird Mission, Early Childhood Development Program. 1981. *Heavenly Recipes*. Beverly, KY: Red Bird Mission. The Red Bird Mission online store lists two cookbooks and a holiday cookbook with similar titles. The mission is now a program of the United Methodist Church.

Saint James Court Association. 1980. *A Walking Tour and Cooking Guide of Saint James Court*. 2nd ed. Louisville, KY: Saint James Court Association. (UKSC). Saint James Court is a historic neighborhood in Old Louisville. The first edition, published in 1976, was produced in conjunction with the Saint James Art Fair and the nation's bicentennial.

Scott County Homemakers Association. 1980. *Martha Barrow Jenks Memorial Cookbook*. Georgetown, KY: Scott County Homemakers. (UKSC).

Sheft, Lori Diane, ed. 1985. *The Park Hills Cookbook*. Olathe, KS: Cookbook Publishers. (Kenton County PL).

Smith, Dorothy W. 1986. *Cooking along the Old Buffalo Trace*. Maysville, KY: Standard Quick Print. (UKSC).

Snider, Laurinda, and Carolyn Goodman. 1983. *Leaves of Gold: Favorite Recipes of the Area (Bloomfield Tobacco Festival)*. Bloomfield, KY: Sutherland and Sons. (Nelson County PL).

Snow, Kimberley. 1980. *The Capall Club Cookbook: Recipes and Observations*. Lexington: Kentucky Horse Center. (UKSC). Kimberley Snow was the chef at the Kentucky Horse Center, where she developed the recipes for this book. *Capall* means "horse" in Gaelic.

Somerset Lioness Club. 1984. *Lions' Favorites*. Somerset, KY: Somerset Lioness Club. (Pulaski County PL).

South Elkhorn Christian Church (Lexington). 1982. *Bicentennial Recipes 1783–1983*. Lenexa, KS: Cookbook Publishers. (UKSC).

Southern Legislative Conference, Kentucky Host Committee. 1988. *Kentucky Sampler: A Collection of Favorite Kentucky Recipes Compiled for the 1988 Southern Legislative Conference*. Lexington, KY: The Committee. (UKSC).

Springfield Woman's Club. 1987. *The Springfield Woman's Club Presents a Tasting Tour through Washington County, Kentucky*. Olathe, KS: Cookbook Publishers. (UKSC).

St. Mark United Church of Christ (Covington). 1988. *St. Mark U.C.C. 80th Anniversary Cookbook*. Covington, KY: St. Mark United Church of Christ. (Kenton County PL).

St. Mary's Episcopal Church, Women. 1984. *Saint Mary's Cookbook*. Middlesboro, KY: St. Mary's Church. (Harlan County PL).

St. Patrick Catholic Church (Mt. Sterling). 1988. *A Collection of Recipes*. Collierville, TN: Fundcraft Publishing. (Montgomery County PL).

Stephensburg Homemakers Club. 1986. *Stephensburg Homecoming Recipes*. 5th ed. Olathe, KS: Cookbook Publishers. (UKSC).

Stone, Martha Jane. 1988. *Life Is so Daily: A Collection of Recipes from the Kitchen of Ada Belle Stewart Stone*. Lexington, KY: Poole Press. (Trigg County PL).

Summit Heights United Methodist Church (Louisville). 1985. *Family Favorites*. Louisville, KY: Summit Heights United Methodist Church. (Miller 2008).

Sutton, Virginia. [ca. 1981]. *Favorite Recipes of Renfro Valley*. Renfro Valley, KY: n.p. (UKSC, EKU). The cookbook contains recipes that are reportedly the favorites of performers at Renfro Valley. For example, the zucchini casserole is cited as the favorite of Lilly May Ledford Pennington.

Telephone Pioneers of America, Kentucky Chapter. 1985. *Kentucky Kitchens*. Vol. 1. Louisville, KY: Southwestern Publishing Group. (UKSC).

———. 1989. *Kentucky Kitchens*. Vol. 2. Louisville, KY: Southwestern Publishing Group. (UKSC).

Tesseneer, Laura F. 1984. *The Wyman Sisters Cookbook*. Crescent Springs, KY: L. F. Tesseneer. (KDLA). This cookbook contains recipes from the eight Wyman sisters (Annie, Ruby, Pearle, Nelle, Alma, Flossie, Cate, and Bernice), who grew up in Lowes, a small town in western Kentucky.

Thomas-Bridges Association. 1983. *The Thomas and Bridges Family Cookbook*. Cadiz, KY: Thomas-Bridges Association. (Trigg County PL).

Tompkinsville Elementary PTA. 1987. *"Another" Cookbook This One by Tompkinsville Elementary PTA*. Olathe, KS: Cookbook Publishers. (Abdmishani).

Transylvania University Women's Club. 1980. *The Bicentennial Cookbook*. Lexington, KY: The Club. (UKSC, Transylvania University).

Trigg County Extension Homemakers Association. 1986. *Sharing Recipes*. Leawood, KS: Circulation Service. (Trigg County PL).

United Church of Christ Women's Guild. 1982. *A Book of Favorite Recipes*. Paducah, KY: Unity Church of Paducah. (McCracken County PL).

United Methodist Temple (Russellville). 1985. *Taste & Tell Again Cook Book*. Olathe, KS: Cookbook Publishers. (WKU).

University of Kentucky Women's Club. 1983. *Stay for Tea . . . and More*. Lexington, KY: University of Kentucky Women's Club. (UKSC). This is part of an irregular series that started in 1948; the most recent volume was published in 2010.

Wallace Woods Neighborhood Association. 1984. *Whooo's in the Kitchen*. Covington, KY: Wallace Woods Neighborhood Association. (Kenton County PL).

Warren County Homemakers Association (Bowling Green). 1981. *Warren County Favorites*. Vol. 2. Bowling Green, KY: Cooperative Extension Service. (WKU).

Wayne County Extension Homemakers. 1987. *Lake Reflections: Favorite Recipes from Our Best Cooks*. Leawood, KS: Circulation Service. This nicely composed collection includes short histories of the local homemaker clubs of Wayne County and a section on microwave recipes. It was reprinted, with additions, in 2000.

Webster County Homemakers. 1986. *Webster County Homemakers Cookbook*. Olathe, KS: Cookbook Publishers. (Webster County PL).

Weisenberger, Phil, and Susan White. [1980s?]. *The Weisenberger Cookbook*. Midway, KY: Weisenberger Mills. (LFPL). Weisenberger Mills produces a wide range of flours and flour-based mixes sold in central Kentucky.

White, Susan. 1989. *Weisenberger Cookbook II*. Midway, KY: Weisenberger Mills. (WKU).

Winchester Fire Department. 1982. *Winchester Fire Dept. Ladies Auxiliary [Cookbook]*. Winchester, KY: Winchester Fire Department. (WKU).

Woman's Club of Louisville. 1984. *Favorite Fare II*. Louisville, KY: The Club. (Department of Defense, Fort Knox). The club originally used the title in 1968.

Woodford County Hospital Auxiliary (Versailles). 1982. *Woodford Recipes*. Versailles, KY: Woodford County Hospital Auxiliary. (UKSC). According to Maruskin, this contains the original cookbook published in 1961; there were supplements in 1967 and 1982.

———. 1986. *Woodford Recipes*. Iowa Falls, IA: General Publishing and Binding. (UKSC).

Wortham, Barbara. 1983. *A Taste from Back Home*. Louisville, KY: Marathon International Publishing. (UKSC, KDLA).

Younger Woman's Club of Berea. 1985. *Berea's Best*. Berea, KY: Berea College Press. (UKSC).

1990s

Ables, Glenda D. C. 1994. *Tastefully Sharing Our Family Roots: The Henson Family Cookbook*. Ashland, KY: Designs on You. (Casey County PL).

Acton Retreat Center, Campbellsville, Kentucky. 1996. *Generations: A Collection of Recipes*. Collierville, TN: Fundcraft Publishing. (Russell County PL).

African-American Heritage Center (Franklin). 1998. *Heritage Cookbook: A Collection of Recipes*. Franklin, KY: African-American Heritage Center of Simpson County. (KHS). This cookbook is listed in the Lupton Collection of African American Cook Books at the University of Alabama. It is available for purchase at the Heritage Center in Franklin.

Agape Lincolnettes. 1995. *Agape Lincolnettes Cookbook*. Middlesboro, KY: Agape Lincolnettes. (Harlan County PL).

Allender, Mary. 1990. *Something Sweet from a Kentucky Kitchen: A Collection of Cookies and Candies*. Columbia, KY: Creations by M. Allender. (UKSC).

Allison-Lewis, Linda. 1998. *Kentucky's Best: Fifty Years of Great Recipes*. Lexington: University Press of Kentucky. (UKSC). Allison-Lewis served as food editor for *Kentucky Living* magazine, published by the Kentucky Association of Electrical Cooperatives.

Applegate, Catherine. 1998. *To Feed Our Flock: Catherine E. Applegate Liver Transplant Club*. Lenexa, KS: Cookbook Publishers. (Mason County PL).

Arnold, Jessie. 1997. *Family and Friends Cookbook: A Cookbook with a Spiritual Flavor, Memories of Yesteryear, and Great Recipes*. Nicholasville, KY: Arnold Publications. (UKSC).

Baker, Brenda. 1998. *Simply Country*. Kearney, NE: Cook Books by Morris Press. (McCreary County PL). This book may focus on McCreary County.

Baldwin Ruritan Club. 1997. *Baldwin Says Let's Eat*. Baldwin, KY: Ruritan Club. (Madison County PL).

Basberg, Lani, and Jeanne Jennings. 1990. *Lexington in Good Taste: A Restaurant Guide with Menus and Recipes*. Kuttawa, KY: McClanahan Publishing House. (UKSC).

Beech Fork Methodist Women (Helton). 1993. *Our Favorites*. Helton, KY: Beech Fork United Methodist Church. (Ebay).

Benham Elementary School (Harlan County). 1991. *Favorite Recipes and Remedies from Benham Elementary School*. Olathe, KS: Cookbook Publishers.

(Miller 2008). The school, which is now a bed-and-breakfast, is located near Benham's Coal Museum.

Bethany Christian Church (Lexington). 1996. *CWF Cookbook*. Audubon, IA: Jumbo Jack's Cookbooks. (UKSC).

Bethel Baptist Church (Frankfort). 1992. *Bethel Baptist Church Recipes*. Waseca, MN: Walter's Cookbooks. (Clark County PL).

Bethlehem Christian Church (Mt. Sterling). 1990. *What's Cooking at Bethlehem*. Mt. Sterling, KY: Bethlehem Christian Church. (Clark County PL).

Birge, Jerry, and Mag Birge. 1996. *The Joanne & Rick Pitino Wildcat Cookbook*. Owensboro, KY: Birge Publishing. (UKSC).

Blue Grass Baptist School (Lexington). 1994. *Taste & See that the Lord Is Good*. Kearney, NE: Cookbooks by Morris Press. (UKSC).

Blue Grass Trust for Historic Preservation, Gratz Park Neighborhood Association. 1995. *The Blue Grass Trust for Historic Preservation's 40th Anniversary Cookbook*. Lenexa, KS: Cookbook Publishers. (UKSC).

Boone County. 1998. *Bicentennial Cookbook, Boone County, Kentucky, 1799–1999*. Lenexa, KS: Cookbook Publishers. (Boone County PL).

Calvary Christian Church (Winchester). 1990. *Calvary Christian Church Cook Book*. Olathe, KS: Cookbook Publishers. (Clark County PL).

Cantrell, Rosemary. 1993. *What's Cookin' on the Bookmobile*. Harlan, KY: Harlan County Public Library. (Harlan County PL).

Castro, Joe. 1999. *Cooking with Chef Joe*. Louisville, KY: Camberley Brown Hotel. (PC). Joe Castro worked as the executive chef of the English Grill at the Brown Hotel.

Cathedral of the Assumption. 1997. *Cathedral Cuisine: A Collection of Recipes Presented by St. Mary's Basilica of the Assumption, Covington, Kentucky*. Kearney, NE: Cookbooks by Morris Press. (UKSC).

Catholic Social Services Bureau. 1999. *Bluegrass Bounty*. Kearney, NE: Cookbooks by Morris Press. (Harlan County PL).

Christian Church Homes of Kentucky. 1991. *Happiness Is Still Homemade*. Nashville, TN: Favorite Recipes Press. (Mercer County PL).

Church of God Cathedral, Ladies Ministries (Winchester). 1995. *A Collection of Favorite Recipes*. Leawood, KS: Circulation Service. (Clark County PL).

Church of the Nazarene, Ladies Fellowship. 1993. *Heavenly Recipes*. Flemingsburg, KY: Church of the Nazarene. (Fleming County PL).

Circle, Alice. 1998. *Heaven's Bounty: 100 Years of Good Cooking*. Paintsville, KY: First Christian Church. (Mason County PL).

Clark County Christian School, Parent Teacher Fellowship. [1994?]. *Clark County Christian School Cookbook: A Book of Favorite Recipes*. Leawood, KS: Circulation Service. (Clark County PL).

Clark County Homemakers. 1995. *Home Cookin'*. Lenexa, KS: Cookbook Publishers. (Clark County PL).

Clark County School Food Service Association (Winchester). 1995. [*Cookbook*]. Lenexa, KS: Cookbook Publishers. (Clark County PL).

Clay County Homemakers. 1992. *Kentucky Bicentennial Cookbook*. Leawood, KS: Circulation Service. (UKSC). This includes some older, traditional recipes.

Clifton, Beth, ed. 1997. *Call to Post: Winning Kentucky Recipes*. Lexington, KY: Lexington Hearing and Speech Center. (Casey County PL). This cookbook includes recipes from chefs, caterers, and home cooks.

Cornett, James W. 1995. *Recipes from the 1800s*. Burnside, KY: Jim Cornett. (Berea College).

Cornett, Jim. 1994. *Stories about Blackey, KY*. Burnside, KY: Jim Cornett. (Berea PL). The Berea College library notes a different title: *Stories about Blackey and Jim's Country Recipes*. Blackey is in Letcher County, and the text has a strong aspect of local color. For example, beaten biscuits are called "beat-up biscuits," and cooks are instructed to "put the dough through a meat grinder five times. (The old way was to give the dough a hundred licks with a flat iron!)" (44).

Cox, Elexene Mastin. 1998. *First Ladies of Jessamine: Their Recipes, Their Homes, Their Histories*. Jessamine County, KY: Jessamine County Bicentennial Committee. (Jessamine County PL).

Crittenden County Extension Homemakers Association (Marion). 1992. *A Book of Favorite Recipes: Heritage Cooking—Crittenden County 1792–1992*. Leawood, KS: Circulation Service. (PC).

Cunningham, Paula, and Meredith Eddy. 1997. *Kentucky: Dining by the Lakes*. Kuttawa, KY: McClanahan Publishing House. (UKSC).

The Cunningham Family Cookbook: Recipes from Our Cousins. 1997. Kuttawa, KY: McClanahan Publishing House. (UKSC).

Cynthiana Christian Church. 1992. *Cynthiana Christian Church Cook Book*. Olathe, KS: Cookbook Publishers. (Clark County PL).

Danville First Church of God, W.C.G. 1991. *Seasoned with Love*. Collierville, TN: Fundcraft Publishing. (Boyle County PL).

DAV Auxiliary, Chapter 25 (Lancaster). 1991. *A Collection of Recipes*. Collierville, TN: Fundcraft Publishing. (UKSC).

Davis, Sandra P. 1990. *That Special Touch, a Maker's Mark Cookbook*. Springfield, KY: Special Touch Publishing. (Jessamine County PL). A website features this cookbook (http://www.makersmarkcookbook.com/orderMakersMarkCookbook.html).

Dexter-Hardin United Methodist Women. 1993. *Cookbook*. Waseca, MN: Walter's Cookbooks. (Marshall County PL).

———. 1997. *Country Cooking.* Dexter, KY: Dexter-Hardin United Methodist. (Marshall County PL).

Dobbs. Verne L. 1998. *Deliteful Lowfat Cooking with Kentucky Author Verne Louise Dobbs.* Kuttawa, KY: McClanahan Publishing House. (LoC).

East Cumberland Avenue Baptist Church (Middlesboro). 1997. *A Matter of Taste: A Collection of Recipes.* Kearney, NE: Cookbooks by Morris Press. (Harlan County PL).

Edmonton–Metcalfe County Chamber of Commerce. 1999. *Celebrity Cooking with the Edmonton–Metcalfe County Chamber of Commerce.* Olathe, KS: Cookbook Publishers. (Miller 2008).

Eliahu Parents' Association (Louisville). 1994. *Passover Potpourri.* Olathe, KS: Cookbook Publishers. (LFPL). These signed recipes, compiled at a Jewish school in Louisville, focus on foods associated with Passover.

Elliot County Woman's Club (Sandy Hook). 1997. *Elliot County Woman's Club 1997 Edition Cook Book.* Waseca, MN: Walter's Publishing. (PC).

Epworth United Methodist Church (Lexington). 1990. *1890–1990 Epworth United Methodist.* Olathe, KS: Cookbook Publishers. (UKSC).

Faith Assembly of God (London). 1995. *Taste and See.* Kearney, NE: Cookbooks by Morris Press. (Miller 2008).

Faith Baptist Church, Women of Faith Sunday School Class (Georgetown). 1991. *A Book of Favorite Recipes.* Leawood, KS: Circulation Service. (UKSC).

Farr, Sidney Saylor. 1995. *Table Talk: Appalachian Meals and Memories.* Pittsburgh, PA: University of Pittsburgh Press. (Jessamine County PL). This volume includes extensive personal recollections from the author and other contributors, as well as recipes from Kentucky and elsewhere.

———. 1997. *Spoon Bread Cookbook.* Berea, KY: Saylor-Farr Publishing. (Clark County PL).

Fayette County Medical Auxiliary. 1999. *Creating a Stir in the Bluegrass and Beyond.* Memphis, TN: Wimmer. (UKSC).

Finchville Baptist Church. 1993. *Heritage Cookbook.* Olathe, KS: Cookbook Publishers. (Ebay).

First Baptist Church (Winchester). 1993. *First Baptist Church Cookbook.* Winchester, KY: First Baptist Church. (Clark County PL).

First Christian Church (Frankfort). 1998. *Feeding the Flock: A Collection of Recipes.* Kearney, NE: Cookbooks by Morris Press. (Paul Sawyier PL).

First Presbyterian Church (Mt. Sterling). 1991. *Special Offerings: The Sequel.* Olathe, KS: Cookbook Publishers. (Montgomery County PL).

First United Methodist Church (Winchester). 1993. *Heavenly Harvest.* Winchester, KY: First United Methodist Church, Winchester. (Clark County PL).

First United Methodist Church, Seekers Sunday School Class (Mt. Sterling).

1995. *Taste & See that the Lord Is Good.* Kearney, NE: Cookbooks by Morris Press. (UKSC).

Flemingsburg Elementary School. 1994. *Fleming County Cooking: A Book of Favorite Recipes.* Leawood, KS: Circulation Service. (Fleming County PL).

Friends of the Owsley House. 1997. *Then and Now: Garrard County, Kentucky, 1797–1997: 200 Years of History, Housekeeping and Recipes: A Bicentennial Publication.* Lancaster, KY: Friends of the Owsley House. (LPL).

Galyen, Sandra, and Muhlenberg County Public Libraries Staff. 1998. *Muhlenberg County Bicentennial Cookbook.* Greenville, KY: Muhlenberg County Public Libraries. (WKU).

Garden Club of Kentucky. 1997. *The Gourmet Gardener.* Kuttawa, KY: Commonwealth Book Company. (UKSC, Campbell County PL). About half the recipes are from Kentucky contributors; the rest are from garden club members from other states. The book is formatted as a menu cookbook.

Glasgow Cumberland Presbyterian Church, Cookbook Committee. 1998. *Our Favorite Recipes.* Glasgow, KY: Jett Press Publications. (UKSC).

Glendale Christian Church, Ladies Circle. 1991. *Treasured Family Favorites.* Olathe, KS: Cookbook Publishers. (Miller 2008).

Glenn, Camille. 1996. *Camille Glenn's Old-fashioned Christmas Cookbook.* Chapel Hill, NC: Algonquin Books of Chapel Hill. (PC). Camille Glenn, a Louisville native, includes Kentucky recipes in this southern-style holiday cookbook.

Godbey, Marty. 1992. *Dining in Historic Kentucky: A Restaurant Guide with Recipes.* Kuttawa, KY: McClanahan Publishing House. (Kenton County PL). The book discusses the history of a number of Kentucky restaurants, in addition to providing recipes from them. Although formatted in a similar way, the 1985 and 1992 editions have different content.

God's Pantry Food Bank. 1998. *The Taste of the Bluegrass.* Lexington, KY: God's Pantry Food Bank. (UKSC).

Grace, Curtis. 1992. *A Little Touch of Grace.* Kuttawa, KY: McClanahan Publishing House. (UKSC). Curtis Grace was the owner of the Ninth Street restaurant in Paducah (now closed).

———. 1998. *Encore: Collection from a Kentucky Cook.* Kuttawa, KY: McClanahan Publishing House. (UKSC).

Grant County Extension Homemakers. 1991. *Grant County Extension Homemakers Bi-centennial Cookbook 1992.* Collierville, TN: Fundcraft Publishing. (Grant County PL).

Grant County Extension Homemakers and Friends. 1992. *A Collection of Recipes.* Grant County, KY: Grant County Extension Homemakers and Friends. (Kenton County PL).

Grant County News Staff. 1998. *Now You're Cooking Grant County!* Grant County News *Cookbook*. Williamstown, KY: Grant County News. (Grant County PL).

G. R. C. Boys' Varsity Cheerleaders. 1994. *Treasured Recipes*. Lenexa, KS: Cookbook Publishers. (Clark County PL). G. R. C. stands for George Rogers Clark High School, named for the American frontiersman.

Green Hill Baptist Church. 1997. *Recipes and Remembrances: A Collection of Recipes*. Kearney, NE: Cookbooks by Morris Press. (UKSC).

Harbin, Alma Louise. 1993. *Fiddlin' in the Kitchen*. Audubon, IA: Jumbo Jack's Cookbooks. (UKSC).

———. 1997. *Fiddlin' in the Kitchen with Alma, Family, and Friends*. Audubon, IA: Jumbo Jack's Cookbooks. (UKSC).

Harlan High School Alumni Association. 1990. *A Book of Favorite Recipes*. Leawood, KS: Circulation Service. (UKSC).

Harmon's Lick Free Pentecostal Holiness Church. 1996. *Cooking with Love & Memories*. Collierville, TN: Fundcraft Publishing. (Madison County PL).

Harrodsburg Historical Society. 1991. *A Taste of Harrodsburg*. Collierville, TN: Fundcraft Publishing. (UKSC).

Hart County Historic Society. 1998. *A Fort Craig Reader: Cooking and History in Hart County Kentucky*. Munfordville, KY: Hart County Historic Society. (KHS, UKSC). This is a handsome and well-presented hardbound community cookbook enhanced by photographs and historical content.

Hazard Christian Academy. 1997. *Unbearably Good: Education with Good Taste—A Collection of Recipes*. Kearney, NE: Morris Press. (Perry County PL).

Hendren, W. S., ed. 1993. *Aunt Ran's Cook Book: Containing 200 Recipes*. Nicholasville, KY: Jessamine County Bicentennial Committee. (Jessamine County Historical Society, LPL). This is a reprint of a 1910 cookbook offered for sale by the county's Historical Society.

Hepburn Avenue Blockwatch (Louisville). 1990. *A Book of Favorite Recipes*. Leawood, KS: Circulation Service. (LFPL).

Hiestand House Museum. 1998. *Taylor County Foods and Homes*. Clinton, KY: Hiestand House Museum. (Taylor County PL).

Howard, Dulsie. 1996. *Treasures from Heaven: A Collection of Recipes from Dulsie Howard*. Collierville, TN: Fundcraft Publishing. (Marshall County PL).

Irvington Woman's Club. 1993. *Our Cookbook*. Olathe, KS: Cookbook Publishers. (UKSC).

Ivie, Dottie A. 1998. *Family Heritage Cookbook: A Collection of Memories and Family Recipes from the Residents of the City of Fort Thomas, Kentucky*. Fort Thomas, KY: City of Fort Thomas. (Campbell County PL).

Jackson Women's Club. 1999. *Kitchen Classics*. Jackson, KY: Jackson Women's Club. (UKSC).

Jessamine County Extension Homemakers. 1990. *More Delicious Recipes.* Collierville, TN: Fundcraft Publishing. (UKSC).

———. 1997. *Heritage Recipes 1997.* Nicholasville, KY: Jessamine County Extension Homemakers. (PC). This collection focuses on historical recipes. For instance, there are recipes for curing pork using brine and for making goetta, a German-inspired product made of pork, pinhead oats, and onions.

Jones, Snake C., and Desmond R. Layne. 1997. *Cooking with Pawpaws.* Frankfort: Kentucky State University Cooperative Extension Program, Pawpaw Research Program Bulletin. (Lupton Collection, University of Alabama). This is a short pamphlet.

Judd, Naomi. 1997. *Naomi's Home Companion: A Treasury of Favorite Recipes, Food for Thought, and Kitchen Wit and Wisdom.* New York: GT Publishing. (LPL). This cookbook is illustrated with photographs and includes comments about the famous country singer's life with her family.

Kabler, Jane Cline. 1999. *Mason County's Greatest Recipes.* Waseca, MN: Walter's Publishing. (Mason County PL).

Kelly Fork Church of God, Ladies Ministries. 1997. *Kelly Fork Church of God Ladies Ministries Cookbook.* Vol. 2. Olathe, KS: Cookbook Publishers. (Perry County PL).

Kentucky State Fair Board. 1996. *Official 1994 and 1995 Kentucky State Fair Blue Ribbon Recipes.* Louisville: Kentucky State Fair Board. (LoC).

Kentucky Wool Festival Cookbook. 1993. Falmouth, KY: Holland Printers. (UKSC).

Kenwood Elementary School (Louisville). 1997. *The Dazzling Delicacies Cookbook: A Book of Family Favorite Recipes and Stories.* Louisville, KY: Dazzling Sunbeam Press. (KHS).

Key Industries (Tompkinsville). 1994. *The Key to Better Cooking.* Glasgow, KY: Jett Press Publications. (UKSC).

Lakeside Presbyterian Church (Fort Mitchell). 1992. *Note'able Recipes.* Olathe, KS: Cookbook Publishers. (Kenton County PL).

Lexington-Fayette Urban County Government, Division of Police. 1995. *Cooking with the Cops: Recipes Compiled by the Lexington-Fayette Urban County Division of Police, Lexington, Kentucky.* Lenexa, KS: Cookbook Publishers. (UKSC).

Lexington Singers. 1998. *Lexington Singers 40th Anniversary Cook Book.* Kearney, NE: Cookbooks by Morris Press.

Linn, Patti, and Donna Neary. 1999. *Riverside Receipts.* Louisville, KY: Jefferson County. (PC). This short pamphlet includes facsimiles of handwritten recipes from the Moreman family that were associated with Riverside, a nineteenth-century farmhouse at Farnsley–Moreman Landing. It was published in conjunction with the reconstruction of the farm's detached kitchen. The authors make it clear that it is not a cookbook.

Lowery, Susan Spicer. 1994. *Susan's Kitchen.* St. Francis, KY: Susan's Kitchen. (LFPL).

Lundy, Ronni. 1991. *Shuck Beans, Stack Cakes, and Honest Fried Chicken: The Heart and Soul of Southern Country Kitchens.* New York: Atlantic Monthly Press. (PC). Ronni Lundy's cookbooks are great for both reading and cooking. This one has a country music theme. Her descriptions of the cooking process are excellent.

———. 1995. *The Festive Table: Recipes and Stories for Creating Your Own Holiday Traditions.* New York: North Point Press. (PC).

———. 1999. *Butter Beans to Blackberries: Recipes from the Southern Garden.* New York: North Point Press. (PC). This is a classic narrative cookbook by an important Kentucky food writer.

Madison County Extension Homemakers (Richmond). 1997. *A Taste of Tradition: A Collection of Recipes.* Kearney, NE: Cookbooks by Morris Press. (Clark County PL).

Magoffin County Historical Society. 1997. *A Joyful Cooking Journey with the Jenkins Family and Friends.* Salyersville, KY: Magoffin County Historical Society. (PC). This book was published for the nineteenth annual Magoffin County Founders' Day celebration.

———. 1998. *Cooking with Memories: Recipes and Stories of Magoffin County Kentucky Past and Present.* Salyersville, KY: Magoffin County Historical Society. This cookbook contains materials relating to family history in the county.

Marion County Bicentennial Group. 1991. *A Tasteful Tour of Historic Homes in Lebanon/Marion County.* Olathe, KS: Cookbook Publishers. (Marion County PL). The library record includes this note: "A collection of recipes and selected histories of various old homes in Lebanon and Marion County. The stories are excerpts from those written by Florence Amelia Edmonds, a local historian and society editor for the *Lebanon Enterprise* a generation ago."

Marshall County High School Concert Choir. 1995. *Noted Recipes from Noteworthy Cooks.* Collierville, TN: Fundcraft Publishing. (Marshall County PL).

May, Carl. 1991. *Cooking with the Cats: The University of Kentucky Sports Cookbook.* Olathe, KS: Cookbook Publishers. (UKSC).

Maysville Younger Women's Club. 1994. *A Taste of Maysville II.* Lenexa, KS: Cookbook Publishers. (Maysville Community and Technical College).

McAlpin's (Lexington). 1993. *McAlpin's: Always "in Good Taste."* Collierville, TN: Fundcraft Publishing. (UKSC).

McCracken County Homemakers Association. 1997. *Best Recipes: McCracken County Homemakers Association.* Paducah, KY: University of Kentucky Cooperative Extension Service. (McCracken County PL). This very large volume is presented in a ring binder.

Messenger-Inquirer (Owensboro). 1997. *Shared Favorites: A Collection of Favorite Recipes Shared by* Messenger-Inquirer *Readers*. Owensboro, KY: Messenger-Inquirer. (Daviess County PL).

Midway Women's Club. 1995. *A Taste of Midway Cookbook*. Waverly, IA: G&R Publishing. (LPL).

Monroe County Extension Homemakers. 1992. *Home Cookin' in Monroe County*. Leawood, KS: Circulation Service. (Abdmishani). The signed recipes are from various communities in this southern Kentucky county.

Montgomery County Homemakers. 1992. *Home Cookin'*. Olathe, KS: Cookbook Publishers. (Montgomery County PL). There is a section on low-fat and low-cholesterol recipes developed under the aegis of the Working to Improve Nutrition (WIN) program of the Cooperative Extension Service of the University of Kentucky.

Morningview United Methodist Church. 1995. *Recipes: From Our House to Yours*. Collierville, TN: Fundcraft Publishing. (Kenton County PL).

Morris Fork Crafts, Cook Book Committee (Breathitt County). 1994. *Morris Fork Crafts Mountain Recipes*. Booneville, KY: Morris Fork Craft Cooperative. (WKU).

Murray Woman's Club. 1991. *Murray Woman's Club Cookbook*. 7th ed. Murray, KY: Quickprint of Murray. (UKSC).

National Sweet Sorghum Producers and Processors Association. 1991. *Sorghum Treasures: A Compilation of Recipes—Old and New*. Audubon, IA: Jumbo Jack's Cookbooks. (PC). This compilation includes recipes contributed by Kentuckians as well as those from other sorghum-producing states.

New Opportunity School for Women. [1994?]. *Recipes from Our House to Yours*. Collierville, TN: Fundcraft Publishing. (UKSC).

Newport Bicentennial Commission. 1995. *Recipes and Remembrances: Newport Bicentennial 1795–1995*. Newport, KY: Morris Press. (Campbell County PL).

Newton, Pat Porter, and Pat Strunk Estes. 1992. *We Remember. . . the Way It Was*. N.p.: n.p. (UKSC).

North Metcalfe Volunteer Fire Department. 1991. *A Book of Favorite Recipes*. Leawood, KS: Circulation Service. (Metcalfe County PL). The recipes are signed. One recipe titled Easy Tupperware Bread includes special instructions for the use of the Fix-N-Mix Tupperware bowl. There is also a section of microwave recipes.

Northeast Area Extension Homemakers (Kentucky). 1999. *From Our Table to Yours: A Collection of Recipes*. Kearney, NE: Cookbooks by Morris Press. (Clark County PL).

Northern Kentucky Extension Homemakers. 1992. *Sharing Recipes*. Leawood, KS: Circulation Service. (Kenton County PL).

Olive United Methodist Church. 1997. *Bread of Life*. Collierville, TN: Fundcraft Publishing. (Marshall County PL).

O'Neal, Mary, and Paula Mueller. 1993. *Cooking with a Light Heart: A Vegan Cookbook*. Lexington, KY: Phoenix Institute. (UKSC).

Owensboro–Daviess County Hospital Volunteer Auxiliary. [1992?]. *Sharing Our Best: Favorite Family Recipes from Owensboro–Daviess County Hospital*. Owensboro, KY: Owensboro–Daviess County Hospital. (Daviess County PL).

Owenton Manor Health Care Center. 1998. *Delights from the Manor's Heart to Your Plate*. Owenton, KY: Owenton Manor. (Owen County PL).

Owingsville United Methodist Church Women. 1994. *Good Methodist Measure*. Collierville, TN: Fundcraft Publishing. (Bath County PL).

Patton, Floy. 1992. *Favorite Foods by Floy*. Hartwell, GA: Calico Kitchen Press. (Morehead State University).

P.E.O. Sisterhood, Lexington. 1994. *Pleasures for Every Occasion*. Kearney, NE: Morris Press. (Kenton County PL).

Pewee Valley Woman's Club. 1997. *The Valley Bountiful: A Collection of Recipes from the Pewee Valley Woman's Club of Pewee Valley, Kentucky*. Lenexa, KS: Cookbook Publishers. (Nelson County PL).

Phi Upsilon Omicron, Iota Chapter, University of Kentucky. 1992. *Campus Cuisine*. Olathe, KS: Cookbook Publishers. (UKSC).

Philpot School. 1992. *Philpot Heritage Cookbook*. Olathe, KS: Cookbook Publishers. (Daviess County PL).

Pikeville By-Pass Church of God. 1993. *Seasoned with Love*. Kearney, NE: Cookbooks by Morris Press. (UPike).

Pikeville Cheerleaders. 1998. *How to Feed a Panther*. Kearney, NE: Morris Press. (Sohn 2005).

Pikeville Main Street. 1997. *Hillbilly Home Cookin', Pikeville, Kentucky*. Iowa Falls, IA: General Publishing and Binding. (UKSC).

Pikeville United Methodist Church. 1993. *Heavenly Fare from Pikeville United Methodist Church*. Olathe, KS: Cookbook Publishers. (Pike County PL, Berea College).

Pleasure Ridge Park Woman's Club. 1999. *Tastes of Tradition, Shades of Yesteryear: A Book of Recipes and History*. Lenexa, KS: Cookbook Publishers. (LFPL).

Port William Historical Society (Carrollton). 1991. *Port William Bicentennial Cook Book, 1792–1992*. Leawood, KS: Circulation Service. (Kenton County PL).

Porter, Joann. 1992. *Home Cookin': Favorite Recipes Put on a Diet*. Olathe, KS: Cookbook Publishers. (Fleming County PL).

Rankin, Jane Lee. 1998. *Cookin' up a Storm: The Life and Recipes of Annie Johnson*. Louisville, KY: Grace Publishers. (LFPL). A second edition was published in 2003.

Rannells, Molly, with Rob Baker and E. Corbin Crutcher. 1996. *The John Jacob Niles Cookbook: With Special Recipes by Mary Tippy Mullins*. Lexington, KY: Watersign Press. (PC). Although John Jacob Niles had a reputation as a fine cook, it is likely that many of these recipes came from Mary Tippy Mullins, the cook and housekeeper at his Clark County home.

Reynolds, Mayme Miracle. 1993. *Cooking with Love and Memories in Kentucky*. Leawood, KS: Circulation Service. (Miller 2008).

Richardson, Shelley, and Bruce Richardson. 1994. *A Year of Teas at the Elmwood Inn: Twelve Months of Menus and Recipes*. Perryville, KY: Richardson. (UKSC).

Richardsville Elementary School (Bowling Green). 1997. *Recipes from the Community*. Glasgow, KY: Jett Press Publications. (UKSC).

Richmond Place: "Our Favorite Recipes." 1991. Lexington, KY: Richmond Place. (UKSC). Richmond Place is a retirement community in Lexington.

Riverpark Center Volunteers, Owensboro, Kentucky. 1997. *From Our Hands to Yours: A Collection of Recipes*. Kearney, NE: Cookbooks by Morris Press. (Daviess County PL).

Ross, Elizabeth. 1996. *Kentucky Keepsakes: Classic Southern Recipes*. Kuttawa, KY: McClanahan Publishing House. (UKSC).

Ruggles, Mildred Sanders. 1990. *The Kitchen Where It All Began*. Lexington, KY: Miss Middie's Ltd. (UKSC).

Russell County Deer Club. 1994. *Recipes*. Waseca, MN: Walter's Cookbooks. (Russell County PL).

Scott, Pearlie B. 1993. *Kentucky Classic Country Recipes*. Nashville, TN: M. C. Art Co. (Pike County PL).

Smith Chapel Free Will Baptist Church. 1994. *Recipes and Remembrances*. Kearney, NE: Cookbooks by Morris Press. (PC). A recipe for the dump cake companion, pig pickin' cake, is included. The recipe starts: "Put cake mix in bowl. Ignore directions on box" (62). The church is located in Webbville in Lawrence County, in eastern Kentucky.

Sohn, Mark F. 1996. *Mountain Country Cooking: A Gathering of the Best Recipes from the Smokies to the Blue Ridge*, with a foreword by John Egerton. New York: St. Martin's Press. (LPL).

South Frankfort Presbyterian Church Youth Group and First Presbyterian Church Youth Groups. 1995. *Our Best Home Cooking*. Collierville, TN: Fundcraft Publishing. (PC). The book was published to help finance the youth groups' travel to a retreat center.

Special Olympics Kentucky. 1998. *Special Tastes: Recipes from Special Olympics Kentucky.* Frankfort: Special Olympics Kentucky. (PC). The recipes were contributed by Kentucky Special Olympics athletes, parents, officials, and administrators.

Springfield Woman's Club. 1992. *A Tasting Tour through Washington County, Kentucky.* Kentucky Bicentennial ed. Olathe, KS: Cookbook Publishers. (UKSC). An earlier version was published in 1987.

St. Elizabeth Ann Seton Parish. 1993. *Good Eatin' with St. Elizabeth Ann Seton Parish.* Olathe, KS: Cookbook Publishers. (UKSC). The history of the parish is reviewed in a short introductory essay. There are relatively few iconic Kentucky recipes.

St. Lawrence Church (Daviess County), 1822–1997: A Journey of Faith: Celebrating 175 Years Community Cookbook. 1997. Waseca, MN: Walter's Publishing. (Daviess County PL).

St. Matthew A. M. E. Church, Lay Organization. [1993?]. *Treasured Recipes: Celebrating Our Roots.* Collierville, TN: Fundcraft Publishing. (PC). St. Matthew African Methodist Episcopal Church was founded in 1860 in Midway, in Woodford County. The Kentucky Historical Society marker notes that St. Matthew served as a recruitment office during the Civil War.

Staton, Vince. 1991. *Jack Daniels's Old Time Barbecue Cookbook.* Louisville, KY: Sulgrave Press. (UKSC). Vince Staton owned a Louisville-area barbecue restaurant and also wrote a very useful guide to barbecue restaurants.

Stone, Barbara, and Mary Graham. 1990. *Barbara and Mary's West Kentucky Recipe Collection.* Cadiz, KY: Authors. (Trigg County PL).

Stone, Michelle. 1998. *Merry Christmas from Kentucky: Recipes for the Season.* Kuttawa, KY: McClanahan Publishing House. (Clark County PL). This was reissued in 2007.

Sts. Boniface and James Parish (Ludlow). 1992. *Denver Sweeties.* Collierville, TN: Fundcraft Publishing. (Kenton County PL).

Sutton Elementary School PTA. 1997. *A Pinch of This—a Pinch of That! A Very Good Cookbook!!!* Owensboro, KY: Sutton Elementary School PTA. (Daviess County PL).

Talcum Ladies Group. 1996. *Talcum Tasties.* Kearney, NE: Cookbooks by Morris Press. (LPL). The group is part of the Mennonite Church in Talcum, a locality in Knott County.

Telephone Pioneers of America, Kentucky Chapter. 1998. *Kentucky Kitchens: I Hear You Calling Me.* Nashville, TN: Favorite Recipes Press. (Miller 2008).

Thomas, Betty. 1992. *Flapdoodle and Other Recipes for Poor People.* Lexington, KY: Vanity Press. (UKSC).

Thomas, Susanna, Virginia Evans, Larrie Curry, and Thelma Linton. 1992. *Thel-*

ma's Treasures: The Secret Recipes of the Best Cook in Harrodsburg. Harrodsburg, KY: Little Barter Press. (UKSC). Thelma Linton was a highly regarded caterer in Harrodsburg and an important leader in the African American community.

Thompson, Sharon. 1993. *Recipes from a Kentucky Blackberry Patch.* Carlisle, KY: WindStone Farms. (LPL). This small-format cookbook is enhanced by illustrations by Susan Brubaker. Sharon Thompson is the food editor of the *Lexington Herald-Leader.*

———. 1998. *A Second Serving: Favorite Recipes.* Lexington, KY: Herald-Leader. (UKSC). This is a supplement to the Sunday paper.

T. J. Samson Hospital, Ladies Auxiliary. 1994. *Our Favorite Recipes.* Glasgow, KY: Jett Press Quick Print. (UKSC).

Transylvania University Women's Club. 1997. *Simply Delicious Recipes.* Waseca, MN: Walter's Publishing. (UKSC).

Trigg County Extension Homemakers Association. 1991. *The Good Cooks' Cook Book: Our Favorite Recipes.* Leawood, KS: Circulation Service. (Trigg County PL).

Trinity Episcopal Church, Women of Trinity. 1993. *What's Cookin' in Danville.* 2nd ed. Danville, KY: Women of Trinity Episcopal Church. (UKSC). The first edition was published in 1988.

Tullar, Patti. 1997. *Miss Patti's Cookbook.* Kuttawa, KY: McClanahan Publishing House. (UKSC). This cookbook is from a Grand Rivers landmark: Patti's 1880s Settlement Restaurant.

Vaughn's Mill Church of God, Powell County. 1992. *A Cookbook of Treasures.* Collierville, TN: Fundcraft Publishing. (UKSC).

Webster County Homemakers. 1996. *Webster County Homemakers* [*Cookbook*]. Kansas City, KS: Cookbook Publishers. (UKSC).

Welcome House of Northern Kentucky (Crescent Springs). 1998. *W.H.O.'s Cooking: A Collection of Heart Warming Recipes.* Edgewood, KY: Inkwell. (Kenton County PL).

Western Kentucky University Home Economics and Family Living Alumni Association. 1992. *The Heritage Collection.* Nashville, TN: Favorite Recipes Press. (WKU).

Whitley County Public Library Bookmobile Service. 1993. *Recipes from Our House to Yours.* Williamsburg, KY: Whitley County Public Library Bookmobile Service. (Whitley County PL).

Winchester Council for the Arts. 1994. *Theatrical Seasonings.* Winchester, KY: Winchester Council for the Arts. (Clark County PL). This includes recipes from the Old South Inn restaurant and from a cookbook produced to support the Bundles for Britain program during World War II.

Winters, Tracy, and Phyllis Winters. 1997. *Another Sunrise in Kentucky: More Recipes from Kentucky's Finest Bed & Breakfast Inns.* Greensburg, IN: Winters Publishing. (UKSC).

Women of Christ Church Cathedral (Lexington). 1996. *Christ Church Classics: 200 Years of Favorite Recipes.* Waseca, MN: Walter's Publishing. (LPL, UKSC).

Women of Trinity. 1993. *What's Cooking in Danville.* Danville, KY: Women of Trinity Episcopal Church. (UKSC).

Woodford County Homemakers. 1999. *Best of the 20th Century Cookbook.* Versailles, KY: Woodford County Cooperative Extension Service. (UKSC).

Woodford County Hospital Auxiliary (Versailles). 1999. *Homemade with Love.* Kearney, NE: Morris Press. (UKSC).

2000s

All Aboard for a Taste of Friendship. 2002. Kearney, NE: Morris Press Cookbooks. (Kenton County PL). This was published for the city of Erlanger.

Allison-Lewis, Linda. 2009. *Kentucky Cooks: Favorite Recipes from* Kentucky Living. Lexington: University Press of Kentucky. (UKSC). Linda Allison-Lewis (now deceased) was the food editor of *Kentucky Living*, the membership magazine published by Kentucky Rural Electric Cooperatives.

Aurora Country Festival Cookbook: The Best of Western Kentucky. 2003. Kearney, NE: Morris Press Cookbooks. (Marshall County PL).

Auxier, Patty. 2008. *Salt and Pepper Memories: Recipes and Stories of Growing up on Trace Fork of Licking River in Magoffin County, with a Little Sojourn in Breathitt County, Now My Feet Are Planted on Puncheon Creek.* Prestonsburg, KY: Williams Publishing. (Rowan County PL). Patty Auxier was involved in various ways with the distinguished Magoffin County Historical Society cookbooks. This is a memoir with recipes rather than a cookbook.

Baker-Nantz, Jamie, ed. 2006. *From Our Kitchen to Yours: The* Grant County News, *Celebrating 100 Years, 1906–2006.* Williamstown, KY: Grant County News. (Grant County PL).

Bath County Agricultural Education and Marketing Center, Bath County Cooperative Extension Service. 2006. *Family Favorites of Bath County Homemakers.* Audubon, IA: Jumbo Jack's Cookbooks. (Bath County PL).

Bed and Breakfast Association of Kentucky. 2008. *Room at the Table: A Collection of Recipes from the Premier Bed and Breakfasts of Kentucky.* Kuttawa, KY: McClanahan Publishing House. (LPL). This features recipes from forty-two bed-and-breakfasts and the photographs of Robin Goetz.

Beech Fork Community Center. 2005. *Taste of Heaven.* Kearney, NE: Morris Press Cookbooks. (Harlan County PL).

Bell Court Neighborhood Association. 2005. *Seasons of Bell Court: A Collection of Recipes and Stories*. Kearney, NE: Morris Press Cookbooks. (LPL). Many of the recipes are accompanied by stories about their sources and other topics.

Bharatiya Temple and Cultural Center. 2005. *Bluegrass Masala: Indo-American Vegetarian Cooking*. Lexington, KY: Bharatiya Temple and Cultural Center. (PC). All the recipes are vegetarian and express the culinary traditions of various regions of India.

Biggerstaff, Pat. 2008. *Pat and Travis in the Back to Basics Kitchen*. Pineville, KY: Pine Mountain Shopper. (Harlan County PL).

Blaine Chapter, Order of the Eastern Star. 2001. *Old and New Family Favorites*. Lenexa, KS: Cookbook Publishers. (PC). Blaine is located in Lawrence County, Kentucky.

Bosley, Patrick. 2005. *Family Favorites from Moonlite: Recipes that Founded a Kentucky Tradition*. Owensboro, KY: Moonlite Bar-B-Q Inn. (LPL). The cookbook is from the legendary Owensboro restaurant.

Bourbon County Extension Homemakers. [2005?]. *Bourbon County Homemaker Clubs Cook Book*. Paris, KY: Bourbon County Extension Homemakers. (Clark County PL).

The Bourland's Feeding the Flock. Vol. 3. 2003. Kearney, NE: Cookbooks by Morris Press. (Marshall County PL). The other volumes of this series are undated.

Bowen, Edward L. 2008. *Entertaining with Bluegrass Winners Cookbook: New Recipes and Menus from Kentucky's Legendary Horse Farms*. Lexington, KY: Garden Club of Lexington. (Kenton County PL). This appears to be a companion volume to the garden club's *Bluegrass Winners* (1985).

Bowling Green Municipal Utilities. 2010. *BGMU Cookbook: 2010*. Bowling Green, KY: Bowling Green Municipal Utilities. (Clark County PL). This is apparently an annual publication.

Bradley Gap Free Will Baptist Church Ladies Auxiliary. 2005. *A Taste of Heaven: A Collection of Recipes*. Kearney, NE: Morris Press Cookbooks. (Lawrence County PL).

Breault, Joseph. [2003?]. *Joseph's Family Recipes*. [Winchester, KY]: Author. (Clark County PL).

Brightside Community Garden Program. 2005. *Brightside Community Garden Cookbook*. Lenexa, KS: Cookbook Publishers. (LFPL).

Britthaven of Tri-Cities. 2005. *Recipes to Remember: Britthaven of Tri-Cities Family Cookbook*. Lenexa, KS: Cookbook Publishers. (Harlan County PL). Britthaven is a chain of nursing homes in North Carolina and Kentucky.

Browning, Reba. 2001. *Reba's Left Handed Cookbook!* Paris, KY: Browning's Country Hams. (Miller 2008). This spiral-bound cookbook is printed so that the pages are in reverse order to accommodate left-handed cooks.

Buffalo Trace Area Agency on Aging. 2006. *Best of Buffalo Trace: A Collection of Recipes*. Maysville, KY: Buffalo Trace Area Agency on Aging. (Robertson County PL).

Burkhart, Greta Hipp. 2001. *Kentucky Always in Season: A Recipe Collection*. Kuttawa, KY: McClanahan Publishing House. (UKSC).

Byrd, Maryann. 2006. *The Biscuit Dive Guide: Restaurants and Recipes*. Breinigsville, PA: Byrdword Productions. (PC). This specialized cookbook includes some Kentucky-sourced biscuit recipes. It is useful because it shows the regional variation in biscuit-making strategies.

Calvert City United Methodist Church. 2010. *The Fruit of the Spirit: A Collection of Recipes by Calvert City United Methodist Church*. Kearney, NE: Morris Press Cookbooks. (Marshall County PL).

Caneyville Community Club. 2008. *Caneyville Community Cookbook: A Collection of Recipes*. Kearney, NE: Morris Press Cookbooks. (Grayson County PL).

The Carpenter's Christian Church (Harrodsburg). 2004. *Tasty Temptations: A Collection of Recipes*. Collierville, TN: Fundcraft Publishing. (Mercer County PL).

Carroll County Public Library in collaboration with Jefferson Community and Technical College–Carroll County Adult Education and Family Literacy Programs. 2008. *Once upon a Thyme II: Bilingual Cookbook*. Carrollton, KY: Carroll County Public Library. (Owen County PL).

Casey County Extension Homemaker Clubs. 2001. *Our Favorite Recipes, Our Best to You: A Collection of Recipes*. Collierville, TN: Fundcraft Publishing. (Casey County PL).

Castro, Joe. 2000. *From Barrel to the Table: Cooking with Classic Kentucky Bourbons*. Louisville, KY: Camberly Brown Hotel. (Ebay). Joe Castro is a noteworthy Louisville chef.

Central Baptist Church, Women's Mission Union (Winchester). 2009. *What's Cooking in the Kitchen?* Vol. 2, *Recipes & Remembrances*. Kearney, NE: Morris Press Cookbooks. (Clark County PL).

Central Baptist Hospital. 2010. *Beyond the Fence: A Culinary View of Historic Lexington*. Lexington, KY: Central Baptist Hospital Foundation Cancer Program. (LPL). This fund-raiser provides a robust narrative featuring horse farms, restaurants, and historic Lexington. The recipes, which include many regional favorites, are presented as seasonal menus.

Central Christian Church (Lexington). 2007. *Feeding Family and Friends of Central Christian Church*. Lexington, KY: Central Christian Church. (UKSC).

Charity League of Paducah, Kentucky. 2000. *Thyme to Entertain: Good Food and Southern Hospitality*. Paducah, KY: Charity League. (McCracken County PL).

Clapp, Wilma, and Mary Davis. 2008. *Bluegrass Treasures: A Guide to Extraor-*

dinary Lodging, Dining & Entertainment. Nicholasville, KY: Sunshine Publications. (Clark County PL). This is primarily a travel guide, but it contains some recipes.

Clark County Public Library. 2007. *Eating Our Words: Clark County Public Library Cookbook.* Winchester, KY: Clark County Public Library. (Maruskin).

Clark County School Food Service Association. 2002. *Recipes to Remember.* Lenexa, KS: Cookbook Publishers. (Clark County PL).

Colombo, Alice S. 2011. *Remember Me? A Collection of Recipes from My Years at the* Courier-Journal. Shepardsville, KY: Publishers Printing. (UKSC). The author edited the long-running "Cook's Corner Recipe Request" column in the *Louisville Courier-Journal.*

Commercial Bank of Grayson Employees, Relay for Life Teams. 2005. *Recipes and Remembrances.* Kearney, NE: Morris Press Cookbooks. (PC). The Relay for Life is an activity organized in local communities to support the American Cancer Society. The cookbook was compiled by the employees of a bank in Olive Hill.

Commodore, Jerry D. 2007. *Feeding the Flock while I Was on the River: A Collection of Recipes by Jerry D. Commodore.* Kearney, NE: Morris Press Cookbooks. (Mason County PL).

Community Action of Southern Kentucky. 2003. *Foster Grandparent Favorites: A Collection of Recipes.* Kearney, NE: Morris Press Cookbooks. (WKU).

Community Christian Church (Richmond). 2002. *Feeding the Flock: A Collection of Recipes.* Kearney, NE: Morris Press Cookbooks. (UKSC).

The Cookbook Ladies. 2003. *A Slice of Kentucky: Sharing Our Recipes.* Kuttawa, KY: McClanahan Publishing House. (UKSC).

———. 2004. *Truly Kentucky, a Culinary Gift from the Bluegrass.* Kuttawa, KY: McClanahan Publishing House. (EKU).

———. 2008. *Another Serving: The* Kentucky Monthly *10th Anniversary Cookbook.* Kuttawa, KY: McClanahan Publishing House. (UKSC).

Cornerstone Church. 2004. *Food & Fun Cookbook: A Collection of Recipes.* Edmonton, KY: Cornerstone Church. (Metcalfe County PL).

Country Cooking at Its Best: A Collection of Recipes by Young Caterers at Heart. 2004. Kearney, NE: Morris Press Cookbooks. (Nelson County PL).

Covington Catholic High School. 2000. *Colonels Culinary Hints.* Covington, KY: Covington Catholic High School. (Kenton County PL).

Crestwood Christian Church. 2002. *Crestwood Cooks.* Lexington, KY: Crestwood Christian Church. (UKSC).

Crittenden County Extension Homemakers Association. 2001. *A Sesquicentennial Celebration Cookbook of Marion, Crittenden County, Kentucky: 150 years: A Collection of Recipes and Memories, by Current and Former Members of the*

Community. Marion, KY: Crittenden County Extension Homemakers Association. (WKU).

———. 2004. *A Taste of Crittenden County: Spotlighting Our Communities.* Kearney, NE: Morris Press Cookbooks. Short descriptions and photographs of Crittenden County communities are included.

Cumberland County Public Library. 2002. *Our Reading Friends Recipes.* Burkesville, KY: Cumberland County Public Library. (McCreary County PL). Located in Burkesville, this library was originally established in 1938 as a Works Progress Administration project. The volume includes a history of the library.

Cunningham, Paula. 2008. *Room at the Table: A Collection of Recipes from the Premier Beds and Breakfasts of Kentucky.* Kuttawa, KY: McClanahan Publishing House. (Kenton County PL).

Cunningham, Paula, Michelle Stone, and Verne Dobbs. 2000. *Derby Entertaining: Traditional Kentucky Recipes.* Kuttawa, KY: McClanahan Publishing House. (UKSC). McClanahan published another book with the same title in 2008.

Cunningham, Paula, and Steve Vest. 2008. *Another Serving: 10th Anniversary Cookbook,* Kentucky Monthly *Magazine.* Kuttawa, KY: McClanahan Publishing House. (Miller 2008).

Daughters of the American Revolution, Louisa Chapter. 2001. *A Taste of Freedom: A Collection of Recipes.* Collierville, TN: Fundcraft Publishing. (Lawrence County PL).

Daviess County Extension Homemakers Association. 2003. *Favorite Recipes of Daviess County Extension Homemakers.* Audubon, IA: Audubon Media. (UKSC).

Delmont Baptist Church (Cadiz). 2003. *Our Favorite Recipes from Our Kitchen to Yours.* Audubon, IA. Jumbo Jack's Cookbooks. (Trigg County PL).

Derby Entertaining: Traditional Kentucky Recipes. 2008. Kuttawa, KY: McClanahan Publishing House. (LPL). McClanahan published a book with the same title in 2000.

Dixon, Dodd D., and Pauline G. Blair. 2004. *Recipes Then and Now.* Winchester, KY: Bluegrass Heritage Museum. (Clark County PL). This was published to commemorate the opening of the Bluegrass Heritage Museum.

Domine, David. 2007. *Adventures in New Kentucky Cooking: With the Bluegrass Peasant.* Kuttawa, KY: McClanahan Publishing House. (UKSC).

———. 2010. *A Feast for the Eyes: Recipes from America's Grandest Victorian Neighborhood.* Kuttawa, KY: McClanahan Publishing House.

———. 2010. *Splash of Bourbon: Kentucky's Spirit.* Kuttawa, KY: McClanahan Publishing House.

Dorton Freewill Baptist Church, Dorton, Kentucky. 2002. *Come and Dine!* Kearney, NE: Morris Press. (Sohn 2005).

East Pine Knot Tabernacle, Church of God. 2006. *Favorite Recipes.* Vol. 4. Collierville, TN: Fundcraft Publishing. Some recipes have symbols signifying "in loving memory," "low-fat," "heritage," or "quick & easy." There is an extended section on preserving blackberries, as well as a history of the church. Pine Knot is located in McCreary County, about five miles from Stearns.

Edmonton Elementary School, 6th Grade Class, Faculty and Staff. 2005. *Sharing Our Best.* Collierville, TN: Fundcraft Publishing. (Metcalfe County PL).

Edwards, Esther. 2001. *Bailey Family Cookbook: In Loving Memory of Opal Bailey.* Waverly, IA: G&R Publishing. (PC). The Bailey family is centered in Magoffin County.

El Bethel United Methodist Church, Winchester, Kentucky. 2005. *Cookbook Album 2005.* Winchester, KY: El Bethel United Methodist Church. (Clark County PL).

Embry Family. 2004. *Recipes and Remembrances: A Collection by the Embry Family, 314 Overland Drive, Richmond, KY 40475.* Kearney, NE: Morris Press Cookbooks. (LPL).

Episcopal Church of Saint Michael the Archangel. 2005. *Sharing Our Table 50th Anniversary: A Collection of Recipes.* Kearney, NE: Morris Press Cookbooks. (UKSC).

Estill County Historical and Genealogical Society. 2004. *Recipes Old and New: A Collection of Recipes.* Kearney, NE: Morris Press Cookbooks. (PC). The recipes are signed, and a few include brief histories of the recipe's source. The ratio of jam cake to stack cake recipes is 2:1. The compilation is enhanced by historical photographs.

Estill County Relay. 2010. *Cooking for a Cure: A Collection of Recipes.* Kearney, NE: Morris Press Cookbooks. (PC). The cookbook supports the Estill County Relay for Life program, affiliated with the American Cancer Society.

Favorite Recipes: 1-320th Field Artillery Regiment Top Gun Family and Friends. 2008. Lenexa, KS: Cookbook Publishers. (Kenton County PL).

First Assembly of God (Flemingsburg). 2005. *Flemingsburg First Assembly of God Cookbook.* Lenexa, KS: Cookbook Publishers. (Fleming County PL).

First Baptist Church Gospel Choir (Frankfort). 2004. *A Taste of Heaven: A Collection of Recipes.* Kearney, NE: Morris Cookbooks. (Paul Sawyier PL).

First Christian Church, Disciples of Christ (Richmond). 2004. *Our Favorite Recipes: A Collection of Recipes.* Kearney, NE: Morris Press Cookbooks. (Madison County PL).

First Christian Church, Disciples of Christ (Winchester). 2006. *Taste of FCC.* Vol. 2. Kearney, NE: Morris Press Cookbooks. (Clark County PL).

First Presbyterian Church (Russellville). 2001. *First Presbyterian Church Bountiful Blessings.* Lenexa, KS: Cookbook Publishers. (UKSC).

First Presbyterian Church, Paris, Kentucky. 2009. *Feeding the Flock: A Collection of Recipes.* Kearney, NE: Morris Press Cookbooks. (PC). This cookbook includes a brief history of the church. The church's women's group published *Housekeeping in the Blue Grass* in 1875—the earliest community cookbook in the state.

First United Methodist Church (Benton). [2000?]. *The Fruit of Our Labor.* Collierville, TN: Fundcraft Publishing. (Marshall County PL).

First United Methodist Church (Mt. Sterling). 2007. *Sharing Our Best.* Kearney, NE: Morris Press Cookbooks. (Montgomery County PL).

First United Methodist Church (Winchester). 2006. *Feeding the Flock: A Collection of Recipes.* Kearney, NE: Morris Press Cookbooks. (Clark County PL).

Fox, Rita Mackin. 2003. *Recipes, Stories, & Photos of the Mackin and Weathers Families of Kentucky.* Paint Lick, KY: Rita Mackin Fox. (Marion County PL). This cookbook was produced for the 2003 Mackin-Weathers family reunion.

Frankfort Younger Women's Club. 2002. *Capital Cuisine II.* Lenexa, KS: Cookbook Publishers. (Pike County PL).

Friends of Sadieville Renaissance. 2010. *A Culinary Train Ride 2010: A Collection of Recipes.* Kearney, NE: Morris Press Cookbooks. (LPL, Scott County PL). This includes four recipes contributed by Ouita Michel, chef at the Holly Hill Inn in Midway.

Fritschner, Sarah. 2004. *Derby 101: A Guide to Food and Menus for Kentucky Derby Week.* Louisville, KY: Butler Books. (UKSC). Sarah Fritschner was the food editor at the *Louisville Courier-Journal.*

———. 2004. *Sarah Fritschner's Holidays: Menus and Recipes for the Fall and Holiday Season.* Louisville, KY: Butler Books. (Miller 2008).

———. 2006. *Sarah Fritschner's Derby: Start to Finish.* Louisville, KY: Butler Books. (UKSC).

Fulton Library. 2003. *Cooking with Friends: Collection of Recipes by Friends of Fulton Library.* Kearney, NE: Morris Press Cookbooks. (Marshall County PL).

Garden Thyme Herb Club. 2004. *Cookin' Thyme: Selected Herbal Recipes from the Garden Thyme Herb Club.* Irvine, KY: Garden Thyme Herb Club. (Maruskin).

Glier's Meats. 2006. *Glier's Goetta Recipe Book: A Guide to Glier's Goetta.* Covington, KY: Glier's Meats. (Boone County PL). Goetta is a ground pork–based product similar to scrapple.

Green, Maggie. 2011. *The Kentucky Fresh Cookbook.* Lexington: University Press of Kentucky. (Estill County PL). This cookbook stresses local sources of food and seasonality.

Green County Public Library. 2002. *Recipes to Remember.* Lenexa, KS: Cookbook Publishers. (Casey County PL). The recipes are signed.

Griggs, Sarah. 2007. *The Bennett House Cookbook of Our Most Requested Recipes*. Richmond, KY: Bennett House Bed and Breakfast. (Madison County PL).

Gruchow, Jeni. 2010. *Fava's Favorites*. Georgetown, KY: Fava's Restaurant. This cookbook was produced in anticipation of the Alltech World Equestrian Event in 2010, held at the Kentucky Horse Park. Fava's Restaurant is on Main Street in Georgetown.

Hardin Church of Christ. 2005. *From the Kitchens of Great Cooks*. Hardin, KY: Church of Christ. (Marshall County PL).

Harper-Bach, Barbara. [2010?]. *From My Mother's Kitchen: Five Generations of Mother's Cooking in Horse Country*. Lexington, KY: Author. This brief collection includes a number of Bluegrass recipes from the 1940s.

———. 2012. *The Pure Kentucky Pie Clinic*. Lexington, KY: Author. (PC). This volume contains extensive instructions for making pie crust, as well as numerous pie recipes.

Hatchett, Louis, ed. 2002. *Adventures in Good Cooking, by Duncan Hines*. Macon, GA: Mercer University Press. This volume and the one below are republications of the original cookbooks by Duncan Hines. *Adventures in Good Cooking* was apparently published periodically, with changes, starting in 1939. Louis Hatchett also wrote *Duncan Hines, the Man Behind the Cake Mix* (2001).

———. 2002. *The Dessert Book, by Duncan Hines*. Macon, GA: Mercer University Press. (LPL). The original version was published in 1955.

Hellier Missionary Baptist Church. 2005. *A Collection of Recipes by Hellier Missionary Baptist Church*. Hellier, KY: Hellier Missionary Baptist Church. (Pike County PL).

Henry County Chamber of Commerce. 2006. *Sharing Henry County's Heritage*. New Castle, KY: Henry County Chamber of Commerce. (Henry County PL).

Hitchens Freewill Baptist Church. 2004. *A Taste of Heaven: A Collection of Recipes by Hitchens Freewill Baptist Church, Hitchens, Ky*. Kearney, NE: Morris Press Cookbooks. (Clark County PL).

Holy Trinity Catholic Church (Fredericktown). 2003. *Feeding the Flock: A Collection of Recipes*. Collierville, TN: Fundcraft Publishing. (Washington County PL).

Hopkins County Genealogical Society. 2011. *Preserving the Past for the Future: Recipes, Family Photos and Historical Tidbits*. Madisonville, KY: Hopkins County Genealogical Society. (PC). In addition to signed recipes, this book includes facsimiles of some local recipes. The narrative covers various topics, such as the recipes' sources, serving ideas, and cooking hints.

Hughes, Lavece. 2003. *Cooking with My Friends: Kentucky Recipes, Tried and True*. Nicholasville, KY: Wind Publications. (UKSC).

———. 2005. *Best Damn Desserts from Bear Wallow to Goosehorn: Delicious Southern Desserts and Delicacies*. Nicholasville, KY: Wind Publications. (UKSC).

James B. Haggin Memorial Hospital Auxiliary. 2006. *Cookbook*. Waverly, IA: G&R Publishing. (Mercer County PL).

Jeffersonville Assembly of God. 2004. *Favorite Recipes*. Jeffersonville, KY: Jeffersonville Assembly of God. (Clark County PL).

Junior League of Louisville. 2000. *Splendor in the Bluegrass, a Cookbook*. Louisville, KY: Junior League of Louisville. (Kenton County PL). This won the Tabasco regional cookbook award.

Junior League of Owensboro. 2004. *Home Again, Home Again*. Owensboro, KY: Junior League of Owensboro. (UKSC). This is a follow-up to the earlier cookbook *To Market, to Market* (1984).

Keeton, Shawn. 2010. *Keeton in the Kitchen*. Morley, MO: Acclaim Press.

Kenton County Public Library (Covington). 2009. *Covington Creations: A Recipe Book Made by and for the Staff of the Kenton County Public Library's Mary Ann Morgan Library*. Covington, KY: The Library.

Kentucky Cook Book. 2008. Phoenix, AZ: Golden West Publishers. (PC). Golden West produces a series of low-cost cookbooks, some of which are state focused. This volume includes many iconic recipes such as burgoo, mint julep, spoon bread, chicken and dumplings, Hot Brown sandwich, and jam cake. The recipes are signed by the contributors.

Kentucky Department of Agriculture. 2002. *Kentucky's Cookin': A Collection of Recipes from the Employees, Families and Friends of the Kentucky Department of Agriculture*. Frankfort: Kentucky Department of Agriculture. (Mercer County PL).

Kentucky Department of Libraries and Archives. 2003. *Sharing Our Best: A Collection of Recipes*. Collierville, TN: Fundcraft Publishing. (KDLA). This project contributed funds to a number of Kentucky charities. The collection includes a recipe for "Dr. Clark's Coconut Cake," which was served at the 100th birthday party of KDLA founder Thomas Clark, held at the department's offices in the Clark-Cooper building in Frankfort. The original recipe is from *Craig Claiborne's Southern Cooking*.

Kentucky Extension Associations of Family and Consumer Sciences. 2003. *Pride of Kentucky: Great Recipes with Food, Farm, and Family Traditions*. Franklin: Kentucky Extension Associations of Family and Consumer Sciences. (UKSC). This was the official cookbook of the 2003 Kentucky State Fair.

Kentucky Federation of Women's Clubs. 2002. *Kentucky Hospitality II: Continuing a 200 Year Tradition since 1775*. Louisville: Kentucky Federation of Women's Clubs. (Pulaski County PL). This is a companion to the 1976 book edited by Dorothea Cooper.

Kentucky Monthly. 2011. *Seasoned Cooking of Kentucky: A Collection of* Kentucky Monthly *Recipes*. Frankfort, KY: Kentucky Monthly. This attractive volume is beautifully illustrated with the food photography of Wales Hunter. Recipe contributors include chefs such as Kathy Cary and David Domine, various restaurants and bed-and-breakfasts, *Kentucky Monthly* recipe competition winners, and cookbooks published by McClanahan. Many of the recipes are iconic Kentucky preparations.

Kosair Children's Hospital Auxiliary. 2002. *Recipes to Remember: A Kentucky Cookbook*. Louisville, KY: Kosair Children's Hospital Auxiliary. (UoL).

Kroger Employees. 2000. *Cooking at Our House: Recipes from Kroger Employees and Our Customers*. Lenexa, KS: Cookbook Publishers. (UKSC).

Lake Cumberland Region Bookmobile and Outreach Service Librarians. 2008. *Our Favorite Recipes*. N.p.: Lake Cumberland Region Bookmobile and Outreach Service Librarians. (Casey County PL).

Line Creek Youth Ministry, Baptist Church (London). 2001. *Recipes and Remembrances: A Collection of Recipes*. Kearney, NE: Morris Press Cookbooks. (UKSC).

Lone Oak High School Band Boosters. 2006. *A "Taste of the Kentucky Colonels Marching Band Recipes": Traditional Kentucky Recipes*. Audubon, IA: Jumbo Jack's Cookbooks. (McCracken County PL).

Lundy, Jonathan. 2009. *Jonathan's Bluegrass Table: Redefining Kentucky Cuisine*. Louisville, KY: Butler Books. (UKSC). Lundy is the chef and proprietor of Jonathan's at Gratz Park, a Lexington restaurant.

Lundy, Ronni, with John Stehling. 2004. *In Praise of Tomatoes: Tasty Recipes, Garden Secrets, Legends and Lore*. New York: Lark Books. (LPL). This book covers many aspects of tomatoes, as well as some recipes. Stehling is the proprietor of the Early Girl Eatery of Asheville, North Carolina. Lundy is a distinguished food writer with Kentucky roots.

Lutheran Women's Missionary League of St. Paul's Lutheran Church (Ashland). [2011?]. *St. Paul's Lutheran Church Heavenly Delights Past & Present*. Kearney, NE: Morris Press.

Lynn, Loretta. 2004. *You're Cookin' It Country: My Favorite Recipes and Memories*. Nashville, TN: Rutledge Hill Press. (UKSC).

Lyons, Benita McCoy. 2006. *Scratch Cooking 2*. Lexington, KY: Real McCoy. (UKSC).

Magoffin County Historical Society. 2000. *Year 2000 Cook Book: Recipes and Stories of Magoffin County, Kentucky*. Salyersville, KY: Magoffin County Historical Society. (PC). This family cookbook was published for the 2000 Magoffin County Founders' Day celebration.

———. 2003. *Circle of Friends Cookbook*. Salyersville, KY: Magoffin County Historical Society. (PC). This noteworthy collection of recipes, family photographs, and history was issued to commemorate the twenty-fifth anniversary of the Magoffin County Historical Society.

———. 2006. *Good Times Cook Book: Now Being Served in Magoffin County.* Salyersville, KY: Magoffin County Historical Society. (PC). Specifically, the focus is "good times" in Magoffin County.

———. 2009. *The Manns Clan Cook Book.* Salyersville, KY: Magoffin County Historical Society. (PC). This family cookbook was published for the 2009 Magoffin County Founders' Day celebration.

The Mahurin Family Cookbook. 2004. Collierville, TN: Fundcraft Publishing. (Scott County PL).

Marshall County Extension Homemakers. 2003. *WCBL & K95 Country Cookin'.* 3rd ed. Audubon, IA: Jumbo Jack's Cookbooks. (Marshall County PL).

Marshall County Public Hospital. 2006. *Bon Appétit: A Collection of Recipes by Marshall County Public Hospital.* Kearney, NE: Morris Press Cookbooks. (Marshall County PL).

Marshall County Service Unit. 2007. *Home and Camping Cookbook.* Collierville, TN: Fundcraft Publishing. (Marshall County PL).

Mary, Queen of Heaven Roman Catholic Church (Erlanger). 2003. *The Queen's Cuisine: A Collection of Recipes.* Collierville, TN: Fundcraft Publishing. (Kenton County PL).

Mason County Cooperative Extension. 2000. *Mason County's Best: Recipes and Reminiscences of Mason County, Kentucky 1937–2000.* Audubon, IA: Jumbo Jack's Cookbooks. (Mason County PL).

Mason County History Center. 2004. *A Taste of the Past . . . : Recipes, Historic Remedies, and Household Tips from the Collections of the Museum Center Archives.* Maysville, KY: Museum Center. (Mason County PL).

Masters, Michael Edward. 2001. *Col. Michael Edward Masters' Hospitality—Kentucky Style: Simply Elegant Cooking and Entertaining.* Bardstown, KY: Equine Writers Press. (UKSC).

———. 2003. *Hospitality—Kentucky Style: Kentucky Heritage Grand Tour: Kentucky Fine Foods and Spirits.* Bardstown, KY: Equine Writers Press. (Washington PL).

Mayfield, Kathy, and Suzy Smith. 2010. *Sterling Bits Cookbook-Sketchbook: Bluegrass Equestrian Experience.* Kuttawa, KY: McClanahan Publishing House. (UKSC).

May's Lick Asparagus Festival. [2011?]. *Asparagus Festival Cookbook.* May's Lick, KY: May's Lick Community Development. (PC).

McCauley, Emilie Hannigan. 2012. *Lunch at the Glitz.* Versailles, KY: Irish Acres. The Glitz is a restaurant located at the Irish Acres Antique Mall in rural Woodford County.

McCreary County Museum (Stearns). 2006. *A Slice of Heaven*. Kearney, NE: Morris Press Cookbooks. (PC). Stearns is near the Big South Fork National River Recreation Area.

———. 2012. *A Taste of History: 100 Years of Cooking Heritage*. Kearney, NE: Morris Press Cookbooks. (PC). Similar in format to *A Slice of Heaven*, this book was published in observance of McCreary County's 100th anniversary. McCreary County was formed from parts of Pulaski, Wayne, and Whitley Counties. The recipes are signed by the contributors, who hail from various communities in McCreary County, the state, and the country. The collection includes regionally iconic recipes such as chicken and dumplings, ethnic dishes such as chicken enchiladas, and classic convenience recipes such as dump cake.

McKee, Gwen, and Barbara Moseley. 2005. *Best of the Best from Kentucky Cookbook*. New ed. Brandon, MS: Quail Ridge Press. (PC). This is an anthology of recipes from various Kentucky sources.

Metcalfe County Extension Homemakers. 2004. *Cooking up a Cure*. Kearney, NE: Morris Press Cookbooks. (Metcalfe County PL).

Midway Christian Church. 2010. *Welcome to the Table: Special Dishes and Memories from a Hometown Congregation*. Kearney, NE: Morris Press Cookbooks. (PC). The cookbook includes a brief history of the church, which was established in 1844. A number of the recipes were contributed by chef Ouita Michel of the Holly Hill Inn and Wallace Station, including "Holly Hill Inn's Extra Creamy Cheese Grits." Listed earlier is a cookbook from the 1940s published by the same church. Midway is in Woodford County, and appropriately, the cookbook includes a recipe for Woodford pudding.

Miller, Nancy. 2003. *Secrets of Louisville Chefs*. Louisville, KY: Tobe Pub. (UoL). This cookbook and the one that follows are products of a television program produced in Louisville and featuring well-known Louisville (and Lexington) chefs. There is also a website: http://louisvillehomezone.com/restaurants.

———. 2005. *Secrets of Louisville Chefs: More than 225 Great Recipes Plus Cooking Tips from the Chefs*. Louisville, KY: Louisville Magazine. (Laurel County PL).

Mitchell, Kim, and Judith Ralph. 2006. *Women, Words & Wisdom: A Kentucky Cookbook*. Reynolds Station, KY: McClanahan Publishing/Hen House Press. (Clark County PL, UKSC).

Mt. Pisgah Christian Church (Morehead). 2007. *Taste and See: That the Lord Is Good—Psalm 34:8*. Kearney, NE: Morris Press Cookbooks. (Clark County PL).

Mt. Zion Baptist Church. 2002. *Recipes and Remembrances: A Collection of Recipes by Mt. Zion Baptist Church*. Kearney, NE: Morris Press Cookbooks. (Grant County PL).

Muhlenberg County Extension Homemakers (Central City). 2000. *Muhlenberg County Extension Homemakers Cookbook*. Audubon, IA: Jumbo Jack's Cookbooks. (Daviess County PL).

Myrtle Chapel Non-Denominational Community Church Ladies Auxiliary. 2009. *Feeding the Flock: The Light at the Top of the Hill*. Kearney, NE: Morris Press Cookbooks. (Grayson County PL).

Napier, Barbara. 2009. *Hot Food & Warm Memories: A Cookbook from Snug Hollow Farm Bed & Breakfast*. Irvine, KY: B. Napier. (Clark County PL). The bed-and-breakfast is located near Irvine in Estill County.

North Middletown Christian Church. 2009. *From Our House to Yours III: A Collection of Recipes*. Kearney, NE: Morris Press Cookbooks. (Clark County PL).

Northpoint Training Center (Danville). 2006. *Recipes to Lock Away*. Kearney, NE: Morris Press Cookbooks. (Mercer County PL). The training center is actually a medium-security prison.

Oakley, Kelli, and Jayna Oakley. 2004. *Kentucky Talegating: Tailgaters' Recipes and Traditions: Stories with Sauce*. Kuttawa, KY: McClanahan Publishing House. (Miller 2008).

———. 2007. *Kentucky Talegating II: More Stories with Sauce*. Sikeston, MO: Acclaim Press. (UKSC).

Ole Gospel Barn Victory Tabernacle. 2002. *Come and Dine with Ole Gospel Barn Victory Tabernacle Family and Friends*. Lenexa, KS: Cookbook Publishers. (Casey County PL).

Owen County Extension Homemakers. 2006. *Recipes from the Heart*. Owenton, KY: Owen County Extension Homemakers/Extension Service. (Owen County PL). This cookbook was published to raise awareness and money to support those with congenital heart defects.

Owensboro Mercy Health Systems, Volunteer Auxiliary. 2003. *Cooking Plain & Fancy*. Owensboro, KY: OMHS Volunteer Auxiliary. (Daviess County PL).

Paris/Bourbon County Chamber of Commerce. 2004. *Paris Winners: A Collection of Recipes from the Paris/Bourbon County Chamber of Commerce*. Paris, KY: Paris/Bourbon County Chamber of Commerce. (Maruskin).

Penn, Sherrie. 2001. *Fancy to Down Home*. Kuttawa, KY: McClanahan Publishing House. (UKSC).

Perryville Homemakers. 2002. *Cooking in Historic Perryville: Past and Present*. Perryville, KY: Perryville Homemakers. (Boyle County PL). This revised edition was produced for the 140th anniversary of Perryville.

Phillips, Teresa. 2011. *Amish Cooking with Sicily Yoder*. Lawrenceburg, KY: CreateSpace. (Boone County PL). Sicily Yoder, the Amish food writer, is also known as Teresa Phillips of Lawrenceburg, Kentucky. This dual identity has led to a number of assertions, including that Yoder is a Canadian cooking show host, writes Amish-themed romance novels and cookbooks, and lives in Toronto and Lawrenceburg. There is also a Sicily Yoder website that mentions Kentucky locations, including Keene and Nicholasville.

Popyach, Barbara. 2004. *Kentucky Authors Cook*. Nicholasville, KY: Wind Publications. (Kenton County PL).

Port William Historical Society. 2009. *Best Dishes from Our Kitchens to Yours: A Masterson House Cookbook*. Fresno, CA: Cookbook Originals. (PC). This cookbook includes a section of "encore" recipes from earlier cookbooks. The historical society is located in Carroll County.

Porter, Juanita. 2007. *Recipes from Porter Hill: A Kentucky Collection*. Falls of the Rough, KY: Porter Hill Press. (Paul Sawyier PL, Grayson County PL).

Providence Montessori School (Lexington). 2004. *Seasons of Taste: Recipes from Families of Providence Montessori School*. Kearney, NE: Morris Press Cookbooks. (PC).

Ralph, Judith, and Kim Mitchell. 2002. *A Kentucky Gathering: Recipes & Remembrances*. Reynolds Station, KY: Hen House Press. (UKSC). All the recipes were contributed by members of a large extended family from western Kentucky. The recipes are enhanced by family stories and photographs.

Rankin, Jane Lee. 2003. *Cookin' up a Storm: The Life and Recipes of Annie Johnson*. Updated 2nd ed. Louisville, KY: Grace Publishers. (PC). I have made a number of recipes from this book. The outcomes were excellent, and the recipes were easy to follow. The book includes a brief foreword by John Egerton and a biography of Annie Johnson, a cook who worked for Rankin's family in Louisville.

Ridenour, Carolyn. 2001. *Inside Miss Jennie's Kitchen: Recipes and Other Gifts from a Distinguished Southern Family*. Kuttawa, KY: McClanahan Publishing House. (Miller 2008).

Robinson Creek Old Regular Baptist Church. 2001. *Robinson Creek Old Regular Baptist Church Cook Book*. Kearney, NE: Morris Press. (Sohn 2005).

Ross, Elizabeth. 2004. *Cornmeal Country: An American Tradition*. Kuttawa, KY: McClanahan Publishing House. (LPL). This is an important single-ingredient cookbook.

Sayre School Parents Club (Lexington). 2003. *Secret Ingredients: Sayre School's Recipes for Success*. Kearney, NE: Morris Press Cookbooks. (UKSC).

Schmid, Albert W. A. 2010. *The Kentucky Bourbon Cookbook*. Lexington: University Press of Kentucky. (LPL). This prize-winning volume was compiled by the chair of Sullivan University's National Center for Hospitality Studies in Lexington.

Sego, Idell. 2004. *Dining at the Whistle Stop: Kentucky Recipes & Reflections*. Glendale, KY: Grapevine Press. (UKSC, Green County PL). The Whistle Stop is a historic restaurant in Glendale in Hardin County.

Shelby Railroad Reunion Homecoming Host Committee. 2006. *Shelby Country Cookin': A Taste of Railroad Past*. Kearney, NE: Morris Press Cookbooks. (Pike County PL).

Simpson, Geneva Ross. 2004. *Granny's Favorite Recipes*. Hazard, KY: C. B. Simpson. (UKSC).

Smart, Rita. 2007. *Bennett House Cookbook: Kentucky Delights*. Richmond, KY: Bennett House Books, in association with McClanahan Publishing House. (UKSC).

Sohn, Mark F. 2005. *Appalachian Home Cooking: History, Culture, and Recipes*. Lexington: University Press of Kentucky. (UKSC). Though not exactly a cookbook, this well-researched book about Appalachian foodways includes many recipes.

Springfield Woman's Club. 2008. *A. Lincoln Legacy Tasting Tour*. Springfield, KY: City of Springfield. (Rowan County PL). This book includes historic photos of Washington County, as well as 800 recipes.

St. Dominic School: Nourishing Minds and Bodies for Seventy-Five Years, 1929–2004. 2004. Olathe, KS: Cookbook Publishers. (Washington County PL).

St. Henry's Catholic Church. 2000. *Angel Food: A Collection of Recipes by St. Henry's Catholic Church*. Kearney, NE: Cookbooks by Morris Press. (Marshall County PL).

St. Hubert's Episcopal Church. 2000. *St. Hubert's Hunt Country Cook Book Revisited*. Lexington, KY: Printing Bids. (UKSC).

St. John's United Church of Christ (Newport). 2007. *Let's Eat and Celebrate: A Collection of Recipes by St. John's United Church of Christ, Newport, Ky*. Kearney, NE: Morris Press. (Kenton County PL).

Stone, Michelle. 2007. *Merry Christmas from Kentucky: Recipes for the Season*. Kuttawa, KY: McClanahan Publishing House. Michelle Stone is the current owner of McClanahan Publishing.

Sullivan-Hackley, Laura. 2000. *Of Menus & Memory: A Memoir of Food & Family: Celebrating a Sense of Family on the Occasion of the Marriage of Susan Sullivan & Doug Bank*. Tallahassee, FL: Harvest Printing. (KHS). This attractive family cookbook has roots in both Frankfort, Kentucky, and Tallahassee, Florida. The recipes are signed by family members and are interspersed with short essays about family experiences.

Sustainable Berea. 2009. *Local Foods Cookbook: Recipes from Berea, KY and the Region*. Berea, KY: Sustainable Berea. (PC). This community cookbook is a compilation of recipes from the first three 100-Mile Potlucks held by the organization. These potluck dinners are based on foods produced within 100 miles of Berea. The effort is part of the local food movement in central Kentucky. The cookbook includes a directory of local producers and suppliers.

Tastes for All Seasons. 2000. Collierville, TN: Fundcraft Publishing. (LFPL).

Tates Creek Christian Church, Woman's Ministry (Lexington). 2003. *Recipes to Remember*. Lenexa, KS: Cookbook Publishers. (Clark County PL).

———. 2008. *Bountiful Heavenly Recipes*. Lenexa, KS: Cookbook Publishers. (PC). The recipes, which are signed, include six for corn pudding and one for Maryim's Grandmother Margaret Moore's Recipe for Pwolkogi (a Korean dish).

Thompson, Sharon. 2006. *Flavors of Kentucky*. Kuttawa, KY: McClanahan Publishing House. (PC). This collection provides contemporary recipes for many iconic Kentucky dishes. Sharon Thompson, food editor for the *Lexington Herald-Leader*, was raised in Clark County, and the selection has a Bluegrass orientation.

Tolson Creek Old Regular Baptist Church. 2002. *Treasures from Heaven: A Collection of Recipes*. Roxana, KY: Tolson Creek Old Regular Baptist Church. (Madison County PL).

Tullar, Chip. 2000. *The Grace of Patti's*. Memphis, TN: Patti's Publishers. (PC).

Turner, Ethel S. 2005. *From Pilot Knob to Main Street: A Collection of Recipes and Stories from Yesterday, Today and Tomorrow*. Bloomington, IN: AuthorHouse. (WKU). Turner is from Crittenden County.

Union County Extension. 2006. *Family Treasures Past and Present: A Collection of Recipes by Union County Extension*. Kearney, NE: Morris Press Cookbooks. (Union County PL).

Unity Cumberland Presbyterian Church. 2007. *Recipes from the Flock*. Kearney, NE: Morris Press Cookbooks. (Marshall County PL).

University of Kentucky Women's Club. 2010. *Stay for Tea, the Centennial Edition*. Lexington: University of Kentucky Women's Club. (PC). This is the most recent version of *Stay for Tea*; the first was published in 1948. It is especially interesting because it includes many recipes from earlier editions that were revised to be healthier.

Wallingford Christian Church Ladies Auxiliary. 2003. *Dinner on the Grounds with Wallingford Christian Church Auxiliary*. Lenexa, KS: Cookbook Publishers. (Fleming County PL).

Walnut Street Missionary Church (Benton). 2003. *Cookbook*. Kearney, NE: Morris Press Cookbooks. (Marshall County PL).

Wayne County Extension Homemakers. 2000. *Golden Memories of Lake Reflections: Favorite Recipes from Our Best Cooks*. Monticello, KY: Wayne County Extension Homemakers. (WKU). In part, this is a reprint of the 1987 *Lake Reflections* cookbook.

Webster County Extension Homemakers. 2002. *Tasteful Treasures*. Collierville, TN: Fundcraft Publishing. (Webster County PL).

West, Gary P. 2007. *Eating Your Way across Kentucky: The Recipes: A Collection of Famous Favorites from the Best Selling Restaurant Travel Guide*. Morley, MO: Acclaim Press. (UKSC). West's guide to restaurants is useful when traveling around Kentucky.

Westbrook, Buddy. 2010. *A Collection of Heirloom Kentucky and Southern Recipes: How Kentuckians Really Fry Chicken at Home*. London, KY: Glenn H. Westbrook (Hotwire). (Laurel County PL). Some sources list alternative titles; for instance, in some cases, the subtitle is listed as the main title. Sample pages are available at the author's website.

Whinnery, Pamela. 2010. *Favorite Recipes of Kentucky Celebrities*. Collierville, TN: Fundcraft Publishing. (Kenton County PL). This was compiled as a fundraiser for DAR projects.

White Oak First Church of God, Ladies Home Mission. 2001. *A Collection of Recipes*. Kearney, NE: Cookbooks by Morris. (UKSC). The church is located in Irvine, Kentucky.

———. 2002. *Recipes and Remembrances: A Collection of Recipes*. Kearney, NE: Morris Press Cookbooks. (PC).

Williams, Charles Dowling. 2004. *Out of Green River Kitchens: A Collection of Family Recipes*. Munfordville, KY: Charles Dowling Williams. (UKSC).

Williams, Lonnie, Jr. 2013. *Remember What Mama Said Recipes: Psalm 121*. Kearney, NE: Morris Press Cookbooks. (PC). This is one of the few contemporary Kentucky cookbooks compiled by an African American author. Reverend Williams is both a minister and a musician.

Winters, Tracy. 2000. *Sunrise to Sunset in Kentucky: A Collection of Kentucky's Finest Bed and Breakfast Recipes*. Greensburg, IN: Winters Publishing. (Boyd County PL).

Woodburn Baptist Church. 2006. *A Taste of Heaven: A Collection of Recipes*. Kearney, NE: Morris Press Cookbooks. (WKU).

Woodford County Woman's Club. 2004. *Recipes and Remembrances: A Collection of Recipes by Woodford County Woman's Club, Versailles, Kentucky*. Kearney, NE: Morris Press Cookbooks. (Owen County PL).

Word of Hope Lutheran Church (Lexington). 2000. *Breaking Bread Together: A Collection of Recipes*. Kearney, NE: Cookbooks by Morris Press. (PC).

Wylie, Sue. 2008. *How to Throw a Great Derby Party*. Lexington, KY: Eclipse Press. (McCracken County PL).

Index